Mind and Mechanism

Mind and Mechanism

Drew McDermott

A Bradford Book
The MIT Press
Cambridge, Massachusetts
London, England

This book was set in Sabon by Interactive Composition Corporation.

Printed on recycled paper and bound in the United States of America.

Library of Congress Cataloging-in-Publication Data

McDermott, Drew V.
  Mind and mechanism / Drew McDermott.
     p.   cm.
  "A Bradford book."
  Includes bibliographical references and index.
  ISBN 0-262-13392-X (hc. : alk. paper)
  1. Mind and body. 2. Artificial intelligence. 3. Computational neuroscience. I. Title.

BF161 .M29   2001
153—dc21   00-066986

For Judy

There are still harmless self-observers who believe that there are "immediate certainties": for example, "I think," or as the superstition of Schopenhauer put it, "I will"; as though knowledge here got hold of its object purely and nakedly as "the thing in itself," without any falsification on the part either the subject or the object.... The philosopher must say to himself: When I analyze the process that is expressed in the sentence, "I think," I find a whole series of daring assertions that would be difficult, perhaps impossible, to prove; for example, that it is *I* who think, that there must necessarily be something that thinks, that thinking is an activity and operation on the part of a being who is thought as a cause, that there is an "ego," and, finally, that it is already determined what is to be designated by thinking—that I *know* what thinking is.... In short, the assertion "I think" assumes that I *compare* my state at the present moment with other states of myself which I know, in order to determine what it is; on account of this retrospective connection with further "knowledge," it has, at any rate, no immediate certainty for me. In place of the "immediate certainty" in which people may believe in the case at hand, the philosopher thus finds a series of metaphysical questions presented to him, truly searching questions of the intellect, to wit: "From where do I get the concept of thinking? Why do I believe in cause and effect? What gives me the right to speak of an ego, and even of an ego as cause, and finally of an ego as the cause of thought?" Whoever ventures to answer these questions at once by an appeal to a sort of *intuitive* perception, like the person who says, "I think, and know that this at least, is true, actual, and certain"—will encounter a smile and two question marks from a philosopher nowadays. "Sir," the philosopher will perhaps give him to understand, "it is improbable that you are not mistaken; but why insist on the truth?"

—Nietzsche (1886), pp. 213–214

Contents

Preface   xi

Acknowledgments   xv

1 The Problem of Phenomenal Consciousness   1

2 Artificial Intelligence   29

3 A Computational Theory of Consciousness   93

4 Objections and Replies   137

5 Symbols and Semantics   167

6 Consequences   215

Notes   243

References   249

Index   259

Preface

There are many reasons to work in the field of artificial intelligence (AI). My reason is a desire to solve the "mind-body" problem, to understand how it is that a purely physical entity, the brain, can have experiences. In spite of this long-range goal, my research has been concerned with seemingly much tinier questions, such as, how might a robot know where it is? How would a computer represent the sort of routine but arbitrary fact or belief that people seem to keep track of effortlessly? (I'm thinking of "facts" such as "If you go swimming too soon after eating, you might get a cramp.") It may seem misguided to pursue tactical objectives that are so remote from the strategic objective, but scientists have learned that in the end finding precise answers to precise questions is a more reliable means to answering the big questions than simply speculating about what the big answers might be. Indeed, scientists who venture to attempt such speculation are often looked at askance, as if they had run out of useful things to do.

Hence, by writing a book on the mind-body problem from a computational perspective, I am risking raised eyebrows from my colleagues. I take that risk because I think the mind-body problem is important, not just technically, but culturally. There is a large and growing literature on novel approaches to the problem. Much of it is quite insightful, and some is totally wrong (in my opinion, of course). Even authors I agree with often fail to understand the role of computational ideas in explaining the mind. Claims like these are often made with only the flimsiest arguments:

· An intelligent computer program would treat every reasoning problem as a deduction.

• There are two computational paradigms to choose from: symbolic computing and neural networks; they are quite different, and have fundamentally different properties.

• People think serially at a conscious level, but are "massively parallel" inside; so it's appropriate to model them with a program only when studying conscious problem solving.

• Whether something is a computer depends entirely on whether a person uses it as a computer.

• When a computer program manipulates symbols, the symbols must have a formal semantics, or the program will do nothing interesting.

• Whether the symbols in a computer mean anything depends entirely on whether people treat them as meaning something.

• A computer could be made to behave exactly like a person, but without experiencing anything.

I will show that all these claims are false, meaningless, or at least questionable.

If these misconceptions mean nothing to you, good; by reading this book first, you will avoid them. Unfortunately, if you've read one or two books on the subject of computation and the mind, you have probably absorbed some of the nontruisms on the list without even noticing it.

I often assume that the mind-body problem is interesting to everyone, but I have discovered, by watching eyes glaze over, that it isn't. One reason is that it is surprisingly difficult to convey to people exactly what the problem is. Each of us has little trouble separating mental events from physical ones, and so we gravitate to a theory that there are two realms, the mental and the physical, that are connected somehow. As I explain in chapter 1, this kind of theory, called *dualism,* though it seems at first obviously true, runs into enough difficulties to move it to the "obviously false" column. This should get anyone interested, because many of us have religious beliefs—important religious beliefs—that presuppose dualism. Hence we have a stake in what theory ultimately replaces it.

Some parts of the book are a bit demanding technically. There is a little mathematics in chapter 2, a survey of the state of the art in artificial intelligence. Chapter 5 addresses the knotty technical issues surrounding the notion of symbols and semantics. I was tempted to leave all these hard bits out, to keep from driving away a large class of intelligent readers who suffer from "mathematics anxiety" or "philosophy narcolepsy." I decided .o leave chapter 2 in to counteract the general tendency in surveys of AI to talk about what's possible instead of what's actually been accomplished. The problem with the former approach is that people have an odd series of reactions to the idea of artificial intelligence. Often their first reaction is doubt that such a thing is possible; but then they swing to the opposite extreme, and start believing that anything they can imagine doing can be automated. A description of how it might be possible to program a computer to carry on a conversation encourages this gullibility, by painting a vivid picture of what such a program would be like, without explaining that we are very far from having one. Hence, throughout the book, I try to differentiate what we know how to build from what we can imagine building.

I left chapter 5 in for a different reason. I think the most serious objections to a computational account of mind rest on the issue of the *observer-relativity* of symbols and semantics, the question of whether symbols can mean anything, or can even be symbols in the first place, unless human beings impute meanings to them. This may not seem like the most serious objection for many readers, and they can skip most of chapter 5. Readers who appreciate the objection will want to know how I answer it.

With these caveats in mind, let me invite you to enjoy the book. The puzzles that arise in connection with the mind-body problem are often entertaining, once you've wrapped your mind around them. They are also important. If people really can be explained as machines controlled by computational brains, what impact does that have on ethics or religion? Perhaps we can't answer the question, but we should start asking it soon.

Acknowledgments

I must thank David Chalmers for writing a great, if totally misguided, book on consciousness that seemed to demand a response. I also thank him for strenuous conversations about the role of qualia in mental life.

Various drafts of this manuscript were read by my siblings (John, Phil, Jim, and Marcia), Will Miranker, two anonymous referees, and my wife, Judy Nugent. Their comments were all very helpful, although there are still plenty of flaws in the book, for which none of these people is responsible.

1
The Problem of Phenomenal Consciousness

Science has pushed man farther and farther from the center of the universe. We once thought our planet occupied that center; it doesn't. We once thought that our history was more or less the history of the world; it isn't. We once thought that we were created as the crown and guardian of creation; we weren't. As far as science is concerned, people are just a strange kind of animal that arrived fairly late on the scene. When you look at the details of how they work, you discover that, like other life forms, people's bodies are little chemical machines. Enzymes slide over DNA molecules, proteins are produced, various chemical reactions are catalyzed. Molecules on the surfaces of membranes react to substances they come into contact with by fitting to them and changing shape, which causes chemical signals to alter the usual flow of events, so that the machine's behavior can change as circumstances change.

Traditionally there was one big gap in this picture: the human mind. The mind was supposed to be a nonphysical entity, exempt from the laws that govern the stars, the earth, and the molecules that compose us. What if this gap closes? What if it turns out that we're machines all the way through?

This possibility may seem too implausible or repugnant to contemplate. Nonetheless, it looms on the horizon. For some of us, it seems like the most likely possibility. The purpose of this essay is to increase the plausibility of the hypothesis that we are machines and to elaborate some of its consequences. It may seem that a wiser or more moral strategy would be to avoid thinking about such a weird and inhuman hypothesis. I can't agree. If we are indeed physical systems, then I get no comfort from the fact that most people don't know it and that I can occasionally forget it.

Mind as Self-Fulfilling Description

I will be arguing that people have minds because they, or their brains, are biological computers. The biological variety of computer differs in many ways from the kinds of computers engineers build, but the differences are superficial. When evolution created animals that could benefit from performing complex computations, it thereby increased the likelihood that some way of performing them would be found. The way that emerged used the materials at hand, the cells of the brain. But the same computations could have been performed using different materials, including silicon. It may sound odd to describe what brains do as computation, but, as we shall see, when one looks at the behavior of neurons in detail, it is hard to avoid the conclusion that their purpose is to compute things. Of course, the fact that some neurons appear to compute things does not rule out that those same neurons might do something else as well, maybe something more important; and there are many more neurons whose purpose has not yet been fathomed.

Even if it turns out that the brain is a computer, pure and simple, an explanation of mind will not follow as some kind of obvious corollary. We see computers around us all the time, none of which has a mind. Brains appear to make contact with a different dimension. Even very simple animals seem to be conscious of their surroundings, at least to the extent of feeling pleasure and pain, and when we look into the eyes of complex animals such as our fellow mammals, we see depths of soul. In humans the mind has reached its earthly apogee, where it can aspire to intelligence, morality, and creativity.

So if minds are produced by computers, we will have to explain how. Several different mechanisms have been proposed, not all of them plausible. One is that they might "excrete" mind in some mysterious way, as the brain is said to do. This is hardly an explanation, but it has the virtue of putting brains and computers in the same unintelligible boat. A variant of this idea is that mind is "emergent" from complex systems, in the way that wetness is "emergent" from the properties of hydrogen and oxygen atoms when mixed in great numbers to make water.

I think we can be more specific about the way in which computers can have minds. Computers manipulate information, and some of this information has a "causative" rather than a purely "descriptive" character. That is, some of the information a computer manipulates is about entities that exist because of the manipulation itself. I have in mind entities such as the windows one sees on the screens of most computers nowadays. The windows exist because the computer behaves in a way consistent with their existing. When you click "in" a window, the resulting events occur because the computer determines where to display the mouse-guided cursor and determines which window that screen location belongs to. It makes these determinations by running algorithms that consult blocks of stored data that describe what the windows are supposed to look like. These blocks of data, called *data structures,* describe the windows in the same way that the data structures at IRS Central describe *you.* But there is a difference. You don't exist *because of* the IRS's data structures, but that's exactly the situation the window is in. The window exists because of the behavior of the computer, which is guided by the very data structures that describe it. The data structures denote something that exists because of the data structure denoting it: the data structure is a wish that fulfills itself, or, less poetically, a description of an object that brings the object into being. Such a novel and strange phenomenon ought to have interesting consequences. As I shall explain, the mind is one of them.

An intelligent computer, biological or otherwise, must make and use models of its world. In a way this is the whole purpose of intelligence, to explain what has happened and to predict what will happen. One of the entities the system must have models of is itself, simply because the system is the most ubiquitous feature of its own environment. At what we are pleased to call "lower" evolutionary levels, the model can consist of simple properties that the organism assigns to the parts of itself it can sense. The visual system of a snake must classify the snake's tail as "not prey." It can do this by combining proprioceptive and visual information about where its tail is and how it's moving. Different parts of its sensory field can then be labeled "grass," "sky," "possibly prey," "possible predator," and "tail." The label signals the appropriateness of some behaviors and the inappropriateness of others. The snake can glide over its tail, but it mustn't eat it.

The self-models of humans are much more complex. We have to cope with many more ways that our behavior can affect what we perceive. In fact, there are long intervals when everything we perceive involves us. In social settings, much of what we observe is how other humans react to what *we* are doing or saying. Even when one person is alone in a jungle, she may still find herself explaining the appearance of things partly in terms of her own observational stance. A person who did not have beliefs about herself would appear to be autistic or insane. We can confidently predict that if we meet an intelligent race on another planet they will have to have complex models of themselves, too, although we can't say so easily what those models will look like.

I will make two claims about self-models that may seem unlikely at first, but become obvious once understood:

1. Everything you think you know about yourself derives from your self-model.

2. A self-model does not have to be true to be useful.

The first is almost a tautology, although it seems to contradict a traditional intuition, going back to Descartes, that we know the contents of our minds "immediately," without having to infer them from "sense data" as we do for other objects of perception. There really isn't a contradiction, but the idea of the self-model makes the tradition evaporate. When I say that "I" know the contents of "my" mind, who am I talking about? An entity about whom I have a large and somewhat coherent set of beliefs, that is, the entity described by the self-model. So if you believe you have free will, it's because the self-model says that. If you believe you have immediate and indubitable knowledge of all the sensory events your mind undergoes, *that's* owing to the conclusions of the self-model. If your beliefs include "I am more than just my body," and even "I don't have a self-model," it's because it says those things in your self-model. As Thomas Metzinger (1995*b*) puts it, "since we are beings who almost constantly fail to recognize our mental models as models, our phenomenal space is characterized by an all-embracing naive realism, which we are incapable of transcending in standard situations."

You might suppose that a self-model would tend to be accurate, other things being equal, for the same reason that each of our beliefs is likely to be true: there's not much point in having beliefs if they're false. This supposition makes sense up to a point, but in the case of the self-model we run into a peculiar indeterminacy. For most objects of belief, the object exists and has properties regardless of what anyone believes. We can picture the beliefs adjusting to fit the object, with the quality of the belief depending on how good the fit is (Searle 1983). But in the case of the self, this picture doesn't necessarily apply. A person without a self-model would not be a fully functioning person, or, stated otherwise, *the self does not exist prior to being modeled.* Under these circumstances, the truth of a belief about the self is not determined purely by how well it fits the facts; some of the facts derive from what beliefs there are. Suppose that members of one species have belief P about themselves, and that this enables them to survive better than members of another species with belief Q about themselves. Eventually everyone will believe P, regardless of how true it is. However, beliefs of the self-fulfilling sort alluded to above will actually *become true* because everyone believes them. As Nietzsche observed, "The falseness of a judgment is ... not necessarily an objection to a judgment.... The question is to what extent it is life-promoting ..., species-preserving..." (Nietzsche 1886, pp. 202–203). For example, a belief in free will is very close (as close as one can get) to actually having free will, just as having a description of a window inside a computer is (almost) all that is required to have a window on the computer's screen.

I will need to flesh this picture out considerably to make it plausible. I suspect that many people will find it absurd or even meaningless. For one thing, it seems to overlook the huge differences between the brain and a computer. It also requires us to believe that the abilities of the human mind are ultimately based on the sort of mundane activity that computers engage in. Drawing windows on a screen is trivial compared to writing symphonies, or even to carrying on a conversation. It is not likely that computers will be able to do either in the near future. I will have to argue that eventually they will be able to do such things.

Dualism and Its Discontents

The issues surrounding the relation between computation and mind are becoming relevant because of the complete failure of *dualism* as an explanation of human consciousness. Dualism is the doctrine that people's minds are formed of nonphysical substances that are associated with their bodies and guide their bodies, but that are not part of their bodies and are not subject to the same physical laws as their bodies. This idea has been widely accepted since the time of Descartes, and is often credited to him, but only because he stated it so clearly; I think it is what anyone would come to believe if they did a few experiments. Suppose I ring a bell in your presence, and then play a recording of the 1812 Overture for you. You are supposed to raise your hand when you hear the sound of that bell. How do you know when you hear that sound? Introspectively, it seems that, though you don't actually hear a bell ringing, you can summon a "mental image" of it that has the same tonal quality as the bell and compare it at the crucial moment to the sounds of the church bells near the end of the overture. (You can summon it earlier, too, if not as vividly, and note its absence from the music.) Now the question is, where do mental sounds (or visual images, or memories of smells) reside? No one supposes that there are tiny bell sounds in your head when you remember the sound of a bell. The sounds are only "in your mind." Wherever this is, it doesn't seem to be in your brain.

Once you get this picture of the relation between mind and brain, it seems to account for many things. I've focused on remembering the sound of a bell, but it also seems to account for perceiving the sound as a bell sound in the first place. The bell rings, but I also experience it ringing. Either event could occur without the other. (The bell could ring when I'm not present; I could hallucinate the ringing of a bell.) So the experience is not the same as the ring. In fact, the experience of the ring is really closer than the physical ringing to what I mean by the word or concept "ring." Physics teaches us all sorts of things about metal, air, and vibration, but the experience of a ringing doesn't ever seem to emerge from the physics. We might once have thought that the ringing occurs when the bell is struck, but we now know that it occurs in our minds after the vibrations from the bell reach our minds. As philosophers say, vibration is a *primary quality* whereas ringing is a *secondary quality*.

Philosophers use the word *quale* to describe the "ringyness" of the experience of a bell, the redness of the experience of red, the embarrassingness of an experience of embarrassment, and so forth. Qualia are important for two reasons. First, they seem to be crucially involved in all perceptual events. We can tell red things from green things because one evokes a red quale and the other a green one. Without that distinction we assume we couldn't tell them apart, and indeed color-blind people don't distinguish the quale of red from the quale of green. Second, qualia seem utterly unphysical. Introspectively they seem to exist on a different plane from the objects that evoke them, but they also seem to fill a functional role that physical entities just could not fill. Suppose that perceiving or remembering a bell sound *did* cause little rings in your head. Wouldn't that be pointless? Wouldn't we still need a further perceptual process to classify the miniature events in our heads as ringings of bells, scents of ripe apples, or embarrassing scenes?

So far I have focused on perception, but we get equally strong intuitions when we look at thought and action. It seems introspectively as if we act after reasoning, deciding, and willing. These processes differ from physical processes in crucial respects. Physical processes are governed by causal laws, whereas minds have *reasons* for what they do. A causal law enables one to infer, from the state of a system in one region of space-time, the states at other regions, or at least a probability distribution over those states. The "state" of a system is defined as the values of certain numerical variables, such as position, velocity, mass, charge, heat, pressure, and so forth—primary qualities. We often focus for philosophical purposes on the case of knowing a complete description of a system at a particular time and inferring the states at later times, but this is just one of many possible inference patterns. All of them, however, involve the inference of a description of the physical state of the system at one point in space and time from a description of its state at other points. By contrast, the reason for the action of a person might be to *avoid* a certain state. A soldier might fall to the ground to avoid getting shot. People are not immune to physical laws; a soldier who gets shot falls for the same reason a rock does. But people seem to transcend them.

This idea of physical laws is relatively new, dating from the seventeeth century. Before that, no one would have noticed a rigid distinction between the way physical systems work and the way minds work because everyone assumed that the physical world was permeated by mental phenomena. But as the universe came to seem mechanical, the striking differences between the way it works and the way our minds work became more obvious. Descartes was the first to draw a line around the mind and put all mental phenomena inside that boundary, all physical phenomena outside it.

Nowhere is the contrast between cause and reason more obvious than in the phenomenon of free will. When you have to make a decision about what to do, you take it for granted that you have a real choice to make among alternative actions. You base your choice on what you expect to happen given each action. The choice can be difficult if you are not sure what you want, or if there is a conflict between different choice criteria. When the conflict is between principle and gain, it can be quite painful. But you never feel in conflict in the same way with the principle of causality, and that makes it hard to believe that it is a physical brain making the decision. Surely if the decision-making process were just another link in a chain of physical events it would feel different. In that case the outcome would be entirely governed by physical laws, and it would simply happen. It is hard to imagine what that would feel like, but two scenarios come to mind: either you would not feel free at all, or occasionally you would choose one course of action and then find yourself, coerced by physics, carrying out a different one. Neither scenario obtains: we often feel free to choose, and we do choose, and then go on from there.

Arguments like these make dualism look like a very safe bet, and for hundreds of years it was taken for granted by almost everyone. Even those who found it doubtful often doubted the *materialist* side of the inequality, and conjectured that mind was actually more pervasive than it appears. It is only in the last century (the twentieth) that evidence has swung the other way. It now seems that mere matter is more potent than we thought possible. There are two main strands of inquiry that have brought us to this point. One is the burgeoning field of neuroscience, which has given us greater and greater knowledge of what brains actually do. The other is the field of computer science, which has taught what machines can do. The two converge in the field of *cognitive science*, which studies computational models of brains and minds.

Neither of these new sciences has solved the problems it studies, or even posed them in a way that everyone agrees with. Nonetheless, they have progressed to the point of demonstrating that the dualist picture is seriously flawed. Neuroscience shows that brains apparently don't connect with minds; computer science has shown that perception and choice apparently don't require minds. They also point to a new vision of how brains work in which the brain is thought of as a kind of computer.

Let's look at these trends in more detail, starting with the brain. The brain contains a large number (10^{11}) of cells called *neurons* that apparently do all its work.[1] A neuron, like other cells, maintains different concentrations of chemicals on each side of the membrane that surrounds it. Because many of these chemicals are electrically charged *ions,* the result is a voltage difference across the membrane. The voltage inside the cell is about 60 millivolts below the voltage outside. When stimulated in the right way, the membrane can become *depolarized,* that is, lose its voltage difference by opening up pores in the membrane and allowing ions to flow across. In fact, the voltage briefly swings the opposite direction, so that the inside voltage become 40 millivolts above the outside voltage. When that happens, neighboring areas of the membrane depolarize as well. This causes the next area to depolarize, and so forth, so that a wave of depolarization passes along the membrane. Parts of the cell are elongated (sometimes for many centimeters), and the wave can travel along such an elongated branch until it reaches the end. Behind the wave, the cell expends energy to pump ions back across the membrane and reestablish the voltage difference.

When the depolarization wave reaches the end of a branch, it can cause a new wave to be propagated to a neighboring cell. That's because the branches of neurons often end by touching the branches of neighboring neurons. Actually, they don't quite touch; there is a gap of about one billionth of a meter (Churchland 1986). The point where two neurons come into near contact is called a *synapse.* When a depolarization wave hits a synapse, it causes chemicals called *neurotransmitters* to be emitted, which cross the gap to the next neuron and stimulate its membrane. In the simplest case one may visualize the gap as a relay station: the signal jumps the gap and continues down the axon of the next neuron. When a neuron starts a depolarization wave, it is said to *fire.* Many neurons have one long branch called the *axon* that transmits signals, and several shorter ones called *dendrites* that receive them. The axon of one neuron will make contact at several points on the dendrites of the next neuron. (A neuron may have more than one axon, and an axon may make contact on the dendrites of more than one neuron.) A depolarization wave travels at a speed between a few hundred centimeters per second and a hundred meters per second, depending on exactly how the axon is configured.

Nowadays we take it for granted that the reason neurons fire is to convey information. That's because we're familiar with the transmission of information in physical forms that are remote from the forms they take when they are first captured or ultimately used. It doesn't strike us as odd that sound waves, disturbances in air pressure, are encoded as little bumps on CDs or electrical impulses in wires. Two hundreds years ago this idea would not have been so obvious, and someone looking at the operation of the brain might have been quite puzzled by the depolarizations traveling through neural membranes. Those who take dualism seriously might demand proof that the signals were actually conveying information. Fortunately, it's not hard to find proof. First, we need to show that as the situation is varied in one place in the brain, the behavior of neurons elsewhere in the brain varies accordingly. This phenomenon has indeed been demonstrated over and over. Light is received by the retina, and neurons in the visual system become active; sound is received by the ear, and neurons elsewhere in the brain respond. Of course, it is not enough to show variation. We must also show that there is a *code* of some kind, so that a piece of information is represented by a consistent pattern of neural behavior that is different from the pattern for other pieces of information. I'll talk about that shortly.

If neural impulses were on their way to a nonphysical mind, one would expect to see neurons transmitting data as faithfully as possible, preserving the content intact until it reached the place where true perception began, and where qualia arose. I've sketched this possibility in figure 1.1. At the point where the interface to the mind appears, one might see neurons with inputs and no outputs. On the "other side" of the mind, one would see neurons with outputs but no inputs, which react to the decisions of the mind by sending impulses to the muscles relevant to the action the mind has decided on. The gap between the last layer of input neurons and the first layer of output neurons might not be so blatant. There might be no spatial gap at all, just a "causality gap," where the behavior of the output neurons could not be entirely explained by the behavior of the input neurons, but would also depend in some way on mental events.

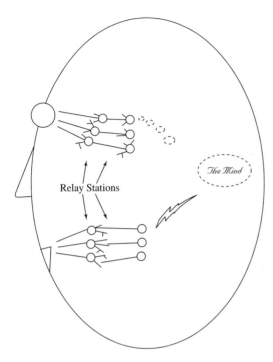

Figure 1.1
The naïve dualist picture

Lest figure 1.1 be thought of as a straw man, in figure 1.2 I have re-produced a figure endorsed by Sir John Eccles, one of the few unabashed dualists to be found among twentieth-century neurophysiologists (Eccles 1970, figure 36, detail). He divides the world into the material domain ("World 1"), the mental domain ("World 2"), and the cultural domain ("World 3"), which I have omitted from the figure. The brain is mostly in World 1, but it makes contact with World 2 through a part called the "liaison brain." The liaison brain is where Eccles supposes the causality gap lies.

Unfortunately for this dualist model, the behavior of neurons doesn't fit it. For one thing, there are few places at which data are simply trans-mitted. Usually a neuron fires after a complex series of transmissions are received from the neurons whose axons connect to it. The signals coming out of a group of neurons are not copies of the signals coming in. They

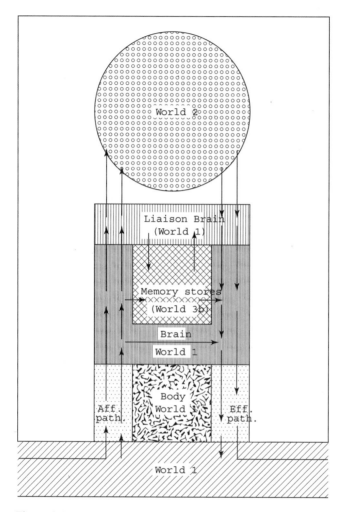

Figure 1.2
From Eccles 1970, p. 167, figure 36

are, however, a *function* of the signals coming in. That is, if there is a nonphysical "extra" ingredient influencing the output of the neurons, its effects must be very slight. As far as we can tell, any given input always results in essentially the same output.

We have to be careful here about exactly how much to claim. Neurons' behavior changes over time, as they must if they are to be able to learn.

However, such changes are reflected in changes of synapses' sensitivity to inputs, so that the output becomes a function of the input plus the state of the synapses, and their state changes as a function of its input and previous state. More subtly, we must deal with the fact that no system ever behaves exactly the same way twice. There is always a tiny variation in the output. Is this a place where mental effects can slip in?

The answer will be no if the variations are irrelevant to the information carried by the neuronal signals. The only way to judge what's relevant is to understand better how neurons encode information. So far, we understand it only partially. In many cases, the information encoded is the average rate at which the neuron fires. For instance, when light strikes a light-sensitive cell in the retina of the eye, the cell responds by firing several times in succession.[2] It behaves for all the world as if the brightness of the light is encoded by the number of depolarization waves that are transmitted per time unit. The size of each depolarization is irrelevant. Indeed, they are all of about the same size. The membrane either depolarizes or it doesn't. Each depolarization, called a *spike* because of its appearance when charted against time, is rapid and complete. What changes is the number of spikes that occur. The greater the stimulation, the faster the firing rate. Some cells can be negatively stimulated, or *inhibited*, in which case they fire more slowly than their normal rate.

Firing rates are not the only coding scheme in the brain. They could not be, because before a neuron fires its dendrites are combining information from several axons using as a medium only the smoothly varying voltages across postsynaptic membranes. In figure 1.3, the axon on the left has fired and caused the membrane voltage to increase, from its normal value of −70 mV to more like −40 mV. However, the axon on the right is connected to this cell by an *inhibitory* synapse, so that as it fires it "hyperpolarizes" the membrane, driving it even more negative than usual. The net effect depends on the geometry, chemistry, and input firing rates, and is not well understood.

Given that any physical quantity is capable in principle of serving as a code for a piece of information, it might seem impossible to determine if a given physical setup is properly described as actually encoding anything. Fortunately, there is another principle we can appeal to. Suppose someone proposes a certain code for some module of the brain. Then we can look

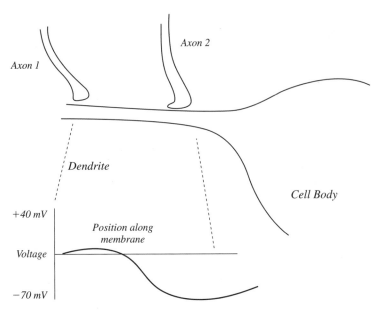

Figure 1.3
Graded action potentials along dendritic membrane

at the data represented by the inputs to that module under the proposal, look at the data encoded by the outputs, and ask whether the output is an *interesting* function of the input, in the sense that one could see why an organism would want to compute that function. If the answer is yes, then that is evidence that the code is real. Such codes are now found routinely. For example, in the visual system of the brain there are arrays of cells whose inputs represent brightness values at all points of the visual field and whose outputs represent the degree to which there is a vertical brightness edge at each point. Such an edge is defined as a brightness profile that changes value sharply along a horizontal line, from light to dark or vice versa. Other arrays of cells are sensitive to edges with other orientations.

Finding edge detectors like this is exciting because there are independent theories of how information might be extracted from the visual field that suggest that finding edges will often be useful. (For example, if the sun goes behind a cloud, all the brightnesses become smaller, but many of the edges stay in the same place.) But what I want to call attention to is that the edges are being found *before* the signals "reach the mind." Edges are not something perceived qualitatively, or at least not exclusively. Here we find edges being found in a *computational* sense that is essentially independent of mind.

At this point we have been led to notice the importance of the second major intellectual strand in the story, namely, the science of computation. We usually use the phrase "computer science" to refer to it, but that doesn't mean it's about laptops and mainframes. It's about physical embodiments of computational processes, wherever we find them, and it appears that one place we find them is in groups of neurons.

Let's turn our attention from neurons for a second and think in terms of artificial systems. Suppose we build an artificial ear. It takes sound waves, analyzes them for different frequencies, and prints out the word "bell" if the frequency analysis matches the profile for a bell, and "not a bell" otherwise. I don't mean to suggest that this would be easy to do; in fact, it's quite difficult to produce an artificial ear that could discriminate as finely as a person's. What I want to call attention to is that in performing the discrimination the artificial ear would not actually experience ringing or the absence of ringing; it would not experience anything. If you doubt that, let's suppose that I can open it up and show you exactly where the wires go, and exactly how the software is written. Here a set of tuning forks vibrate sympathetically to different frequencies; here an analog-to-digital converter converts the amplitude of each vibration to a numerical quantity; there a computer program matches the profile of amplitudes to a stored set of profiles. There's no experience anywhere, nor would we expect any.

Hence it should give us pause if the structures in the brain work in similar ways. And in fact they do. The ear contains a spiraling tube, the cochlea, different parts of whose membrane vibrate in resonance with different frequencies. These vibrations cause receptor cells to send trains of spikes of different frequencies, the frequency of a spike train encoding the amplitude of a particular sound frequency. The overuse of the word "frequency" here is confusing, but also illuminating. One physical quantity, the rate at which a neuron fires, is being used to encode a completely different quantity, the magnitude of a certain frequency in the spectrum of a sound, just as voltages are used in digital computers to represent entities that have nothing to do with voltages. The representations feed further computations in each case, leading to the extraction of richer lodes of information, such as the phonemes and words hidden in a stream of sounds. What they apparently don't lead to is any experience of anything.

The problem is that every time we find information being extracted computationally, that's one less job for the mind to do. If we find that color discriminations can be done by nonminds, that is, by sensors and computers, and we find the brain doing it the way a nonmind would do it, where does the mind come in? The traditional dualist presupposition was that the brain does almost nothing except prepare raw sensory data to be passed to the mind. That's not the case, so we have to find some other way for the mind to be present.

One possibility is that the mind is still lurking there, it just requires a bit more preprocessing than we used to think. In other words, it receives not raw brightness data, but data already helpfully analyzed into colors, edges, texture analysis, matchings of the images from the two eyes, and so forth. What the mind does is *experience* all these things. Another possibility is that experience inheres in the brain as a whole; in addition to performing computation, the collection of molecules has a quite different function, namely, to provide qualia for some of the discriminations made by the computations.

The question that now arises is what role these experiences play in determining behavior. Dualism maintains that they are crucial. If we trace out the events happening in neurons, we will (at least in principle) find places where what happens cannot be explained purely in terms of physics and chemistry. That is, we would find a gap where a physical event P_1 caused a nonphysical experience N, which then caused another physical event P_2. For example, consider the behavior of a wine taster. She sips a bit of 1968 Chateau Lafitte Rothschild, rolls it around her tongue, and pronounces "magnifique." Dualism predicts that if we were to open up her brain and take a peek, we will see neurons producing spike trains that represent various features of the wine. These spike trains apparently would go nowhere, because their sole function is to interface with the intangible dualist mind. Other neurons would produce impulses sent to the mouth and vocal cords to utter the word "magnifique," but these impulses would apparently not be a function of anything. As discussed above, the gap might be much smaller than depicted in figures 1.1 and 1.2, but it would have to be there, and the link across it would be nonphysical.

It is possible that we will encounter such a linkage in the brain, but almost no one expects to. Eccles (1973, p. 216) proposes that his "liaison brain" is located in the left hemisphere, because the speech center of most people is located in the left hemisphere. Needless to say, despite intense research activity, no such linkage has appeared. Of course, if it existed it would be very hard to find. The network of neurons in the brain is an intricate tangle, and there are large sections as yet unexplored. Almost all experimentation on brains is done on nonhuman animals. Probing a person's brain is allowed only if the probing has no bad or permanent effects. The failure to find a liaison brain in a nonhuman brain might simply indicate that such brains are not conscious. On the other hand, if an animal is conscious, it might be considered just as unethical to experiment on its brain as on one of ours. So we may be eternally barred from the decisive experiment. For all these reasons it will probably always be an option to believe that dualistic gaps exist somewhere, but cannot be observed. However, failing to find the causal chain from brain to mind and back is not what the dualist must worry about. The real threat is that neuroscientists will find another, *physical* chain of events between the tasting of the wine and the uttering of the words.

Suppose we open up the brain of a wine taster and trace out exactly all the neural pathways involved in recognizing and appreciating a sip of wine. Let's suppose that we have a complete neuroscientific, computational explanation of why she utters "magnifique!" instead of "sacre bleu!" at a key moment. Even if there is an undetected dualist gap, there is nothing for it to do. Nothing that occurs in the gap could affect what she says, because we have (we are imagining) a *complete* explanation of what she says.

One further option for the dualist is to say that experience is a nonphysical event-series that accompanies and mirrors the physical one. It plays no causal role, it just happens. This position is called *epiphenomenalism*. This is a possibility, but an unappealing one. For one thing, it seems like an odd way for the universe to be. Why is it that the sort of arrangement of molecules that we find in the brain is accompanied by this extra set of events? Why should the experiences mirror what the brain does so closely? Keep in mind that the dualist holds that there is no physical explanation of this link, so it is difficult to point to physical properties of the molecules in the brain that would have anything to do with it. The interior of the sun consists of molecules that move around in complex ways. Are these motions accompanied by experiences? When an ice cube melts, its molecules speed up in reaction to the heat of the environment. Does the ice cube feel heat? It can't tell us that it does, but then you can't tell us either. You may *believe* that your utterance of the words "It's hot in here" has something to do with your experience of heat, but it actually depends on various neurophysiological events that are no different in principle from what happens to the ice cube. The experience of heat is something else that happens, on the side. Difficulties such as these make epiphenomenalism almost useless as a framework for understanding consciousness, and I will have little to say about it.

Most scientists and philosophers find the problems with dualism insurmountable. The question is what to replace it with. A solution to the problem of consciousness, or the *mind-body* problem, would be a purely physical mechanism in the brain whose behavior we could identify with having experience. This is a tall order. Suppose we filled it, by finding that mechanism. As we peered at it, we could say with certainty that a certain set of events was the experience of red, that another set was a kind of pleasure, another an excruciating pain. And yet the events would not be fundamentally different from the events we have already observed in brains.

Furthermore, if the brain really is just an organic information-processing system, then the fact that the events occur in neurons would just be a detail. We would expect that if we replaced some or all of the neurons with equivalent artificial systems, the experiences wouldn't change. This seems implausible at first. We think of living tissue as being intrinsically sensitive in ways that silicon and wire could never be. But that intuition is entirely dualistic; we picture living tissue as "exuding" experience in some gaseous manner that we now see isn't right. At a fine enough resolution, the events going on in cells are perfectly mechanical. The wetness disappears, as it were, and we see little molecular machines pulling themselves along molecular ropes, powered by molecular springs. At the level of neurons, these little machines process information, and they could process the information just as well if they were built using different molecules.

This idea seems so unpalatable to some that they refuse to speculate any further. Consciousness is evidently so mysterious that we will never understand it. We can't imagine any way to build a bridge between physics and mental experience, so we might as well give up. (Colin McGinn is the philosopher most closely associated with this position; see McGinn 1991.) This is an odd position to take when things are just starting to get interesting. In addition, one can argue that it is irresponsible to leave key questions about the human mind dangling when we might clear them up.

Modern culture is in an awkward spot when it comes to the mind-body problem. Scientists and artists are well aware that dualism has failed, but they have no idea what to replace it with. Meanwhile, almost everyone else, including most political and religious leaders, take dualism for granted. The result is that the intellectual elite can take comfort in their superiority over ordinary people and their beliefs, but not in much else. Is this a state of affairs that can last indefinitely without harmful consequences?

I realize that there is a cynical view that people have always accepted delusions and always will. If most people believe in astrology, there can't be any additional harm in their having incoherent beliefs about what goes on inside their heads. I suppose that if you the view the main purpose of the human race as the consumption of products advertised on TV, then their delusions are not relevant. I prefer to think that, at the very least, humans ought to have a chance at the dignity that comes from understanding and accepting their world. Our civilization ought to be able to arrive at a framework in which we appreciate human value without delusions.

Nondualist Explanations of Consciousness

The field of consciousness studies has been quite busy lately. There seem to be two major camps on the mind-body problem: those who believe that we already have the tools we need to explain the mind, and those who believe that we don't and perhaps never will. McGinn is in the pessimistic camp, as is Nagel (1975) and others. I'm an optimist.

Some theorists (notably Bernard Baars 1988, 1996) focus on explaining the function of consciousness and how this function might be realized by the structures of the brain. Although this is an important area, it won't be my main focus. I agree with Chalmers's assessment (Chalmers 1996) that the "hard problem" of consciousness is to explain how a physical object can have experiences. This is the problem of *phenomenal consciousness*. It is a hard problem for all theories, but especially for computational ones.

Like everyone else, I can't define "phenomenal consciousness." It's the ability to have experiences. I assume that anyone who can read this knows what it means to experience something (from their own experience!); and that everyone knows that thermostats don't have experiences, even though they can react to temperature differences.

The difficulty of defining consciousness has led some to propose that there is no thing as consciousness. The standard citations are to Churchland (1990) and Rorty (1965). This position is called *eliminativism*. The idea is to replace the concept of consciousness with more refined (more scientific?) concepts, much as happened with concepts like "energy" and "mass" in past scientific revolutions. It seems plain that a full understanding of the mind will involve shifts of this kind. If we ever do achieve fuller understanding (which the pessimists doubt), any book written before the resulting shift, including this one, will no doubt seem laughably quaint. However, we can't simply wait around for this to happen. We have to work on the problems we see now, using the tools at hand. There is clearly a problem of how a thing, a brain or computer, can have experiences, or appear to have what people are strongly tempted to call experiences. To explain how this is conceivable at all must be our goal.

O'Brien and Opie (1999) make a useful distinction between *vehicle* and *process* theories of phenomenal consciousness:

Either consciousness is to be explained in terms of the nature of the representational vehicles the brain deploys, or it is to be explained in terms of the computational processes defined over these vehicles. We call versions of these two approaches VEHICLE and PROCESS theories of consciousness, respectively.

A process theory is one that explains experience in terms of things the brain does, especially things it computes. A vehicle theory explains experience as a property of the entity doing the computing. O'Brien and Opie themselves propose a vehicle theory in which experience is identified with (or correlated with?) stable activation patterns in networks of neurons. Another example, much vaguer, is that of John Searle (1992), who appeals to unknown "causal powers" of brain tissue to explain experience.

Then there is the theory of Stuart Hammeroff (1994; Penrose 1994), which explains consciousness in terms of the quantum-mechanical behavior of brain cells, specifically their microtubules. I don't know how this approach fits into O'Brien and Opie's dichotomy, because the details are so fuzzy. But if the theory is a process theory, it's a theory of an unusual kind, because the processes in question cannot, by hypothesis, be explained mechanistically. Instead, the proposal seems to be that the ability of the mind to arrive at sudden insights is explained in the same way as the sudden collapse of wave functions in quantum mechanics. Grant that, and perhaps you may be willing to grant that phenomenal consciousness gets explained somehow, too.

The problem with all these theories besides their vagueness is that they are vulnerable to subversion by competing process theories (McDermott 1999). This is a flaw they share with dualism. As I explained above, any dualistic or "vehicular" explanation of the mind will have to accommodate all the facts that mundane process models explain, a set of facts that one can expect to grow rapidly. Every time we explain a mental ability using ordinary computational processes, we will have to redraw the boundary between what the vehicle theory accounts for and what the process theory accounts for. There are only two ways for this process to be arrested or reversed: either the vehicle theorists must explain more, or the process theorists must fail to explain very much. In the first case, the vehicle theory must compete with process theory on the process theory's home field, explaining how particular behaviors and competences can result from implementing a computation in one medium rather than another. That's hard to picture. In the second case, the vehicle theory will get a tie by default; no one will have explained consciousness, so the vehicle theory will have explained it as well as anyone.

If process theory doesn't fail, however, vehicle theory will be left in an odd position indeed. Suppose we have two entities E_1 and E_2 that behave intelligently, converse on many topics, and can tell you about their experiences. Their similarity is explained by the fact that they implement the same computational processes. However, the one implemented using vehicle $V_{genuine}$ is, according to the theory, conscious. The other, implemented using vehicle V_{bogus}, is only apparently conscious. When it talks of its experiences, it's actually making meaningless sounds, which fool only those unfamiliar with the theory. Unfortunately, no matter how elegant the theory is, it won't supply any actual *evidence* favoring one vehicle over the other. By hypothesis, everything observable about the two systems is explained by the computational process they both instantiate. For instance, if you wonder why E_1 is sometimes unconscious of its surroundings when deeply involved in composing a tune, whatever explanation you arrive at will work just fine for E_2, because they implement exactly the same computational processes, except that in the case of E_2 you'll have to say, "It's 'apparently conscious' of its surroundings most of the time, except when its working on a new tune, when it's not even apparently conscious."

Vehicle theories are thus likely to be a dead end. This is not to say that the explanation of consciousness may not require new mechanisms. The point is, though, that if they are required they will still be *mechanisms*. That is, they will explain observable events. Phenomenal consciousness is not a secret mystery that is forever behind a veil. When I taste something sour, I purse my lips and complain. A theory must explain why things have tastes, but it must also explain why my lips move in those ways, and the two explanations had better be linked.

Many critics of computational theories reject the idea that phenomenal consciousness can be explained by explaining certain behaviors, such as lip pursing, or utterances such as "Whew, that's sour." But even those who believe that explaining such behavior is insufficient must surely grant that it is *necessary*. We can call this the Principle of the Necessity of Behavioral Explanation: No theory is satisfactory unless it can explain why someone having certain experiences behaves in certain characteristic ways. Naturally, process theories tend to explain behavior well and experience not so well, whereas vehicle theories tend to have the opposite problem.

Process theories tend to fall into two groups, called *first-order* and *higher-order* theories. The former are those in which in some contexts the processing of sensory information is "experience-like" in a way that allows us to say that in those contexts the processing *is* experience. Higher-order theories, on the other hand, say that to be an experience a piece of sensory information must itself be the object of perception. First-order theories include those of Kirk (1994) and Tye (1995).

Shapiro (2000) sketches what might be considered the "primordial" first-order theory:

> Why not think of our perceptual experiences as sometimes entering a channel that makes us phenomenally aware of what they represent and other times bypassing this channel? When I'm driving around town thinking about a lecture I need to prepare, my perceptions of the scenery bypass the phenomenal awareness channel. When, on the other hand, I need to attend more closely to the world, to heighten my awareness of the world, I elect (perhaps unconsciously) to make my perceptions of the world conscious. Accordingly, my perceptions of the world get funneled through the phenomenal awareness channel. Phenomenal awareness, on this picture, requires no higher-order representational capacities.

He says this model is pure speculation, so I don't suppose he would defend it if pressed, but it makes a convenient target in that its obvious flaw is shared by all first-order theories. The flaw is that nothing is said about what makes events in one channel conscious and those in another channel unconscious. In Kirk's version, sensory data that are presented to the "main assessment processes" (1994, p. 146) are experienced, whereas other sensory data are not. Why not, exactly? Just as for dualist theories and vehicle theories, first-order computational theories suffer from a disconnection between the hypothesized process and its visible effects. The theories tend to treat "conscious" as a label stuck onto some signals in the brain, without any explanation of how this labeling causes people to be able to report on those signals (while being unable to report on those without the label).

Second-order theories do not have this flaw, because they say exactly what the labels consist in: computational events whose topic is the sensory processes being labeled. Here the labels are as concrete as data structures in a computer, so there is no difficulty following the chain of causality. The difficulty is convincing anyone that the resulting system has real experiences.

I will be pursuing a second-order theory in the rest of the book. Chapter 2 is a survey of the present state of research in artificial intelligence. Chapter 3 is a detailed explanation of my theory of consciousness. Chapter 4 deals with various objections, including those alluded to in the previous paragraph. The most serious objections are based on the observation that a computational theory of mind can't be correct because concepts such as "computer" and "symbol" are ill defined. Chapter 5 deals with this issue. Chapter 6 deals with various consequences of the theory, including the impact on religion and ethics.

One feature that will strike many readers is how little I appeal to neuroscience, unlike a great many recent theories of consciousness (Flanagen 1992; Crick and Koch 1998; Churchland 1986, 1995). One reason neuroscience is so popular is that it has produced some detailed, interesting proposals for how the brain might work. Many people won't be satisfied with an explanation of thinking and consciousness that doesn't ultimately appeal to the facts of neurophysiology.

But another reason is a prejudice that the basic case of phenomenal consciousness is the quivering bit of protoplasm in contact with the cruel world. The brain feels, in the end, because it is made of living, feeling parts. I have the opposite intuition: that feeling has nothing to do with being alive. The great majority of living things never feel anything. When evolution invented feeling, it stumbled onto a phenomenon that can be elicited from a living system, but not just from living systems. A theory of phenomenal consciousness must reflect this neutrality.

Another way to put it is this: Different organisms sense vastly different things. We rely primarily on visual inputs and so we receive completely different data about the world than a bat would at the same point in space and time. But gathering data and having experiences are two different things, and it may be that adding phenomenal consciousness to data processing is always a matter of adding the same simple twist to the system. If we ever find life on other planets, we will probably find that the data they gather from their environment, and the anatomical structures they use to process them, are specific to that environment and their needs; but if they're conscious it will be because of the same trick that our brains use. *What* they're conscious of will be different, but *the way* they're conscious may be the same. The same conclusions would apply to conscious robots.

This book is mainly about philosophical questions, but I confess that I do not always feel comfortable using the usual philosophical tools to approach them. Usually this is owing to differences in training and disposition. I hope those who would feel more at home in a discussion conducted in the pure philosophical style will nevertheless bear with me, in spite of my neglect of some of the problems and issues that philosophers focus on.

For example, philosophers spend a lot of time arguing about *functionalism*. This term has several meanings. Some people treat it as synonymous with *computationalism,* the doctrine that the mind can be explained entirely in terms of computation. Since I'm defending a version of computationalism, to that extent I'm defending functionalism, too. However, there are also other meanings assigned to the term, which reduces its utility. One version may be summarized thus: what mental terms and predicates refer to is whatever fills certain causal roles in a functional description of the organism involved. For example, a statement such as "Fred is in pain" is supposed to mean, "Fred is in state X, where X is a state with the properties pain is supposed to have in a worked-out functional description of Fred, e.g., the property of causing Fred to avoid what he believes causes X." Actually, stating the full meaning requires replacing "believe" with a functionally described Y, and so forth.

The purpose of this version of functionalism is to show that, in principle, mental terms can be defined so that they can be applied to systems without making any assumptions about what those systems are made of. If pain can be defined "functionally," then we won't be tempted to define it in terms of particular physical, chemical, or neurological states. So when we find an alien staggering from its crashed spaceship and hypothesize that it is in pain, the claim won't be refutable by observing that it is composed of silicon instead of carbon.

I am obviously in sympathy with the motivation behind this project. I agree with its proponents that the being staggering from the spaceship might be in pain in spite of being totally unlike earthling animals. The question is whether we gain anything by clarifying the definitions of terms. We have plenty of clearcut mental states to study, and can save the borderline cases for later. Suppose one had demanded of Van Loewenhook and his contemporaries that they provide a similar sort of definition for the concept of life and its subconcepts, such as respiration and reproduction. It would have been a complete waste of time, because what Van Loewenhook wanted to know, and what we are now figuring out, is *how life works.* We know there are borderline cases, such as viruses, but we don't care exactly where the border lies, because our understanding encompasses both sides. The only progress we have made in defining "life" is to realize that it doesn't need to be defined. Similarly, what we want to know about minds is *how they work*. My guess is that we will figure that out, and realize that mental terms are useful and meaningful, but impossible to define precisely.

In practice people adopt what Dennett (1978a) calls the "intentional stance" toward creatures that seem to think and feel. That is, they simply *assume* that cats, dogs, and babies have beliefs, desires, and feelings roughly similar to theirs as long as the assumption accounts for their behavior better than any other hypothesis can. If there ever are intelligent robots, people will no doubt adopt the intentional stance toward them, too, regardless of what philosophers or computer scientists say about the robots' true mental states. Unlike Dennett, I don't think the success of the intentional stance settles the matter. If a system seems to act intentionally, we have to explain *why* it seems that way using evidence besides the fact that a majority of people agree that it does. People are right when they suppose babies have mental states and are wrong when they suppose the stars do.

So I apologize for not spending more time on issues such as the structure of reductionism, the difference between epistemological and metaphysical necessity, and the varieties of supervenience. I am sure that much of what I say could be said (and has been said) more elegantly using those terms, but I lack the requisite skill and patience. My main use of the philosophical literature is the various ingenious thought experiments ("intuition pumps," in Dennett's phrase) that philosophers have used in arguments. These thought experiments tend to have vivid, intuitively compelling consequences; that's their whole purpose. In addition, the apparent consequences are often completely wrong. I believe in those cases it is easy to show that they are wrong without appeal to subtle distinctions; if those familiar with the philosophical intricacies are not satisfied, there are plenty of other sources where they can find the arguments refuted in the correct style. In particular, Daniel Dennett (1991), David Rosenthal (1986, 1993), Thomas Metzinger (1995a), and William Lycan (1987, 1996) defend positions close to mine in philosophers' terms, though they each disagree with me on several points.

Several other nonphilosophers have proposed second-order theories of consciousness. Marvin Minsky is especially explicit about the role of self-models in consciousness (Minsky 1968). Douglas Hofstadter's proposals (Hofstadter 1979; Hofstadter and Dennett 1981) are less detailed, but in many ways more vivid and convincing. Michael Gazzaniga (1998) bases his ideas on neuroscience and psychology.

Adding another voice to this chorus may just confuse matters; but perhaps it may persuade a few more people, and perhaps even clarify the issues a bit.

2
Artificial Intelligence

Cognitive science is based on the idea that computation is the main thing going on in the brain. Cognitive scientists create computational models of the sorts of tasks that brains do, and then test them to see if they work. This characterization is somewhat vague because there is a wide range of models and testing strategies. Some cognitive scientists are interested in discovering exactly which computational mechanisms are used by human brains. Others are interested primarily in what mechanisms could carry out a particular task, and only secondarily in whether animal brains actually use those mechanisms.

This discipline has been around for about half a century. Before that, psychologists, linguists, neuroscientists, and philosophers asked questions about the mind, but in different ways. It was the invention of the digital computer that first opened up the possibility of using computational models to explain almost everything.

It is possible to approach cognitive science from various points of view, starting from psychology, neuroscience, linguistics, or philosophy, as previous authors have done (Jackendoff 1987; Dennett 1991; Churchland and Sejnowski 1992). My starting point is going to be computer science. The application of computer science to cognitive science is called *artificial intelligence,* or *AI.* AI has been used as a platform for a more general discussion before (Minsky 1986; Hofstadter and Dennett 1981), but rarely in a way that takes philosophical questions seriously.[1]

One misapprehension is that artificial intelligence has to do with intelligence. When the field started, it tended to focus on "intellectual" activities such as playing chess or proving theorems. It was assumed that algorithms for hard problems like these would automatically apply to other areas requiring deep thought, while "lower level" activities like walking or seeing were assumed to be relatively straightforward applications of control theory. Both of these assumptions have been abandoned. There turns out to be no "General Problem Solver"[2] that can solve a wide range of intellectual problems; and there turns out to be no precise boundary line between lower-level activities and high-level "thinking." There are plenty of boundaries between *modules,* but no difference in computational mechanism between peripheral and central modules, and no clear support for the notion that as you penetrate deeper into the brain you finally reach an area in which you find "pure intelligence."

It would be better, therefore, if AI had a different name, such as *cognitive informatics.* Since we can't wave a magic wand and cause such a terminological revolution, we will keep the old label for the field, but let me repeat: AI will have a lot to say about what role computation plays in thinking, but almost nothing to say about intelligence.

People tend to underestimate the difficulty of achieving true machine intelligence. Once they've seen a few examples, they start drawing schematic diagrams of the mind, with boxes labeled "perception" and "central executive." They then imagine how they would carry out these subtasks, and their introspections tell them it wouldn't be that hard. It doesn't take long for them to convince themselves that intelligence is a simple thing, just one step beyond Windows 98. The truth is that boxes are much easier to label than to fill in. After a while, you begin to suspect the boundaries between the boxes were misdrawn. Fifty years into the AI project, we've become much more humble. No one would presume any longer to draw a schematic for the mind. On the other hand, we have more concrete ideas for solving particular tasks.

Some of the topics in this chapter may be familiar to some readers. I urge them not to skim the chapter too hastily, though, because when I allude to computational mechanisms later in the book, I'm thinking of mechanisms such as the ones I describe here. That's not to say that there won't be plenty of new algorithms and data structures discovered in the future. I'm just not assuming the need for, or predicting the discovery of, any powerful new ideas that will revolutionize the way we think about computation in the brain. There is nothing up my sleeve.[3]

Computer Chess

To get a feel for what artificial intelligence is trying to do, let's look at a particular case history, the development of computer programs to play games such as chess. Playing chess was one of the first tasks to be considered by researchers, because the chessboard is easy to represent inside a computer, but winning the game is difficult. The game has the reputation of requiring brains to play, and very few people ever get good at it. There is no obvious algorithm for playing chess well, so it appears to be a good domain for studying more general sorts of reasoning, or it appeared that way at first. In the 1950s, Allen Newell, Clifford Shaw, and Herbert Simon wrote some papers (Newell et al. 1958) about a program they designed and partially implemented, which used general-purpose symbolic structures for representing aspects of chess positions. However, over the years chess programs have become more and more specialized, so that now there is no pretense that what they do resembles human thinking, at least not in any direct way.

Almost all chess programs work along the lines suggested in early papers by Claude Shannon and Alan Turing (Shannon 1950*a*, 1950*b*; Turing 1953), which build on work in game theory by von Neumann and Morgenstern (1944). A key feature of chess is that both players know everything about the current state of play except each other's plans. In card games a player is usually ignorant of exactly which cards the opponent has, which adds a dimension we don't need to worry about in chess, where both players can see every piece. We can use this feature to construct a simple representation of every possible continuation from a chess position. Imagine drawing a picture of the current position at the top margin of an enormous blackboard. Assuming it is your turn to move, you can then draw all the possible positions that could result from that move, and join them to the original position by lines. Now below each such position draw a picture of every position that can be reached by the opponent's next move. Continue with your move, and keep going until every possible position reachable from the original position has been drawn. (This had better be a really big blackboard.) The process will go on for a long time, but not forever, because at any position there are only a finite number of available moves and every chess game must come to an end. The resulting

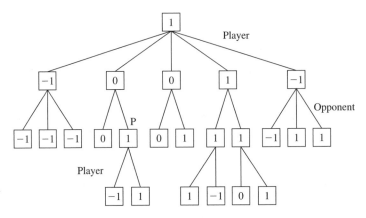

Figure 2.1
Game tree

drawing is called a *game tree* (figure 2.1). Each position is indicated by a square. Pretend the square contains a chess position reached at a certain point in a game; I'll explain the numbers shortly. The *root* of the tree is at the top and the *leaves* at the bottom. It looks more like a tree if you turn the picture upside down, but it's called a tree even though it's usually drawn with the root at the top. The root is the original position, and the leaves are the final positions, where the game has ended and no further moves are possible.

We now label the leaves with 0, 1, or −1, depending on whether the game is a draw, a win for you, or a win for your opponent, respectively. To describe what happens next I need to introduce another definition. Let the *children* of a position B refer to the positions reachable by making one move in B. (I apologize for the mixing of a family-tree metaphor with the botanical-tree metaphor.) Now pick a position P that has only leaves as its children, that is, a position in which no matter what move is made the game is over. Suppose that at that position it is your turn to move. If there is a child position labeled 1 (meaning "you win"), then you can win in position P by making the corresponding move. Hence P can be labeled 1 as well. If no child is winning, then if there is a child labeled 0 (draw), you can at least draw, so P should be labeled 0. Otherwise, no matter what you do you will lose, so P is lost, and should be labeled −1. Actually, this is impossible in chess; the last person to move can't lose. We include this possibility for completeness, because we're going to see the same pattern elsewhere in the tree: at any position where it's your turn to move, the position should be labeled 1 if any child is labeled 1; 0 if no child is labeled 1 but some child is labeled 0; and −1 if every child is labeled −1. In other words, at every position where it's your turn to move, you should label it with the maximum of the labels attached to its children. At positions where it's the opponent's turn to move, you should, by a similar argument, place a label equal to the *minimum* of the labels attached to the children.

If we continue in this way we will eventually label every position. The original position will be labeled 1 if you can force a win, −1 if your opponent can, and 0 if neither of you can. This claim may not seem obvious, so let's consider in more detail the strategy you can follow if the label is 1. There must be some child position labeled 1, so pick one and make the move that gets you there. At this position it is the opponent's turn to move, so if it's labeled 1 then every child position must be labeled 1. So no matter what the opponent does, you will be in a situation like the one you started with: you will have a position with at least one child position labeled 1. You will be able to make the corresponding move, and then wait for the opponent to pick among unappetizing choices. No matter what happens, you'll always have a position labeled 1 and can therefore always force a situation where the opponent must move from a position labeled 1. Sooner or later you'll get to a position one step from a leaf, where you have a move that wins.

This idea was first made explicit by von Neumann and Morgenstern. It sounds like a surefire recipe for winning at chess (and any other board game with complete information about the state of play and no random element such as dice or roulette wheels). Of course, no person can play the game this way, because the equipment (an enormous blackboard) is too unwieldy, and it would take way too long to work out the whole game tree. But computers can get around these problems, right? They can use some kind of database to represent the tree of positions, and use their awesome speed to construct the tree and label all the positions.

No, they can't. There is no problem representing the board positions. We can use a byte to represent the state of a square, and 64 bytes to represent the board.[4] It's not hard to compute the set of all possible moves from a position. There are a finite number, and there are unambiguous rules that determine how each piece can move. The problem is that there are just too many possible positions. At the start of the game White (who always moves first) has 12 possible moves, and Black has 12 possible replies. As the game progresses, the number typically grows, then shrinks again when lots of pieces are off the board. A game can go on for a long time, but some games are over quickly. An accurate estimate of how big the game tree is would have to deal with these factors of varying width and depth of the tree, but we will neglect all complexities in the interest of getting a quick but crude estimate. For simplicity, let's just assume there are 10 possible moves at each position and that the entire tree is 100 ply deep. A *ply* is a move by one player, so a 50-move game corresponds to 100 ply. The total number of positions after one ply is 10; from each of those we can reach 10 more, so the number reachable in two ply is 10×10, or 100. After three ply the number is $10 \times 10 \times 10 = 1000$. Past this point writing out the multiplications gets tedious, so we use the abbreviation 10^3, or, after n ply, 10^n. This number, written out, is 1 followed by n zeroes. The number of leaves in the tree is, therefore, about 10^{100}. This is a huge number. If the computer could examine a billion positions (10^9) a second, and it was started when the earth first formed about 5 billion years ago, it would have examined only about 10^{26} positions so far. If it lasts another 50 billion, it will get to 10^{27}. Furthermore, the result of the search would have to be stored somehow. We need to know the first magic move, and then for each possible reply we have to store at least one winning move. That means that at positions where the opponent moves we must represent all the possibilities, while at positions where you move we need represent only one. That cuts the stored tree down to a size of only 10^{50}. A ten-gigabyte hard disk can store 10^{10} bytes. We will need 10^{40} ten-gigabyte disks to store all the positions in the tree. Suppose each hard drive is 1 cm on a side. The volume of the earth is about 10^{12} cubic meters, so if the earth were hollowed out and used to hold hard drives it could hold 10^{18} of them. So we'll need 10^{22} earth-sized planets to hold all the data. I belabor all this because it is easy to misjudge just how large these numbers are. Once you grasp their size you realize why it is that no two chess games are alike; there is always a large amount of uncharted territory that one or both of the players can push the board into.

It is unlikely that a computer could ever be built that could construct more than a small fragment of the game tree for chess. But perhaps a small fragment is all that is necessary. As first suggested by Shannon, a computer could construct all the positions reachable in, say, five ply. At that point it could apply a *position-evaluation function,* which would look at factors like the number of remaining pieces belonging to each player, pawn structure, piece mobility, king safety, and so on in order to come up with an estimate of which player is winning. The numbers wouldn't have to be 1, 0, or −1. We could use numbers like 0.3 to indicate a slight advantage for White, or −0.9 to indicate a big advantage for Black. The computer can then use the same labeling idea, taking the maximum of child labels at a position where it is to move, the minimum where its opponent is to move.

This idea underlies almost all chess-playing programs. There are a lot of possible enhancements. The position-evaluation function can be tuned differently for middle game and end game. There are ways of pruning the tree slightly, so that once a good move has been found the computer can skip examining some of the other branches. One can streamline data structures and optimize move-generation algorithms. Good openings can be prestored so that the computer just plays them, doing no game-tree generation at all, just as a grandmaster does. If a position can be reached by two different sequences of moves, the computer can avoid exploring it twice. You can also buy a faster computer. One way to do that is to use several computers to explore the game tree in parallel. However, by itself this step doesn't get you very far, as the numbers above suggest.

Another possible line of attack is to observe how human experts play chess and try to duplicate their skills. This was what Newell and Simon tried. They were interested in questions such as, what do human players look at when they look at a board? What hypotheses do they form about key features of the current position? They thought that answers to these questions might give them ideas they could incorporate into computer programs. However, even though a few things were learned about human play, none of this knowledge is used in the design of today's programs. Nonetheless, these programs play very well, as was shown dramatically in 1997 when a computer, Deep Blue, constructed and programmed by programmers from IBM, beat Garry Kasparov, who is probably the best human chessplayer. Deep Blue used a combination of parallelism and an excellent position-evaluation function to beat Kasparov.

When this happened, it made headlines all over the world. Every newspaper and magazine ran opinion pieces. Most of the writers of those pieces argued that the computer's victory should not be a threat to our position as the most intelligent species on the planet. There were several main lines of argument. Some pointed to the fact that the methods used by Deep Blue are very different from the methods used by human players. Some argued that Deep Blue's narrowness meant that it wasn't really intelligent; sure it could win the game, but it couldn't even see the board, and when you come down to it, it didn't care whether it won or not. Some believed that the fact that Deep Blue had to be programmed meant that its programmers were intelligent, not the machine itself. And some pointed out that chess is a finite world, so computers were bound to become fast enough to search enough of its ramifications to win.

I don't think these arguments are as strong as they seem at first. But before I address them, let me point out that the evolution of chess programs has been similar to the evolution of AI systems in general. In the early days, researchers in the field tended to assume that there were general algorithmic principles underlying human thought, so that (a) these could be embodied as all-purpose intelligent algorithms, and (b) these algorithms would resemble humans in their style of thinking. As time has gone by, systems have gotten more and more specialized. A researcher in computer vision, which is defined as the attempt to extract information from visual images, deals with completely different issues from those explored by computer-chess researchers, or researchers working on understanding natural language, scheduling resources for companies, and proving mathematical theorems. Within these specialties there are subspecialties. People working in stereo vision (comparing information from two eyes to estimate depth) do not use the same methods as people studying processing images over time. If there are general principles of reasoning, they don't play a role in most of what gets studied nowadays.

In addition, the principles of computer reasoning don't seem much like the principles of human reasoning, at least not those we are introspectively aware of. A chess master will explore a tree of moves, but not every legal move, only those that make sense. Computers usually look at every move at a given position. This is a pattern that we see a lot: the computer is good at exhaustively sifting through possibilities, while the person is good at insight and judgment. It is this striking difference that many people adverted to in the reassuring editorials that appeared after Deep Blue beat Kasparov.

I think this reassurance is illusory, for the following reasons:

1. Insight and judgment are not the names of techniques used by the brain; they are words used to praise the brain's output.

2. The method used by the brain to arrive at insightful results might, when implemented on a computer, involve a lot of exhaustive sifting.

These points are frequently misunderstood, and explaining them further will be one of my main goals in this chapter.

People often find the digital computer to be a ridiculous model of the human brain. It executes a single instruction at a time, pulling small chunks of data in from memory to a central processing unit where various tiny little operations are done to them, and pushing the results back out to memory, all of this happening repeatedly and repetitively, billions of times a second. What in the brain or mind looks like that? The answer is: nothing. There is no way that a brain can be thought of as a digital computer.

This fact is, however, completely irrelevant. Our hypothesis is that the brain is using neurons to do computation. The hypothesis implies that what's important about a neuron is not the chemicals it secretes or the electrical potentials it generates, but the content of the information encoded in those physical media. If you could encode the information in another set of physical properties, and still do the same computation, you could replace a neuron with an equivalent computational device in another medium, and it wouldn't make any difference. You could replace *all* the neurons in a brain with one or more digital computers simulating them, and the brain would be just as good. The point is that the digitalness of the computer is a red herring. Animals need things to be computed in the same sense that they need blood to be circulated. There are many different technologies that can carry out these computations. Each technology will approximate the answer slightly differently, and thereby introduce slightly different errors, but as long as the errors are small these discrepancies will be irrelevant. Neurons are wonderful biological computers, but there is nothing magical about them. Digital computers are just as good in some ways. Above all, they are much more flexible. We can reprogram them overnight. For that reason they are a superb tool for exploration of hypotheses about what it is neural systems are trying to compute.

The question I raised above is whether the methods used by Deep Blue are intrinsically less insightful and more exhaustive than the methods used by Garry Kasparov and other grandmasters. The answer is that nobody knows. There has been some work on the psychology of chess playing (deGroot 1965; Chase and Simon 1973), but it really doesn't tell us what good chess players are doing. If you ask them, they can give you lots of fascinating advice. Here is the "thinking technique" recommended by Silman (1993):

1. Figure out the positive and negative imbalances for *both sides*.
2. Figure out the side of the board you wish to play on....
3. Don't calculate! Instead, dream up various fantasy positions, i.e., the positions you would most like to achieve.
4. Once you find a fantasy position that makes you happy, you must figure out if you can reach it. If you find that your choice was not possible to implement, you must create another dream position that is easier to achieve.
5. Only now do you look at the moves you wish to calculate....

This may superficially appear to be an algorithm. Each step appears to call a subroutine,[5] and there's even a little loop from step 4 back to step 3. However, this is an illusion. Although Silman gives some further elaboration of each step, such as listing the different kinds of imbalance one is to look for in step 1, it remains true that you can't even begin to follow his advice until you are a pretty good chess player. He's basically telling you how to "get organized." The details are up to you. You might ask, how does a good chess player find "imbalances" in a position? Why does a grandmaster find imbalances better than a mediocre player? Unfortunately, no one really knows. The literature cited above seems to indicate that a grandmaster has a huge store of previously seen positions that he or she can access. Given a new position, two or three relevant positions from this collection come to mind. How are they stored and how are they accessed? No one knows. The key point for us, however, is that looking up these positions in memory requires a lot of work by a lot of neurons. Each neuron is performing a tiny piece of the job. Each piece involves no insight or judgment at all. If we implemented the process on a digital computer, it would look a lot like exhaustive sifting. So the fact that Deep Blue does a tremendous amount of "brute force" computation is, in itself, irrelevant to the question of whether it is intelligent; we know from our own example that insight can be the result of millions of uninsightful computations.

One can still be reassured by one of the arguments I mentioned above, that Deep Blue is too narrow to be truly intelligent. For the time being, we can expect programs to solve a handful of well-defined tasks and be completely oblivious to other demands of a situation. But the other arguments are mirages. The fact that it took intelligence to program the computer says nothing about the mental capacity of the resulting program. The fact that a game or other problem domain is finite does not imply that eventually computers will become fast enough to solve them. Deep Blue embodied many algorithmic advances, as well as being quite fast. There are plenty of "finite" but enormous domains that computers will never conquer merely by running faster. Finally, the argument that Deep Blue's methods are "exhaustive" in a way that people are not is, as I have shown, based on a quick jump to a conclusion that cannot withstand serious examination.

Neural Nets

I have argued that digital computers are useful for studying mental processes because mental processes are ultimately computational, and digital computers are the Swiss Army knife of computation. This account of where they fit into the explanatory landscape of the brain and its activities seems pretty straightforward to me. However, there is a competing story, which goes like this: There was once a field called Good Old Fashioned Artificial Intelligence (GOFAI, to use an acronym coined by John Haugeland 1985). It was based on a model of mind as a symbol-manipulation system. In this framework, the beliefs of the mind are represented as expressions in a formal language not unlike the language of mathematical logic. The central processor of this mind takes groups of expressions and derives new expressions from them. The expressions have a formal *denotational semantics;* each symbol denotes an object or relationship in the world the computer is reasoning about. The inputs to the system are expressions describing the objects and events in the mind's vicinity, as revealed by the senses; the output is a series of expressions telling the muscles (or computer screen) what to do. Exactly what it means to derive an expression from some precursor expressions is not clear, but the ideal case is deduction, where the derived expression must be true if the precursor expressions are.

This paradigm is usually described in order to be contrasted, often unfavorably, with more recent paradigms, especially the use of artificial neural networks, which are supposed to transcend some of the limitations of GOFAI. Neural networks are made of units that mimic some of the operations of real neurons, as described in chapter 1, but they are simpler. I will use the word "neuron" to refer to these units, but bear in mind that the real thing is more complex, in ways we don't really understand yet. The artificial neurons are connected to each other by links. A neuron will have several input links and one output link, although the output can split and connect to the inputs of several other neurons. The output is typically a number between 0 and 1, 0 corresponding to inactivity in a biological neuron, and 1 corresponding to maximum output (maximum rate of firing). The inputs are weighted and summed. That is, if neuron T receives input from neurons A, B, and C, then the net input is $w_A V_A + w_B V_B + w_C V_C$. The output is high (close to 1) if the net input is over a threshold t, and low if it is under the threshold (figure 2.2a). The neuron's behavior is entirely described by specifying its weights and threshold.

There are many variations on this theme. Sometimes cycles in the net are allowed, so that a neuron's output impacts on neurons whose outputs eventually come back to the original neuron's input. In other cases there are no cycles, but instead there is a distinct input layer of neurons that feeds a second layer, and so forth, until we reach an output layer. In any case, the overall net must ultimately receive input from outside the net, and send output somewhere else as well (figure 2.2b).

At first glance this seems like a very different model of computation from the computers we are used to, with their CPUs, instruction streams, and formal languages. These differences have caused many philosophers to view neural nets as a fundamentally different paradigm for computation from the standard digital one. They have endorsed the phrase

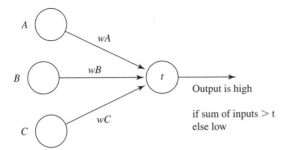

(a) Single neuron

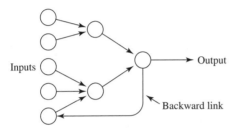

(b) Network of neurons

Figure 2.2
Neural nets

connectionism as a tag for the doctrine that millions of small units sending small signals over wires is better than the "good old-fashioned" research paradigm. This whole theory is based on exaggeration of superficial differences. Anything that can be computed by a neural net can also be computed by a digital computer. In fact, no one actually bothers to build neural nets; they're all simulated on ordinary computers. The reason should be obvious: it's much easier to experiment with software than with hardware, and you don't lose any meaningful accuracy by simulating with a digital computer.

One reason neural nets have attracted so much attention is that they suggest a model of learning that is close to the way brains appear to learn. In brains learning can occur by alterations in the strength of synapses, and in the sensitivity of membranes to stimulation. In the artificial model, the corresponding changes are to the weights and thresholds. After every computation, the weights can be changed a little bit so that the next time the result will be slightly more accurate. After many such "training" sessions, the net can become quite good at some tasks. For example, the TD-gammon program of Gerald Tesauro (1995) learns to play the game of backgammon. It does not construct a game tree, because backgammon involves throwing dice, which makes the number of possible positions too large to search. Instead, it tries to recognize patterns that tell it which side is winning in any particular position. It can then make a move by picking the move that appears to improve its chances the most. The program was trained by having it play hundreds of thousands of games against itself. It eventually became the strongest backgammon program in the world.

I use the word "program" here because TD-gammon, like almost every other neural network, never existed as a piece of hardware, that is, as a collection of neurons. It was a garden-variety program with one data structure representing the weights, another representing the outputs, and so forth. A subroutine determined the output given the current input and weights, and another program figured out how the weights should change after every move. Once again, the digital computer is playing the role of "universal computational solvent" that makes it so useful for so many applications.

One difference often claimed to separate GOFAI systems from neural nets is that the former are "symbolic" and the latter are "nonsymbolic." Sometimes the word "subsymbolic" (Smolensky 1988) is used to describe neural nets, as though symbols were slow, rare creatures whose graceful flights above the mental landscape were supported by invisible neural monorails. I will discuss symbols in depth in chapter 5, but it's important to dispel these misconceptions immediately. There are symbols all over the place in just about any computational system. Some of them are used to denote objects outside the system, but many are simply computational placeholders, like the little digits you write above a column of numbers you are carrying into.

Neural nets can have both kinds of symbol. Consider the case of the visual system of the frog. One of the major functions of this system, as is well known (Lettvin et al. 1951), is to detect small flying insects. When the visual image of a small object passes rapidly across the frog's retina, signals are sent from the retina to the brain that cause the frog to orient to the small object and jump toward it while opening its mouth and whipping out its tongue. The system works no matter what part of the retina the small object appears on; which part it appears on determines which way the frog points. Obviously, the visual system is condensing the information on the retina, extracting the small nugget of information that the frog needs. Somewhere between the retina and the muscles of the tongue there is a signal that causes the frog to attack; this same signal is produced by a wide variety of retinal subsystems. Hence we can identify the symbol structure "attack in direction D" as the state of the retinal subsystems that initiates the attack and orients it toward D (Fodor 1986).

There must be millions of examples of symbols of this kind in complicated mammalian brains. We can often plausibly argue for the presence of a symbol even when we lack any neurophysiological evidence for how it is implemented. Suppose an animal sees a predator at a certain range and distance. We can tell a story similar to the one we told about the frog (with the opposite sign: retreat rather than attack). But I want to focus on what happens when the prey sees the predator for only an instant, after which it is seen to disappear behind a hedge. After that point, the visual system is reporting "hedge" about that part of the visual field. But the prey animal does not relax. It continues to react in much the same way as it would if a predator were in plain view. There must be some internal state of the prey animal that preserves the information about the approximate location of the predator. This state is a symbol that stands for the predator.

The conventional wisdom is that *this* kind of symbol is not the kind that GOFAI made use of. Unfortunately, it is hard to find programs that actually used symbols in the way that conventional wisdom so fondly remembers. Just about every program ever written violates the supposed constraints on "good old-fashioned" systems, which are supposed to manipulate a formal language with a denotational semantics, deriving one expression from another in a way that is paradigmatically deductive.

Here is how Stevan Harnad characterizes "symbolic" computation:

A symbol system is:

1. a set of arbitrary "physical tokens," scratches on paper, holes on a tape, events in a digital computer, etc. that are

2. manipulated on the basis of "explicit rules" that are

3. likewise physical tokens and strings of tokens. The rule-governed symbol-token manipulation is based

4. purely on the shape of the symbol tokens (not their "meaning"), i.e., it is purely syntactic, and consists of

5. "rulefully combining" and recombining symbol tokens. There are

6. primitive atomic symbol tokens and

7. composite symbol-token strings. The entire system and all its parts—the atomic tokens, the composite tokens, the syntactic manipulations both actual and possible and the rules—are all

8. "semantically interpretable": The syntax can be systematically assigned a meaning e.g., as standing for objects, as describing states of affairs).

... All eight of the properties listed above seem to be critical to this definition of symbolic. (Harnad 1990)

If these properties are critical, then there has never been a symbolic computation system. In particular, the requirements that symbol manipulation be governed by explicit rules, that symbols be combined only into strings, and that symbols be semantically interpretable are never (or almost never) satisfied.

Consider the chess program again. It manipulates a vector of bytes representing a chess position. It is tempting to say that this vector obviously has a rigid formal meaning, but the temptation is misguided. It's true that the programmer knows what the data structures mean, in the sense that the program is not gibberish, but the same can be said of any data structures, including the ones implementing a neural network. The hypothesis that there was something special about GOFAI revolved around some specific theories of meaning that were developed by mathematical logicians in the first half of the twentieth century, notably Alfred Tarski (1956) and Rudolf Carnap (1942, 1947). Under these theories, a formal language is a purely syntactic object until it is given an *interpretation*, a mapping of its expressions to objects in some universe. Originally the theory focused on universes of mathematical objects, because the main purpose of the theory was to understand the foundations of mathematics. But Carnap and others (such as Richard Montague and Donald Davidson) thought that the theory might shed light on human languages and their meanings, and they tried hard to apply it to them.

Whether they succeeded or not, the fact is that it's very hard to apply their theory to a chess program. At first glance it seems obvious that, say, the code −1 might occur somewhere to indicate that a black pawn is on a certain square, and that therefore "−1" denotes "black pawn." Fair enough, but notice that matters are not quite so straightforward. If I ask you to point to the object being denoted, you probably can't. Suppose the game is being displayed on the screen of your terminal. Is it a particular picture of a pawn that the symbol denotes? Not really. If you turn the screen off, the picture ceases to exist but the pawn does not. Suppose you set up the pieces physically. Does the −1 in cell ⟨0, 1⟩ of the array denote the black pawn on square a2? Maybe. But suppose you are carrying on a correspondence game, and the computer's opponent has his or her own physical board set up in another city. Does the symbol denote both black pawns? If your board is set up only between the time you receive the opponent's next move and the time you respond with the computer's, and the opponent's board is set up only when he or she is contemplating a move, what does the data structure denote the rest of the time (assuming the computer keeps running all the time)?

These questions may seem silly, but the key point is that they obviously have nothing at all to do with the way the program works. The person who wrote the program never thought about the issue. It's part of the flexibility of a digital computer that no one *ever* has to think about it. The computer doesn't care what the symbols mean, so they can mean anything or nothing. The only important question is whether the program does something useful.

I raise these difficulties in connection with a case that ought to fit the GOFAI paradigm perfectly if there were such a thing as GOFAI, in order to show that there isn't. As soon as we turn to almost any other data structure we find these issues of semantics getting worse and worse. For example, what do the labels on the positions represent? Recall that we label positions with positive numbers if they appear to be good for the computer, and negative if they appear to be good for the opponent. So what do they denote? "Goodness"? To claim so is to claim that goodness is something that exists in the world whether it's noticed or not, so that the computer can have a symbol denoting it. That might be true, but if so the symbol doesn't denote real goodness, but only an approximation to it. (And, of course, exactly the same kind of number is manipulated by TD-Gammon, which is supposed to follow a completely different paradigm.)

It is possible, by sufficient contortion, to find a sense in which a chess program is actually deducing something about a position. We might say: It's deducing that *if* the goodness of all those leaf positions are as stated, *then* the proper move at this position is such-and-such. And *to the extent* that piece count, pawn structure, king safety, and such are the only factors in goodness, *then* the goodness of the position is the computed number.

Computers don't deduce conclusions about things; they perform computations about them. Whether or not the results of the computations constitute inferences requires a separate analysis for each case. The symbols manipulated during the course of the computation may or may not denote anything; they can be useful computational markers even if they denote nothing at all. If symbols do denote anything, it's because they are connected by the right kind of causal chains to the things they denote. *These facts are just as true for neural networks as for any other sort of computer.* I will return to these issues in chapter 5.

There is one other point to make about the underlying similarity between neural nets and game-tree-search programs. Tesauro quotes Kit Woolsey, a world-class backgammon player, as making the following appraisal of TD-Gammon's abilities:

> There is no question that its positional judgment is far better than mine. Only on small technical areas can I claim a definite advantage over it.... I find a comparison of TD-Gammon and the high-level chess computers fascinating. The chess computers are tremendous in tactical positions where variations can be calculated out. Their weakness is in vague positional games, where it is not obvious what is going on.... TD-Gammon is just the opposite. Its strength is in the vague positional battles where judgment, not calculation, is the key. There it has a definite edge over humans.... In particular, its judgment on bold vs. safe play decisions, which is what backgammon really is all about, is nothing short of phenomenal.

The conclusion I want to draw your attention to is this: In the details of the operations they perform, TD-Gammon and Deep Blue are indistinguishable. Any observer, looking at the microsteps of their computations, would see roughly the same mundane things: additions, multiplications, conditional branches. But step back, and in one system one style of play becomes visible, in the other something quite different. The moral is that knowing that each step a process takes is "mechanical," or that the number of steps is so astronomical as to constitute "brute force," tells you nothing about the properties of the overall process, and in particular nothing about the insight and judgment it manifests.

Vision

So far we have considered applications of AI to game playing, which may require intelligence but probably have little bearing on behavior in the real world. This is *not* because of some intrinsic limitation on search and neural nets, but just because it seemed simpler to start with the kind of closed, well-defined world created by the rules of a game.

Getting a computer to thrive in the real world immediately raises the problem of getting information into the computer and allowing its behavior to change the things around it. Getting information in is the problem of *sensing;* behaving is the problem of *robotics.* To these we now turn. We will focus on computer vision. This is the sense modality most thoroughly studied, presumably because scientists are primates and have excellent vision themselves.

Biological vision systems are very good at finding moving objects in images. Indeed, the primitive visual systems of frogs and similar animals see very little except moving objects. Since the work of the psychologist J. J. Gibson, many have used the concept of *optical flow* to think about processing changing images. Imagine capturing the state of the image over a small time interval and watching where each part of the image moves. For example, imagine you're on a roller coaster, zooming down the track. Everything in the image is moving, except a point directly in front of you, the point you're headed toward. But if you're rounding a corner, then nothing in the image is stationary. At each point in the image, draw an arrow in the direction that piece of the image is moving, and make the arrow longer if that piece is moving faster. When I say "point," I mean mathematical point, so there is an infinite number of arrows; this is an abstract vector field. The flow field is useful in a couple of ways. If you are moving, the stationary point, if there is one, tells you what your immediate target is. Points nearer by are moving faster, so the field tells you the approximate distance of objects. If you are not moving, then the flow field tells you what is moving; if you're a frog, a small moving object is lunch. See figure 2.3a, showing the flow field a person might see as she exits a building.

It is possible to state a precise relationship between the way the image changes as you move across it spatially and the way it changes at a particular point over time. An example appears in figure 2.3b. Suppose

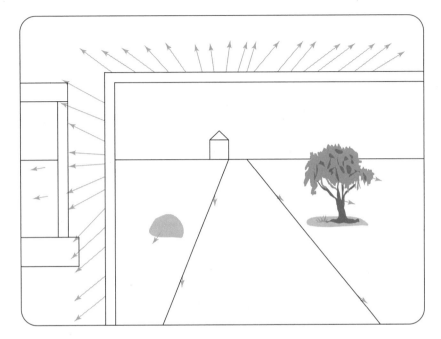

Figure 2.3a
Optical flow

Figure 2.3b
Moving patch

an image consists of a dark patch moving over a white background. The patch is not uniform, but is a darker gray in the middle than at the edges. Consider what happens at a point P as the right edge of the patch moves over it. At one instant the brightness is $I(P, 0)$; after the patch has moved

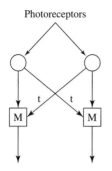

Photoreceptors

"t" indicates short time delay

Figure 2.3c
Two motion detectors (from Sekuler et al., fig. 1C)

for a short length of time t, the brightness is reduced to $I(P, t)$. But if the dark patch doesn't change as it moves, it is possible to predict this change by looking at the piece that's coming. Letting v be the velocity of the patch, it will travel distance vt over the time interval t, so the brightness value that's at point vt to the left of P now will be over P after the interval. Calling this value $I(P - vt, 0)$, we can conclude

$$I(P, t) = I(P - vt, 0).$$

In other words, if we know v we can predict the change in brightness value at P by "peeking" to the left to see what's coming. However, what we want to do is the opposite: figure out the value of v by matching up the temporal brightness change at a single point in the image (the left side of the equation) with the spatial brightness change at a single point in time (the right side of the equation). The flow field is just the value of v at every point.[6]

Actually computing the field requires coping with the fact that we can't really list the value of the field at the infinite number of points in the image and points in time. One way to cope is to approximate by laying a grid over the image, and finding the value several times a second at every square of the grid. If the grid is fine enough, the resulting approximation will give you all the information you need. Not surprisingly, both the biological vision system and the digital vision system use such an approximation. The digital system represents the image and the flow field as arrays of numbers, and the biological system represents them by the activity levels of arrays of cells in the retina of the eye and visual cortex of the brain. The computer's arrays are more regular, but that's a detail. The computer solves the equation numerically by performing repeated numerical operations at every grid square, or *pixel,* of the image. The brain of an animal solves it by allowing a neuron reacting to the brightness level at one place to compare it to the recent brightness stored at a neighboring neuron (Reichardt 1961, Sekuler et al. 1990). In figure 2.3c, two motion-detection cells, labeled "M," are connected to two nearby receptor cells with delays (labeled) in between. As a pattern moves across the two receptors, the M cells are able to compare the brightness at a point with the recent brightness at a nearby point. This is the biological system's way of comparing $I(P, t)$ with $I(P - vt, 0)$.

The key point is that both schemes rely on approximations of the underlying abstract mathematical objects. They work because the approximations are close enough. The details of the hardware, whether cells or silicon, are not important, provided they don't get in the way.

There are obvious differences between the two cases. The visual system must have many pairs of cells, one for each possible position, orientation, and velocity of a patch moving across the eye. A given motion detector can only tell you the motion at a certain point, in a certain direction, and at a certain speed.[7] To compute the whole field you have to provide a stupendous number of cells, each of which does a tiny bit of the computation. The digital computer may employ a stupendous number of silicon memory chips, but all the numbers pulled from those chips go through a small number of CPUs, each working blindingly fast. The digital computer exhibits what is called a *von Neumann architecture;*[8] the neural system has a *connectionist architecture,* because every interaction between two computations must be manifest in an explicit connection between the neural structures that perform them. But, as I have argued already, this is a difference that makes no difference, a matter of minor economic constraints on the materials at hand.

Another difference is that the computer implementation is the result of a deliberate attempt by vision researchers to solve an equation, whereas the biological system was designed by evolution—that is, not designed at all. So we must be cautious in claiming that the equation explains the structure of the biological system. Nonetheless, this kind of claim is not that unusual. Suppose that we are trying to explain photosynthesis, and we produce a thermodynamic analysis that shows that the maximum amount of energy that can be extracted from sunlight is X. Then we find a mechanism in plants that comes close to extracting that amount. The existence of the mechanism is explained by pointing out the need and the analysis. Of course, many gaps are left. We have to explain how the mechanism can have arisen from a series of mutations. We have to argue that the energy required to create and sustain the mechanism is less than X. We might even have to argue that the mechanism confers no other large benefit on the plant, whose existence might lead us to a different or complementary explanation of its evolution. This is a topic I will return to (in chapter 5).

Robotics

Vision and other sensor systems give an organism information about the world around it. The main use of this information is to guide the organism's motion through the world. The word "robot" is used to refer to a mechanical analogue: a creature that uses motors to control the motion of its body and limbs.

The problem of controlling motion using sensors is difficult for several reasons. One is that robots are more complex than traditional machines. An automobile engine contains many moving parts, but they're all moving along fixed trajectories. A piston goes back and forth in exactly the same way millions of times, causing the crankshaft to rotate the same way on each occasion. But consider an arm consisting of a shoulder, an elbow, a wrist, a hand, and several fingers. When the elbow and wrist are extended, the arm is the shape of a beam, and the shoulder must support the movement of a beam. If the arm is extended and holding a heavy object (such as a bag of garbage), the beam's physical characteristics change completely, but the shoulder muscles must still control its motion. When the elbow is bent, the same shoulder is the pivot for an object of an entirely different shape. When the elbow is bent and the hand is positioned near a table (to do some work on a watch, for instance), then the shoulder and elbow must move in such a way as to keep the hand near its position while allowing the fingers to manipulate things. So the general motion problem is to move some parts of the arm-hand system in a desired motion, carrying loads of different sizes, while other parts obey constraints on their possible locations and velocities.

That's one bundle of difficulties. Another is that the world imposes constraints on the possible locations of the parts of the system. If you're working on an automobile engine, your arm must fit around the contours of the engine and its compartment.

But the worst problem is that it is not easy to obtain from the sensors the information required to control motion. We saw in the last section how hard it is to compute the optical flow. We are now asking for something much more precise: the exact three-dimensional structure of, say, an automobile engine. Extracting this information is possible, but it's not clear that you can get everything you need to guide an arm. There are several methods for extracing three-dimensional structure from an image. One is to use two eyes, and use the slight differences between the two images to compute depths of points; another is to shine a laser at different points of an object and measure how long it takes for the pulse to return. Obviously, the former method, *stereoscopic vision,* is used by animals (including us), and the latter, *laser rangefinding,* is not. There are less obvious techniques, such as noticing how texture and shadows change as a surface curves away from the eye. Optical flow gives depth information; objects that are closer tend to move faster across the eye. Using these techniques one can recover a *depth map,* which gives the distance from the eye of every pixel in the image. This is almost the same as a three-dimensional model of the object; it represents that shape from the point of view of the eye, and it's a straightforward mathematical operation to transform it to represent the shape from any other desired point of view.

Unfortunately, except for laser rangefinding, all of these techniques tend to yield inaccurate depth maps, and in any case a depth map is not a complete representation of the three-dimensional shape of the object being seen. It's almost one but not quite. By definition it says nothing about pieces of the object that are not visible, which includes at least half of it. (See figure 2.4, which shows the depth map generated from a 3/4 view of a bucket.) The eye can move to take in more of the object, but that requires knitting together depth maps taken from more than one point of view.

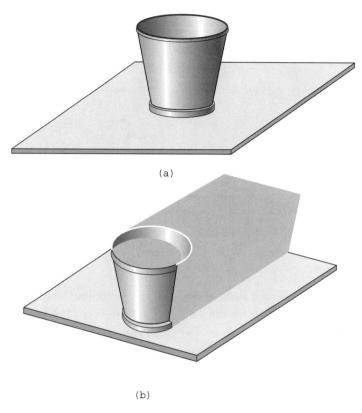

(a)

(b)

Figure 2.4
(a) Bucket. (b) Depth map from (a) (seen from the side)

It may be possible to solve these problems, but it may also be unnecessary. There isn't much hard evidence that the human visual-motor system constructs an accurate three-dimensional model of the objects in view before beginning to interact with them. As we interact with an object, we keep looking at it and are constantly acquiring new views of it. As we move our hands close to a part of the object, we can see our fingers getting closer to it without knowing exactly where either the object or the hand is. And, of course, we have our sense of touch to tell us when the hand (or the elbow) has bumped into something, whether we see the collision or not.

We can use the same approach in a robotic system, on a more modest scale. Suppose we want the robot to align a screwdriver with a screw. The screw is sticking up out of a surface, and the robot is supposed to

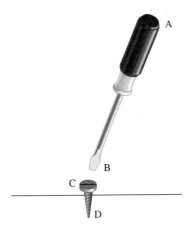

Figure 2.5
Screwdriver control

screw it down flush with the surface (figure 2.5). This requires lining up four points: the place where the screw enters the surface, the head of the screw, the blade of the screwdriver, and the handle of the screwdriver (points A, B, C, and D in figure 2.5). These four points are really defined in three-dimensional space, but all the robot knows is where they are in the image, a two-dimensional space. Under the expected range of motions, these four points will not change their appearance very much. So we can define them as visual patterns that the vision system should keep track of as the hand moves. Now our control algorithm can work as follows: Draw line segments $A'B'$ and $C'D'$, joining the centers of the visual patterns corresponding to points A and B, and C and D, respectively. If the two line segments are not collinear, move the screwdriver a little bit (the exact motion depends on the discrepancy in direction of $A'B'$ and $C'D'$, as well as how far the line containing $A'B'$ is from the line containing $C'D'$; the details are beyond the scope of this book). After the motion, take another picture. Presumably $A'B'$ is closer to the line containing $C'D'$, so the operation is repeated, until the two segments are collinear.

This procedure will not guarantee that the physical points A, B, C, and D are collinear. If they lie in a plane, and that plane is parallel to the line of sight, then they will look collinear no matter what their true alignment. Any variation in position in that plane will be invisible to the camera. However, if we use *two* cameras looking from slightly different directions, then it is possible to align the screwdriver with the screw using only measurements in the image (Hager 1997), without ever having to infer the three-dimensional position of any of the objects involved.

A very different problem in robotics is the problem of map learning. Many animals do an amazingly good job of getting from one place to another. Bees find their way to flower beds, birds find their way south in the winter, and many mammals, including humans, roam a large territory without getting lost. The field of *map learning* has the goal of giving robots a similar set of skills.

The word "map" may have misleading connotations. One pictures a folded piece of paper with a schematic picture of the world on it. Such a picture might indeed be a necessary component of a map, but it omits an important factor, namely, what a point on the map looks like when you're there. Without this information, you will know which way to turn at every point on the trip, but you won't know when you're at that point. The only reason a road map is usable is that it shows the names of streets and roads, and, if you're lucky,[9] there are street signs displaying the same names. That's normally all you need to know about what the place looks like. In environments less structured than street networks, you must store more and different information about what the places look like when you're there.

Animals use a variety of techniques for figuring out where they are (Gallistel 1990; Muller et al. 1991). One technique is *dead reckoning,* in which the animal keeps track of every step and turn it takes after leaving home, adding up all those little motions to figure out what its net motion from home has been. It can then find its way back by turning in the direction of home and heading straight there. Robots can do this, too, but not as well. They do it by counting things like the number of times their wheels have turned. A typical robot changes its heading by having one wheel rotate more than the other, so a difference in the rotation counts for the two wheels translates into a change in the direction the robot is moving. Unfortunately, even though the robot can measure fairly small fractions of a wheel rotation, slight errors in the measurement translate into significant errors in the robot's estimate of its heading. Every time a robot turns it loses track of its orientation by a couple of degrees, so a few

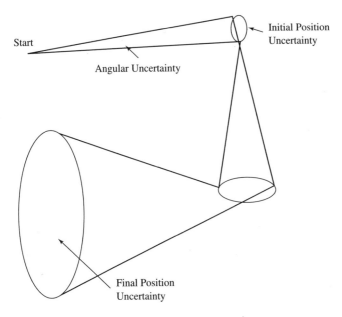

Start

Initial Position
Uncertainty

Angular Uncertainty

Final Position
Uncertainty

Figure 2.6
Positional uncertainty due to angular uncertainty

turns leave it rather disoriented. If the robot travels a long distance in an uncertain direction, a seemingly small direction uncertainty can translate into a large position uncertainty. In figure 2.6, the robot has no uncertainty at all about the distance it travels, and it knows the amount it turns to within 10 degrees. Nonetheless, after three turns and moves, its positional uncertainty (represented by an ellipse surrounding all the places where it might be) is enormous.

Hence a robot cannot rely entirely on dead reckoning to tell it where it is. It must visit locations more than once, and remember what they look like, or how they appear to nonvisual sensors. Then, if dead reckoning tells it that it might be at a previously visited location, it can compare its current appearance with the stored picture (or sonar recording) to verify.

Much of the research in this area uses sonar to measure the shape of the robot's immediate environment. Pulses of ultrasound are sent out and the time required for the pulse to bounce off something and return is recorded. The idea is that if there is an object in front of the sonar, the time recorded tells the robot how far away that object is. Sonar has the advantage that it is cheap and simple. Many commercially available robots come equipped with rings of sonars so that signals can be sensed in all directions simultaneously. The quality of the information sonar returns is not very good, however. A sonar beam is 30 degrees wide, so getting a pulse back tells you there is an object but gives its direction to within only 30 degrees. The time it takes to record a pulse depends in complex ways on the composition and shape of obstacles.

Vision potentially provides a lot more information. A medium-sized black-and-white image can contain over 10,000 pixels, each encoded with a byte of information. A ring of 16 sonars provides about 16 bytes. A sonar recording of the environment is a low-resolution, one-dimensional row of dots. A picture is worth ..., well, you get the idea. Many places look pretty much alike to a sonar. Every place looks different to a camera.

The problem is that the *same* place looks different to a camera. If you take a picture of a place, then come back and take another picture, they will look different. For one thing, some of the contents of the image will be different. The lighting may have changed. But the biggest changes will be due to the fact that the camera will not be in exactly the same place. Many of the lines will be at different angles. Objects will be foreshortened differently.

An algorithm developed by Hemant Tagare (Tagare et al. 1998) can cope with some of these problems. The idea is to treat the change in an image due to the change in camera position as a random perturbation of the image. If the camera hasn't moved too far, then there are limits to how the image can have changed. Let's assume that the camera is mounted horizontally and is located in the same plane now as when the picture was taken. Let's also assume that the lighting conditions haven't changed much. These assumptions are reasonable for indoor scenes taken from a robot rolling around on a flat, horizontal floor. Under these conditions, there are three ways the scene can be perturbed: (1) the camera axis won't be parallel to its orientation when the picture was originally taken; (2) the camera will be closer to or further from the objects in front of it; (3) some objects may have been added or removed; in particular, even if the same objects are present, some objects in the foreground may block different parts of the background image than they did originally (figure 2.7a,b).

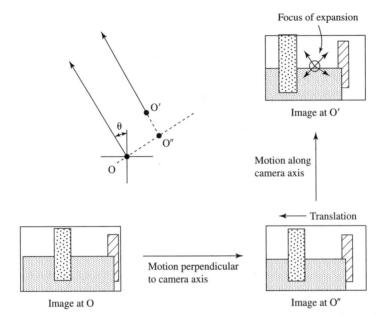

Figure 2.7a
Camera shift

The first kind of perturbation is handled by taking a wide-angled picture when a location is first visited. We don't use a wide-angled camera, but instead take a series of ordinary pictures and "glue" them together. If the resulting *panorama* spans 160 degrees, and the camera's field of view is 30 degrees, then the later picture can be taken with the axis rotated by up to 50 degrees (left or right) and it will match some part of the panorama.

The second kind of perturbation is more tricky. We don't know if the camera moved away from or toward the objects in the scene. Even if we did, the amount that a pixel would shift depends on the distance of the object whose surface it occurs on. In fact, this is a variant of the optical-flow problem we considered earlier, the difference being that we don't get to track pixels over time; if the camera had moved smoothly and directly from its old to its new position, we could compute the flow, but all we have is two snapshots. Nonetheless, for each pixel in one image, we can place constraints on the pixels it "could have flowed from" in the other. We call this set of pixels the *source region* for that pixel. If we maintain

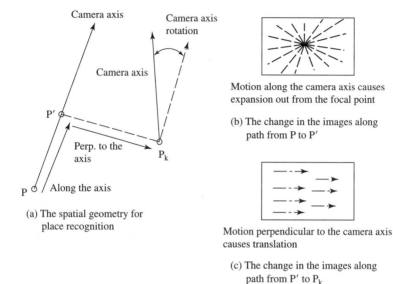

Camera axis

Camera axis rotation

Camera axis

P′

Perp. to the axis

Along the axis

P

P_k

(a) The spatial geometry for place recognition

Motion along the camera axis causes expansion out from the focal point

(b) The change in the images along path from P to P′

Motion perpendicular to the camera axis causes translation

(c) The change in the images along path from P′ to P_k

Figure 2.7b
Image perturbations due to camera shift

the idealized picture of the camera rotating and then moving in or out, and we correctly guess the rotation, then the pixel in the center of the image will be the same as in the old image; its source region is one pixel. As we look at pixels further from the center, the optical geometry of the camera means that the source regions get bigger. We can draw a diagram that gives, for some representative pixels, the source region in the other image (figure 2.8). For each point with a cross-hair over it, the enclosing quadrilateral with curved side gives the source region for that point.

The third kind of perturbation is unmodelable. Some pixels in the two images simply don't correspond to each other. We call these *outliers*. The more there are, the harder it is to see the similarity of the two images.

We put all this together by providing an estimate for the probability that the image can have arisen as a random perturbation of a slice of the panorama. For each pixel, we look at the pixels in its source region. If they are all of roughly the same gray level, then this pixel's brightness had better be close to it. If they exhibit a wide range of gray levels, then this pixel's brightness must fall in that range. The algorithm examines every

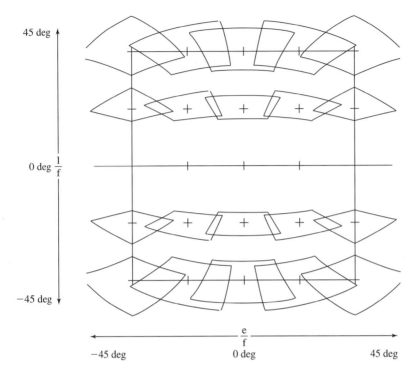

Figure 2.8
Pixel source regions (from Tagare and McDermott 1998)

pixel, and computes the square of the difference between it and the middle of the range as a proportion of the size of the range. If the difference is very high, then the algorithm classifies the pixel as an outlier. When every pixel has been examined, we arrive at two numbers that characterize how good the match is between two images: the outlier count, and the average difference between nonoutliers. If both these numbers are low, then the chances are good that the new image was taken from about the same place as the panorama.

This algorithm is not foolproof. There cannot be a foolproof algorithm in a world where some pairs of locations look very similar. But it often provides a strong clue to a robot that it has returned to a previously visited location. With enough such clues the robot can build a map.

There have been several approaches to robot map building (Kuipers and Byun 1991; Mataric 1990; Kunz et al. 1997; Engelson and McDermott

1992; Kriegman and Taylor 1996). A recent piece of work (Thrun et al. 1998) relies, like many recent research efforts in AI, on the theory of probability. That's because the inputs to the system yield "clues" to the shape of the world but not perfect information. It turns out that such clues can be modeled well using the language of *subjective probability*, in which propositions are assigned "degrees of belief" between 0 and 1. A proposition with subjective probability 1 is believed to be true with certainty; one with probability 0 is believed to be false with certainty; if you believe a proposition with degree p, you should be willing to bet p dollars against $1 - p$ dollars that the proposition is true (Savage 1954).

Thrun et al. represent a map as an assignment of probabilities of the presence of landmarks at every point in an area. A *landmark* is a recognizable entity; the case of there being no landmark at a point is treated as the presence of a special "null landmark" there. For example, in figure 2.9a, after some exploration a robot might assign probability 0.99 to the presence of the null landmark at every point except those near the two indicated points. At one of these the robot identified a coatrack, at the other a floor lamp. It is more certain of the exact location of the coatrack, so there is a smaller cluster of higher probabilities there. In figure 2.9b we see a more realistic example, in which the space consists of a set of corridors. Many areas cannot be visited at all, because they are blocked by walls and unopened doors. The landmarks in this case consist of panoramas that are matched at various points.

A robot can use a map like this in a couple of ways. One is for *route planning*. Given a destination and an origin, the robot can compute a path through the map that will allow it to get to the destination. Another is *location estimation*. As the robot moves, it can update its position by comparing what it sees with the map. Because the map is represented probabilistically, we can think of this as the problem of finding the location L such that the following quantity is maximized:

$P(\text{robot at } X \,|\, \text{map } M \,\&\, \text{observations } D)$,

where $P(A \,|\, B)$ is the *conditional probability* of proposition A given proposition B. X is a location, M is a probabilistic map, and D is a set of data from observations taken as the robot moves around, including dead-reckoning data and the landmarks seen along the way. Conditional

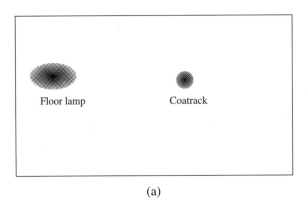

(a)

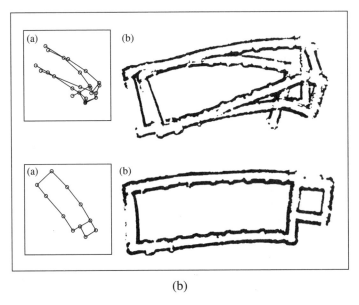

(b)

Figure 2.9
(a) Simple probabilistic map. (b) More complex map (from Thrun et al. 1998)

probability is a convenient way of representing changes in judgments of the plausibility of various beliefs as information is gathered. The probability that your ticket will win the lottery, $P(win)$, might be $\frac{1}{1,000,000}$; but after several digits have been selected, and they all match your ticket, you're justified in getting excited, especially if your ticket survives until there's just one digit left to select. At that point the relevant number is $P(win|all\ but\ one\ digit\ match)$, which is $\frac{1}{10}$.

Sometimes the robot is just given the map to begin with, but it can also use probability techniques to learn a map by wandering around and noticing landmarks. We pose this problem as that of finding a map M so as to maximize

$P(map\,M\,|\,observations\ D)$,

where now D is the set of observations collected as the robot wanders.

Conditional probability is related to unconditional probability by the following relationship

$P(A\,|\,B) = P(A\&B)/P(B)$.

For instance, in the case of our lottery, the probability $P(all\ but\ one\ digit\ matched) = \frac{1}{100,000}$, so that

$$P(win\,|\,all\ but\ one\ digit\ matched) = \frac{\frac{1}{1,000,000}}{\frac{1}{100,00}} = \frac{1}{10}.$$

Given this relationship between conditional and unconditional probabilities, we can infer:

$P(A\&B) = P(A\,|\,B)\,P(B) = P(B\,|\,A)\,P(A)$

and hence

$$P(A\,|\,B) = \frac{(P(B\,|\,A)\,P(A))}{P(B)}.$$

This equation is known as Bayes's Theorem. It is very handy when you want to compute $P(A\,|\,B)$ and you happen to know $P(B\,|\,A)$. In our map example we can apply Bayes's Theorem to derive this:

$$P(map\ M\,|\,observations\ D) = \frac{P(D\,|\,M)\,P(M)}{P(D)}$$

The term $P(D\,|\,M)$ is the probability of observations given the map. Because the map specifies more or less where everything is, it turns out that this is not too hard to compute; it corresponds to asking, what would I see if I stood at a given point in the map and looked in a certain direction? $P(M)$ is the *prior probability* of a map. Some maps might be considered less plausible than others even if you had no data. For instance, you might not know where an acquaintance's house is, but you might rate it as unlikely that the house is in the river (although not impossible). $P(D)$ is the probability, over all possible maps, of the data that we happened to observe. These two quantities may sound difficult to compute, but we can get around the difficulties. The exact form of $P(M)$ is not too important. Perhaps some simple rule would suffice that assigns higher probability to maps with landmarks spaced at a certain ideal distance. $P(D)$ doesn't depend on M at all, so if we want the M that maximizes $P(M|D)$ and don't care about the exact *value* of $P(M|D)$, we can just leave $P(D)$ out. (I have omittted many technical details.)

Thrun et al. tested their algorithm by moving the robot around by hand for fifteen minutes, telling it where various landmarks were. They then ran their algorithm to find the map that maximized the probability of making the observations that were actually made. The map that resulted was accurate to within inches.

Language

How well do computers solve the problem of language use?

Before we can ask that question, we have to decide whether there *is* a problem of language use, and if so, what it might be. If the problem is to get computers to understand spoken commands, then it is often quite easy to define, at least in principle. Given the set of all possible commands, and a particular utterance, then the question is, which command was intended by that utterance? If there are just two possible commands, as might happen with an automated balloon guidance system that need only respond to *Up* and *Down,* then the problem is to figure out whether a certain yell sounds more like one than the other. If there is essentially an infinite number of commands (say, strings of coordinates given to a more elaborate navigation system), then, as we shall see below, the problem gets somewhat more complicated.

But suppose the problem is simply to "understand" an ordinary English utterance. Historically this has been the ultimate problem of the field of "natural language processing," or perhaps of AI in general. For example, consider these two sentences (due to Winograd 1972):

The city council refused the demonstrators a parade permit because they advocated violence.
The city council refused the demonstrators a parade permit because they feared violence.

In the first sentence, one sees instantly that "they" refers to the demonstrators. In the second, it is obvious that "they" refers to the city council members. If you saw either sentence without the other, it would probably never occur to you that there was an ambiguity, especially if the sentence occurred in the context of a coherent story about a political squabble. Whatever else you may say about sentence understanding, it's clear that you don't understand sentences such as these unless you can successfully infer what "they" and other pronouns refer to.

Unfortunately, although it is not hard to enumerate inferences that a language-understanding program ought to be able to make, such an enumeration does not really pin down what problem such a program is supposed to be solving. There is an infinite number of possible inferences; which ones need to be found in order to understand a sentence?

At one time it appeared that there was a natural answer to this question. Suppose there is an *internal notation* system in which thoughts are expressed. (Fodor 1975 calls it the "language of thought.") The brain keeps track of a proposition it believes by, in essence, writing down the expression for that proposition in the internal notation, and tagging the expression with a "B" for "believed." It infers new beliefs from old ones by processes akin to the manipulations of a formal deductive system. Just as a formal deductive system allows you to conclude Q from P and *If P then Q*, so the brain concludes "the butler did it" from "this is a mystery set in an English country house" and "no one else but the butler could have done it." If you don't quite see how to make the leap from the inference involving *If P then Q* to the inference involving the butler, you're not alone; but perhaps part of the difficulty is that we don't yet understand how the internal notation works.

The nice thing about the internal-notation proposal is that, if it could be carried out, it would tell us what inferences need to be drawn in understanding a sentence, namely, just those required to recover the proper internal representation of it. The problem of pronoun interpretation fits neatly here. The internal representation of a sentence should presumably not contain any pronouns. If there is a term X_1 that is the proper translation of "the city council," and another, X_2, that is the proper translation of "the demonstrators," then the internal representation of either of the example sentences given above contains either X_1 or X_2 in the expression about the cause of X_1's decision regarding X_2's permit. Pronouns make sense as abbreviatory devices in speech, but expressions in the internal notation are going to be stored for a long time and used in many different contexts, so it's hard to see how such abbreviations could be useful. If someone tells me "Go see Ms. Smith in Accounting. She has something for you," what I want in the internal representation of "She has something for you" is some label for the bundle of facts I know about her. For instance, if I am engaged in looking for Ms. Smith, my visual system must have ready access to information about what she looks like. A pointer to this bundle of facts is very different from the pronoun "she."[10]

Assuming you are convinced by this argument, you will then agree that you can't translate the sentences about granting the demonstrators a parade permit unless you can make inferences about the motives and likely behavior of city councils and demonstrators. If we make similar arguments about other aspects of the sentences, we might eventually wind up with a formal representation of the second sentence that looks something like this:

```
group(d3, person) /* d3 is a group of persons */
city_council(c4, city8) /* c4 is the city council of some city */
hypothetical_event(e66, parade(d3, city8)
              & 0 < time_interval(e65, e66) < 1 month)
event(e65,
      request(d3, c4,
              permission(e66)))
```
/* e65 is the event of d3 requesting permission for a parade in the city
   in the near future */

```
event(e67,
      deny(c4, d3, e65))
```
/* e67 is the event of c4 denying the request referred to as e65 */

```
reason(e66, fear(c4, violent(e66)))
```

Note that "they" has vanished, replaced by c4, the term denoting the city council. Note also that I have made several other facts explicit that were only implicit in the sentence, including the fact that the violence the council was afraid of would be associated with the planned parade.

Unfortunately, the internal-representation theory is not as healthy as it used to be. There are two problems: how to recover internal representations from sentences (and other inputs), and what to do with them once they have been recovered. The first problem may sound harder, but in fact the second is worse. Many of the solutions to the first problem don't work until you've solved the second. One such solution is to choose the internal representation that minimizes contradictions with what you already know; but this requires being able to tell when a set of beliefs in the internal notation is inconsistent.

One problem is that it appears there is no way to make inferences efficiently using the sorts of complex symbolic structures that the theory posits. If we restrict our attention to deductive systems, then most inference problems can be shown to be intractable in the worst case. "Intractability" is a technical property of a problem, and it is difficult to explain exactly what its consequences are. (I will explain it a bit further in chapter 5.) For our purposes, a problem is intractable if any algorithm that solves every instance of it will take a very long time on some instances, and in particular if the delay grows much faster than the size of instances of the problem. For every problem size larger than some low threshold there is an instance of that size that the algorithm will take more than a billion years to solve on any conceivable computer. Such problems are not out of bounds to AI; in fact, many problems of interest to AI are intractable. It may sound crazy to try to solve an unsolvable problem, but there are some loopholes: it may be useful to solve *some* problems of large size, even if not all can be solved; it may be useful to find a near-solution when no solution can be found; and, in some cases, even though a problem class is intractable there is a special subclass that can be solved efficiently.

The problem is that no has proposed anything like a special subclass of the problem of making inferences from internal language representations that (a) is big enough to include the representations of all sentences people are likely to utter (or think about); and (b) supports efficient inference algorithms.

However, the absence of an efficient deductive inference algorithm is not the biggest obstacle to the success of the theory. The biggest obstacle is that most inferences we make are not deductive, and there is no general theory of nondeductive inference (McDermott 1987). A deductive inference is an inference that must be true if its premises are. If you hear that your older brother got more jellybeans than your younger brother, and that your younger brother got more jellybeans than you, then you can be sure of the inference that your older brother got more than you, so long as you don't doubt either of the two premises you heard. This is an example of a deductive inference. They are hard to find outside of geometry class. If you vote for Jones because she is a Republican and therefore will support a balanced budget, you must be prepared for disappointment. That's an obvious example, but consider something much more straightforward: you go to class at 9:30 on Wednesday because the class meets Monday, Wednesday, and Friday at 9:30. It's very likely that the class will meet on this occasion, but it's not definite. There are many reasons why it might not. That's life.

There is no problem in principle with a computer making deductive or nondeductive inferences. If a robot arrives at a plan for going to a destination based on a map inferred from sensory data, the plan might or might not work. The inference to the plan can be wrong for all sorts of reasons, even if the premises are true (i.e., the input data were accurately sensed). Even in the case of something as straightforward as the calculation done by the IRS to determine whether you get a refund or must pay more taxes, it is not always obvious if the inference is deductive. Suppose the IRS computer is figuring the taxes of a consultant, and sees three income items, one for $5467, one for $1076, and one for $1076.39. Is the inference that the total income = $7619.39 a deductive inference? A human accountant might wonder if the second two figures were the same amount reported twice, by two different channels. Is he doubting the premises, and if so what are they?

The point is one I made above: computers don't deduce, they calculate. Whether the conclusions they draw are deductive or not is seldom an issue. The problem is not with getting computers to draw nondeductive conclusions; they do it all the time. The problem is to get them to do it with an arbitrary formula in the internal notation. The IRS computer can represent facts about tax returns. The map-building robot can represent facts about the layouts of buildings. What's missing is a general theory of inference that will tell us what we are justified in inferring from an arbitrary collection of facts. In the first half of the twentieth century, philosophers like Carnap worked hard on finding such a theory, and instead found many reasons to doubt that such a theory exists (Putnam 1963).

It could turn out that there is some marvelous computational engine in the brain that can manipulate the sorts of expressions exemplified above, making nondeductive inferences rapidly, smoothly, and fairly accurately without turning a hair—but I doubt it. My guess is that life tends to present us with a series of stereotypical problems, for which our brains have specialized solution techniques. Information is not stored in a general-purpose notation, but in a set of notations specialized for the algorithms that will be used to solve them. For instance, there might be one representation system for maps, a different one for manipulable objects in the immediate vicinity, and another for faces of people we are acquainted with.

Language appears to be the big counterexample to this proposal, because we can apparently hear a sentence on any topic and immediately assimilate the information it contains. But this appearance might be misleading. It is now accepted that any normal person can perform a purely *syntactic* analysis of an arbitrary novel sentence with no conscious effort. Syntactic analysis—or *parsing*—segments a sentence so that the phrases it contains are properly grouped. For example, in a sentence like "The man Fred yelled at was more helpful," we know immediately that Fred yelled at the man and that the man was more helpful (and not, for instance, that the man yelled at Fred or Fred was more helpful). The question is what happens to the word groups after such syntactic parsing. Consider a riddle such as this one: "If a plane crashes right on the border between the United States and Canada, where would they bury the survivors?" Or this one: "A train leaves New York headed for Albany at 80 miles per hour, and simultaneously another train leaves Albany headed for New York at 40 miles per hours. When they collide, which one is closer to New York?" A significant number of people perform such a shallow analysis of these seemingly simple questions that they get the meanings wrong. What model of semantic processing would account for that?

Fortunately, we can learn a lot about language without solving the problem of what it means to understand an arbitrary sentence. For instance, consider the problem of *information extraction,* in which the computer's job is to extract data from sources such as newspaper stories or commercial message traffic. Suppose we are interested in tracking the occurrence of terrorist incidents around the world. We could hire people to read newspapers and summarize all the stories about terrorism. But we can provide a more precise description of the job: scan every story; if it doesn't describe a terrorist incident, discard it. Otherwise, figure out who attacked whom, on what date, in what location, with what weapons, and what damage was done. In other words, the crucial data about each story can be fit into a simple table:

Date: _____
Location: _____
Terrorist: _____
Victim: _____
Weapon: _____

Furthermore, each blank can be filled in with something simple. The date and location can be in standard formats. The terrorist can be one of several anticipated organizations (the IRA, the Shining Path, the PLO—the usual suspects), and if we can't extract a familiar name, we can just include whatever phrase was used in the article.

The point is that by focusing on this task we can sidestep the question of true understanding and replace it by the question: can computers perform this task as well and as cheaply as people?

Another example is the problem of translating from one language to another, possibly in a restricted domain. Suppose I want to translate computer-software manuals from Japanese to English. I can hire a person to do it, or I can write a computer program. In the case of a person, I would assume that a prerequisite to doing the job is the ability to understand both Japanese and English. But that's not strictly part of the definition of the problem. There might be rules that enable me to select the right syntactic structures and word choices in the target language without understanding what the words mean.

Then there is the problem of translating spoken speech into written words. Like many skills we usually take for granted, it seems effortless but is really extremely difficult. If you have ever tried to understand a native speaker of a language you have been exposed to only in school, you have an idea of how hard it is to extract words from what sounds like a rapid stream of meaningless babble. However, this problem does have the advantage of being well defined. A string of speech sounds does usually correspond to a single string of words, and all we have to do is extract it.

In all three of these cases, we can view the computer as a proxy. It is extracting information, or translating text, or capturing spoken words, so that eventually a human being can look at them. Hence, with a couple of reservations, we can postpone the task of getting the computer to understand the words.

One reservation is that you probably can't do any of the tasks I described *perfectly* without actually understanding the words being manipulated. In the 1960s, Yehoshua Bar-Hillel wrote a paper arguing that you can't translate properly without actually understanding what you're translating (Bar-Hillel 1960). In the two sentences:

The ink is in the pen
The pig is in the pen

it's impossible to translate the word "pen" without understanding what's being described, because in most languages the word for "writing instrument" and the word for "enclosure for animals" are not the same. He concluded that translation would be impossible without first solving the understanding problem. (Then he went on to conclude that translation was impossible because the understanding problem was impossible.) But this argument is not airtight. For one thing, it may be possible to get the right translation of "pen" from the mere presence of "ink" or "pig" in the vicinity. With enough statistical knowledge of the patterns of discourse in English one might be able to fake understanding. But even if there are examples that absolutely require understanding, we can still ask whether it is possible to automate the process so that the computer costing X/hour makes about as many errors as a person costing X/hour would (or fewer)? After all, people aren't perfect at information extraction, translation, speech transcription, or anything else. Can computers compete?

The other reservation is that in the long run we will have to say more about what it means to understand language. Fortunately, the problem doesn't seem particularly urgent. If machines have no thoughts about city councils and parade permits, getting them to talk about those things is a sterile exercise. What I expect to happen is that as people and machines have an increasing need to communicate in areas they are collaborating on, the machines will begin speaking and understanding some very minimal subsets of natural language, and these will gradually grow. At the same time we may gain greater insight into what really happens when people speak and understand.

Since that day has not yet come, let's look in some detail at what computers can do with natural language now. We start with speech recognition. If a speech signal were presented as a stream of consonants and vowels, then the problem would be to figure out how to group them into words. But the speech signal is actually just a time-varying sound, and the problem for the human ear and the computer is to extract the consonants and vowels—or *phonemes*—before it can even look for words.

Sound waves consist of slight pressure disturbances traveling through the air. A transducer, such as the human ear, converts these vibrations into a form suitable for information processing. A key fact about waves is that they can be summed, or *superposed*. If you throw two rocks into a pool at slightly different places, the two wave patterns expand forward together, and the net effect at any given point on the pool is the sum of the effects of the two rocks. Similarly for sound waves. Suppose we transmit a sound consisting of just two pitches. Each pitch corresponds to a wave of a different frequency. The two combined yield a wave that is the sum of the individual waves (figure 2.10). To hear the two pitches (as we in fact can), the ear must take the summed wave and decompose it into the two waves that it comprises. This is called a *frequency analysis* or *Fourier analysis* of the wave.

Real sounds tend to have contributions at all the frequencies over a range. When your mouth forms the sound "s," it is generating a large variety of frequencies, but only for the duration of that sound. In the word "so," the frequency bundle, or *spectrum,* of "s" is immediately followed by a different but equally complex spectrum for "o." Specifying a frequency bundle requires more than just specifying its component frequencies. We must also specify their strengths, that is, *how much* of each frequency to mix in. It turns out that as the mouth is shaped to produce

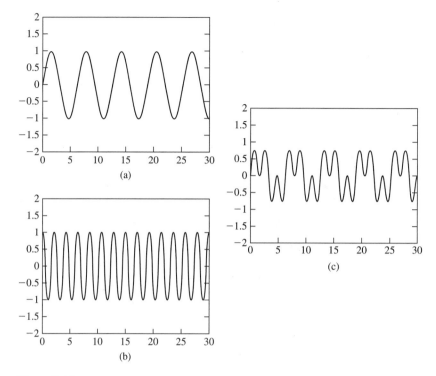

Figure 2.10
(a) Low-frequency signal. (b) High-frequency signal. (c) Sum of (a) and (b)

different vowels, it takes on different resonant frequencies. A *resonance* is a natural mode of vibration of an object. If an object is stimulated by vibrations at different frequencies, it will respond most vigorously to vibrations at its resonant frequency. The air inside the vocal passage has several resonances at any given moment. When stimulated by the sound from the vocal cords, it tends to pass the resonant-frequency components through and mute the others. The resonant frequencies associated with a particular vowel sound are called the *formant frequencies* of that vowel (Denes and Pinson 1973). We are, of course, completely unaware of this level of analysis. When we hear a vowel in our native language, we hear it as a single distinctive sound without any components. Vowels in foreign languages sound like weird versions of the vowels we are familiar with. Figure 2.11 shows the sound pattern of the sentence "Kids

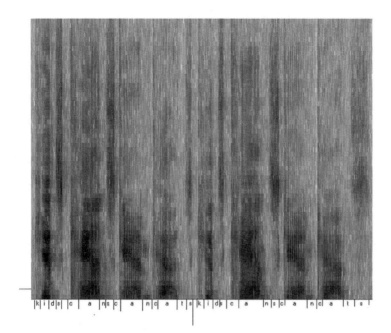

Figure 2.11
Spectrogram of sentence "Kids *can* scan cats" uttered twice

can scan cats" as spoken twice by a native of the American midwest. (The word "can" is emphasized so that it contains the same vowel as "scan.") The sentence is repeated to show that the variation between words is greater than the variation between different utterances of the same word. The vertical axis shows the amount of energy present at different frequencies as different sounds are produced. A darker patch indicates more energy at the corresponding frequency. Vowel sounds ("i" and "a" in this example) are longer than consonants, and have a distinctive pattern of dark, irregularly horizontal bands; the bands occur at the formant frequencies.

Consonants are more difficult to define than vowels. Although "s" has a distinctive spectrum, a typical consonant like "k" or "t" is defined as a transition in one of the formant frequencies. The transition is very fast and hard to spot in speech diagrams. Furthermore, what sounds like the same consonant in different words is actually a varying sound pattern that depends on the context. A "k" before an "a" is a different pattern than a "k" before an "i" (figure 2.11).

So it seems that what we have to do in order to recognize speech is (a) break the sound stream into small segments and do a frequency analysis of each segment; (b) scan a catalog of phonemes to find the one that matches most closely. Unfortunately, it is hard to create such a catalog, because a given phoneme will correspond to many different frequency patterns, depending on the phonemes on either side of it, the exact shape of the speaker's mouth, the amount of background noise, and so on.

At this point we must resort to a probabilistic analysis of the speech data, using statistical techniques to find the most likely interpretation of a stream of sounds, the same techniques that are so useful in map learning and in other areas. What we are interested in is finding a word string W, such that

P(speaker said W | heard sound stream S)

is as large as possible. This quantity is the conditional probability that the speaker said W given that the hearer heard sounds S. Just as in map learning, we are interested in the hypothesis (W) that will maximize this probability, once we have gathered the evidence (S).

For instance, suppose the sound stream were something like, "Write before the game was tidy through an intersection." Of course, by using English words to describe this sound stream I am being (deliberately) misleading. What I should do instead is indicate it purely phonetically, perhaps this way: "R ie t b ee f or dh uh g ai m w uh z t ie d ee th r ue a n i n t ur s e k sh uh n," using one- or two-letter combinations to indicate sounds. (The sound "dh" is a voiced "th"; the word "this" starts with "dh," where as the word "thespian" starts with "th." You may never have noticed the difference, which just illustrates the point that it's easier to hear the senses than the sounds of your own language.) Call this sound stream S_1. Now consider these two possible word strings:

W_1 = Right before the game was tied he threw an interception

W_2 = Write before the game was tidy through an intersection

There are, of course, many other candidates (such as, "Write bee four the game ..." etc.). Most speakers of American English, at least those familiar with American football, would rank $P(W_1 | S_1$ higher than

$P(W_2 \mid S_1)$. Although this hypothesis requires the assumption that the fourth-from-last sound was actually a "p" and not a "k," it is hard to imagine anyone saying W_2. We might assign probabilities as follows: $P(W_1 \mid S_1) = .98$; $P(W_2 \mid S_1) = .005, \ldots$ The sum of the probabilities for all the candidates has to be 1, so the remaining .015 is divided among the other candidates. In principle, there could be a lot of them, with very tiny probabilities, but perhaps we can neglect most of those, as long as we always find the most likely candidates.

Now comes the hard part: getting a computer to compute the probabilities correctly. Over the past twenty years, there has been steady progress. The most successful programs are based on the idea of hidden Markov models of speech signals. A *hidden Markov model,* or HMM, is a way of characterizing all the different ways a word (or sentence) can be uttered, and assigning a probability to each pronunciation. Such a model is a network of *states* whose links are joined by *links* labeled with probabilities and outputs. A word is generated by starting in the special *initial state* of the HMM, then moving to a state along a link, then to another state, and so on, generating outputs as the links specify. If a link is labeled with *p*, this means that the link is followed with probability *p*, and when it is followed the output symbol *s* is generated. Output symbols are patterns of spectral energy, of short enough duration that every speech sound can be characterized as a sequence of such patterns.

For concreteness suppose we have a single HMM for each word. If we run it repeatedly, we will get a variety of symbol sequences out, each corresponding to a different pronunciation of the word. The more likely pronunications will be generated more often. So the model characterizes fairly directly the following conditional probability:

$P(\textit{sound stream } S \mid \textit{word } W)$.

But what we want is the opposite, $P(W \mid S)$. Fortunately, we can use Bayes's Theorem again to estimate this quantity given a set of HMMs representing words. We can combine statistical models of the way sounds make up words with statistical models of the way words occur in sentences to produce models for recognizing words in context. In case you're wondering where all these models come from, the answer is that they can be inferred automatically from samples of speech. Consult Jelinek (1997)

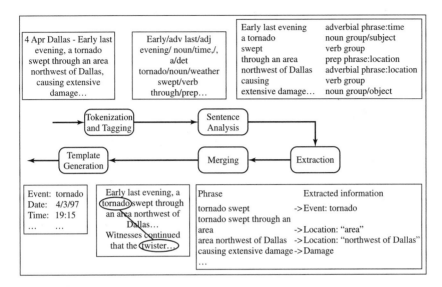

Figure 2.12
Architecture of an information-extraction system (from Cardie 1997, fig. 2)

or Rabiner and Juang (1993) for details, but be prepared to get through some fairly high-powered mathematics.

Today speech-recognition systems are becoming commercially available. They are reliable for isolated words, somewhat less so for recognition of continuous speech. One company claims 95% accuracy in recognition of continuous speech at 160 words per minute. Typically, to achieve this kind of performance the system must be getting sound input only from the speaker, without any loud distracting noises in the background. Still, these are very impressive figures.

Let's turn our attention now to *information extraction,* in which texts are scanned to find fragments that fill slots in an output template. Figure 2.12 shows the architecture of a typical information-extraction system. In the first two phases the sentence is analyzed syntactically. (These systems usually start with printed words, so no speech recognition is necessary.) As I implied above, this parsing process requires assigning the correct syntactic structure to the whole sentence (Jackendoff 1987), but information extractors usually don't try to do that. One reason is that sentences often have several different possible syntactic analyses, which we are normally unaware of. Another is that some inputs use bad grammar, and so have no complete syntactic analysis, or no correct one. To sidestep these problems, information extractors do "partial parsing," in which only phrases whose analysis is fairly certain are found. For example, in a sentence like "The Liberation Front blew up the Minister with his bodyguards," it is obvious only after semantic analysis that "with his bodyguards" does not modify "blew up." (Contrast "The Front blew up the Minister with grenades.") But we can extract the phrases "The Liberation Front," "blew up," "the Minister," and "with his bodyguards" with fair confidence that they are at least constituents of the correct analysis.

In the next phase, the phrases found are used to generate pieces of information that may ultimately be part of the answer. This phase relies on domain-specific relations between phrases. If "blew up" is followed by a noun phrase, then in the terrorism domain it is probably giving us two slot fillers: the victim of a terrorist act (the noun phrase) and the weapon used (explosives). Any phrase that doesn't fit an extraction pattern is ignored, the hope being that it is not relevant to the target domain.

However, the program can't just throw the information so gathered into the output template. There may be more than one such template, so it is important to figure out how the fragments fit together. This calculation is done during the merge phase of information extraction. The key step is to realize when different noun phrases and pronouns probably refer to the same entity. This is a generalization of the pronoun-reference problem I discussed at the beginning of this section. In this situation the program has to infer that, for instance, "the tornado" and "the twister" refer to the same entity. It does so by merging any two expressions that could be synonyms and have no contradictory properties.

The performance of an information-extraction program is measured using two quantities, recall and precision. *Recall* is the fraction of relevant facts in a text that the program actually finds. *Precision* is the fraction of facts the program finds that are correct. Suppose a program for extracting information about terrorist incidents fills its template as follows:

Date: July 15, 1998
Location: ??
Terrorist: the French Press

Victim: General Francois Mercredi
Weapon: ??

The original story might have been:

The French government revealed yesterday that General Francois Mercredi was the victim of a terrorist incident last month. Gen. Mercredi was last seen on July 15. His body was found just yesterday, with two bullet holes to the head, and a note in the pocket from the Aquarian Liberation Front. He had had a rocky career, having been repeatedly attacked by the French Press, but seemed to be vindicated after being made Commander of the Fifty-Fifth brigade. He was last seen leaving his villa on the way to work.

In this case there are four pertinent facts specified in the article (the victim, the date, the terrorist group, and the weapon). The program has found two of them and also surmised that the terrorist was the "French Press." Hence the recall is 2/4 = 50%. Of the three "facts" the program found, two are correct, so the precision is 2/3 = 67%.

Several information-extraction programs have been written, notably those produced by the contestants in the Message Understanding Competitions sponsored by the Defense Advanced Research Projects Agency in the early 1990s. Since then programs have been written to extract information from other kinds of text, such as medical records (Soderland et al. 1995). Getting a program to work in a given domain requires careful analysis of the concepts, words, and phrases in that domain. In a typical case one can achieve recall rates of about 50% and precision rates of about 70% (Cardie 1997). These rates may not sound very impressive, but the rates for people are not that close to 100% either, and, moreover, people take longer. For many applications, such as doing a fast scan through thousands of articles for relevant information, it might be better to employ a computer than a person.

It is not clear how much programs like this have to say about the way people process language. Some of the assumptions they make appear to be obviously wrong. For example, it has been known since the 1950s (Chomsky 1957) that Markov models are not powerful enough to represent the grammar of a real human language, so it may seem crazy to rely on them so heavily in speech recognition. However, the role they play in speech recognition is to account for variations in data, not for grammar as such. Besides, there are ways of incorporating similar ideas into more powerful grammatical mechnanisms, yielding probabilistic phrase-structure grammars (Charniak 1993).

Even if such technical objections can be dealt with, it seems as if little progress has been made on actually "understanding" natural language. The information-extraction model seems unable to account for humans' ability to hear something unexpected, something that would fall outside the range of the templates it is trying to fill in. And the theory is silent on the question of why and how sentences are generated in the first place.

These criticisms are reasonable but not conclusive. It is an open question how novel a sentence can be and still be understood by the average person the first time he or she hears it. Conversations often involve fairly formulaic topics. Perhaps after syntactic analysis people troll through a sentence looking for material relevant to the current topic, extract enough morsels of information to advance the conversation a bit, and discard the rest. In any case, the alternative—that an arbitrary content can be generated, placed in one's mental model, and used without further ado—seems very dubious for reasons outlined above.

Mathematical Reasoning

In the next chapter I will try to demonstrate that if AI is possible, that is, if cognitive science succeeds, a theory of consciousness follows fairly clearly. However, if AI is impossible this argument will be irrelevant. Many people think AI has dubious prospects at best, and some think it is provably impossible.

People who think AI is unlikely to succeed must grant that machines can play chess, control simple robots, find anticipated patterns in visual images, and so forth, because these skills have been demonstrated. What they doubt is that this little cluster of skills is going to grow and improve until the equivalents of full human intelligence and creativity are reached.

Such doubts are entirely reasonable. Progress so far in AI does not provide much evidence of a theory of general intelligence. On the contrary, the history of the field has been a progression from attempts to find general theories to success at finding narrow theories of particular mental faculties. In other words, one of AI's main game plans has been to move the goalposts closer. In AI's defense, however, neuroscientists and psychologists have made similar moves in their theorizing about how humans think. Some modules of the brain appear to handle unexpectedly specialized functions, such as recognition of familiar human faces (Desimone 1991; Bruce 1991). When we understand everything our specialized modules do, it is not at all clear what will remain. It's true that it's hard to imagine how Mozart's mind could be the result of the interaction of ordinary human brain modules, but perhaps most of what the average person does could be.

In spite of hand waving of this sort, the real argument AI people have in mind is the what-else-could-it-be argument. The more we understand about the brain, the more its operation resembles computation. What else could it be? Many people feel instinctively that it could be a lot of other things. Unfortunately, they can't come up with a convincing list. In this book, as a working hypothesis—or a dogma accepted on faith—I usually assume that there's nothing else it could be. There's a danger that by adopting this hypothesis we are blinding ourselves to alternatives, but as long as only a minority are blinded the danger doesn't seem too great. Besides, a truth can become widely accepted only if someone is willing to believe it before it is widely accepted.

Some people find the idea of intelligence as computation so abhorrent that they look for proofs that it is impossible. One of the most influential is John Searle, whose arguments are best looked at in the context of the theory of consciousness I present in chapter 3. Another strong proponent of such an argument is Roger Penrose (1989, 1994), building on the work of Lucas (1961). This is the argument from Gödel's Theorem (Nagel and Newman 1958). What Gödel showed (as rephrased by Turing) is that it is impossible to build a computer, or write a computer program, that can prove every theorem a human mathematician can. Hence, Penrose concludes, what human mathematicians do can't be captured completely by an algorithmic process.

This sounds impressive until you look at the details. What Gödel actually proved was this: Let M be a program that takes a mathematical statement P (in a suitable formal language) and either runs forever or stops eventually and says, "P is a theorem," and, when it stops, is always correct in its assertion that P is a theorem. Then it can be shown, although it's certainly not obvious, that there exists a $P*$ that is true if and only if M does not stop if given $P*$ as input. This statement can't be false, or M would stop given $P*$ as input, thereby certifying that $P*$ is true. But if it's true, M never says it is. Hence M fails to conclude, as we conclude, that $P*$ is true. Hence M fails to capture what human mathematicians do. Since M is an arbitrarily chosen theorem-proving machine, the conclusion follows for *any such machine.*

That paragraph is way too short a summary. For details, consult Penrose (1989, 1994). The technically difficult part of the proof, the part Gödel deserves the credit for, is showing that there must exist such a $P*$. Its content is, in essence, "M does not stop if given me as input," and it is amazing that you can say that in even very simple formal languages.

It may sound odd to require that M stop only if P is a theorem. Wouldn't it be more useful to have a machine that occasionally concluded P was not a theorem and, when it did, stopped and said so? Yes, but if there were a machine M' with this behavior we could easily modify it to become M, or incorporate it into an M, and any gap in the ability of M would have to be shared by M'.

Alas for the argument from Gödel's Theorem, it convinces almost no one. There are technical problems with it, which are reviewed exhaustively in LaForte et al. (1998) and *Behavioral and Brain Science* **13** (1990).[11] What I want to point out here is that it is completely irrelevant to cognitive science. Suppose we succeeded in building an intelligent mathematician. Would it be a program that ran for a while, maybe until we lost patience with it and pulled the plug, or maybe until it stopped and printed "Theorem" or "Nontheorem"? No, of course not. If it was intelligent, it would carry on conversations with other mathematicians, give and get inspiration, and go down many blind alleys. It would occasionally make mistakes, and print utter falsehoods as if it believed they were true. We hope, of course, that it would eventually realize its errors, certainly if they were pointed out to it. Such a machine would not be in the same genus as M.

Penrose believes that inside any such computer program an M would have to lurk. I believe his reasoning is as follows: A computer program is an algorithm, that is, a formal system, isomorphic to the formal languages Gödel's Theorem concerns itself with. We could disguise its output with various conversational red herrings, but a close inspection of the listing would smoke it out. This is an example of the most pervasive fallacy in philosophizing about computers, namely, to assume that the formal system embodied by a computer must be the same as that of the formal domains the computer reasons about. We can call this the "formalism fallacy." It sneaks in here because of an ambiguity in the word "algorithm." An algorithm is defined in elementary computer-science textbooks as a "precise specification of a behavior," but often it is used in phrases like "greatest-common-divisor algorithm," meaning "procedure for computing the greatest common divisor." An algorithm *for* something is guaranteed to do that something. If you give a greatest-common-divisor algorithm two positive integers, it will always find their greatest common divisor.

Many useful algorithms are not algorithms *for* anything. A chess program is completely algorithmic, that is, specified precisely enough to be executed by a computer. But it is not guaranteed to play a good game of chess.[12] It just seems to do so fairly often. Similarly, if automated mathematicians ever exist, they will be algorithms, but not algorithms *for being mathematicians.* They just have to succeed often enough to be useful.

Another way to put this is that there is always a "hermeneutic" problem in interpreting the output of an intelligent system. The precise meaning of its utterances will not always be obvious or even well defined. Suppose that a machine prints out "Newsflash! Fermat's Last Theorem is false!" How do we know it's serious? Perhaps it's trying to confuse us for some unknown motive. Or it's subject to odd compulsions. Or it's in possession of a flawed counterexample to Fermat's Last Theorem. Examining its listing may settle the matter, but it may not. Deciding if an arbitrary program is lying or mistaken is surely as difficult as deciding if an arbitrary statement is a theorem or not, and there is no reason to think that people have a special ability in this regard.

If you watch *Star Trek,* it may have occurred to you that one way to tell if a computer is mistaken is to see if it crashes or if smoke comes pouring out of it when it comes upon a contradiction. Less fancifully, it seems as if we run into the following problem: In any formal deductive system, if you conclude P and *not-P* for some proposition P, then you can conclude any proposition whatever. Since robots are formal deductive systems, don't they become useless as soon as they draw a conclusion and its negation?

Not necessarily. This argument hinges on the formalism fallacy I discussed earlier, that a computer's conclusions must be describable by some formal system. It's just not true, and it cannot possibly be true if computers are to be able to reason nondeductively. To take a trivial example, I can program a computer to print out "The world is flat" and "The world is not flat," and then go on to make arbitrary inferences without using these two premises. Of course, there is some doubt whether this counts as the computer's actually "believing" these two contradictory facts, but then there will always be some doubt about what the computer believes. That's the hermeneutic problem I talked about.

It's worth pausing here to talk about another recent feat of AI researchers. In 1996 the EQP program of Argonne National Laboratory (McCune 1997) proved a theorem that answered a conjecture that had been open for over 60 years. This was the first time a computer proved a theorem that human mathematicians had failed to prove, and it got a fair amount of publicity. As usual, in explaining what the program did I run the risk that of removing some of the glamor from it, but it's a good way to get a sense of what computers are currrently capable of.

Suppose we have an algebraic operation that we denote with "+". Forget that this usually stands for addition; we are going to let it stand for some unknown operation about which we know only that it is commutative and associative:

$$x + y = y + x$$
$$(x + y) + z = x + (y + z),$$

and one more fact, which explains the interaction between an operation $n(x)$ and $+$:

$$n(n(n(x) + y) + n(x + y)) = y.$$

The unary operation "n" is again an unknown operation. Note that all three axioms are making statements about all values x, y, and z. That means we can substitute arbtirary expressions for the variables. The axioms are said to be *universally quantified*.

The following theorem was proved in 1997 by a program called EQP developed by William McCune at the Argonne National Laboratory, a center for work on automated theorem proving:

From the three equations above you can deduce an equation of the form $c + d = c$, for two expressions c and d. (The expressions are written in the same language as the axioms, that is, using variables, parentheses, and the symbols $+$ and n.)

From this theorem you can then prove various other things, including the tidy conclusion that the algebras that satisfy these equations, called *Robbins algebras,* are exactly the *Boolean algebras,* the algebras of truth and falsehood that play such a crucial role in designing the circuits of digital computers.

The program worked by using a single inference rule, a generalized version of substitution of equals for equals. From the third equation we can infer

$$n(n(n(n(x) + y) + n(x + y)) + n(n(x) + y + n(x + y))) = n(x + y)$$

by substituting $n(x) + y$ for x and $n(x + y)$ for y. The underlined portion is now identical to the left-hand side of the third equation, so we can substitute the right-hand side, which is just y, yielding

$$n(y + n(n(x) + y + n(x + y))) = n(x + y).$$

This is the tenth equation generated by the program in one of its searches for a proof. A typical way to use the EQP program is to choose values for the parameters that control which way it searches, let it run for a while, see what direction it goes in; then change the parameters slightly and let it try again. For example, there is a parameter that limits the length of the equations generated by substitution, so that long equations are discarded. In the course of the "attack" on the Robbins problem, the limit on the length was set initially at 36, then raised by stages to 80 (McCune 1997). On the run that proved the theorem, the program generated thousands of equations. The actual proof of the theorem takes just twelve steps, but the twelfth step of the proof is the 8,871st equation found:

$$n(n(x + x + x) + x) + x + x = x + x$$

This equation solves the problem, by demonstrating expressions c and d such that $c + d = c$, to wit:

$$c = x + x$$

$$d = n(n(x + x + x) + x)$$

The program had to come up with 8,871 substitutions of the sort described above, of which 8,859 were completely irrelevant. One could argue that a human would be much more "insightful" in arriving at a proof, but of course no human ever did. It may just be that this theorem has no short intuitive proof. One might also argue that EQP deserves only half the credit for the theorem, since the parameter tuning done by McCune was so vital.

However, anyway you look at it this result shows how far automated mathematics still has to go. The method the program uses to search for the theorem is not exhaustive, but it is mind-numbingly literal. It does not attempt to find a more abstract model for the algebra, but instead just grinds away at the equations. There have been many other research projects that have given computers more interesting ways to prove things. One of them is proof by mathematical induction, in which a statement is proven true for all nonnegative integers by showing that it is true for 0, also showing that it is true for $i + 1$ if true for all integers between 0 and i inclusive. Proving a statement P by mathematical induction requires finding an *induction hypothesis,* a statement that implies P but also involves integers in the way required by induction.

The Architecture of the Mind

The long-range goal of cognitive science is to explain everything about the mind. So far it has explained only bits and pieces, and sometimes the bits and pieces seem to be bits and pieces of something else entirely. In some cases, as in vision, we can find close analogues between computational analysis and neurophysiological structure. In other cases, the analogy is highly suspect, as in the way computers play chess. In others the issue is obscure. It is well known that Markov-style state-transition models are incapable of accounting for the syntactic structure of human languages (Chomsky 1957), but that doesn't necessarily imply that the entire edifice of speech recognition is wrong. There are ways of incorporating the insights of Markov theorists into more powerful models, such as context-free grammars (Charniak 1993). Perhaps one such model is psychologically real. One may be put off by all this disorder, or see it as a lot of smoke disguising a rout on the battlefield. I don't agree. It seems to me that cognitive science and AI in particular are progressing quite nicely. It is true that some early hopes that a small number of good ideas would explain all of thinking have not panned out. As a result, researchers take the modularity of the mind much more seriously. We're not going to conquer the heartland before scaling the coastal ranges, that is, before mastering vision, speech recognition, natural-language syntax, motor activity, spatial localization, map learning, and other areas whose existence we didn't notice until recently.

One topic I have neglected in this chapter is learning, which I touched on only in connection with neural nets and robot map learning. I run the risk of giving the impression that learning is terra incognita, or, even worse, that there is a module in the brain labeled "Learning," into which flow experiences and out of which flows wisdom. In fact, in learning as in everything else, the main result of fifty years of research is that there is no general theory. For every mental skill there are techniques for improving that skill, but the techniques for improving one skill do not carry over to another. Language learning is the classic example. There is excellent evidence (reviewed in Pinker 1994) that language is learned by a system, possessed by every normal child, that starts with strong innate constraints on the possible human languages and learns the language spoken by the child's community by finding the unique allowed language that fits what it hears. Now consider the phenomenon that when you meet people of an ethnic group that is new to you, at first the members of the group are easy to confuse with one another; they all "look alike." Over time, the members of the group become as easy to distinguish as members of a familiar group. Obviously, your face-recognition module has learned something. Just as obviously, such learning is unlikely to be performed by the same module that learns the grammar of a language.

It might seem as if my bias toward modularity in this chapter has been extreme. Other discussions of cognitive science, such as Jackendoff (1987), have argued, often cogently, for the existence of certain kinds of representation in the human brain, based purely on the fact that people can grasp a certain kind of distinction. The typical result of such an argument is a suggested representational structure that is expressive enough to make the distinctions people make. When such an exercise is taken to its logical end, we wind up with elaborate systems of "knowledge representation" in which anything at all can represented (Davis 1990; Lenat and Guha 1990). The problem with these arguments is that they don't say much about how the knowledge is manipulated. Indeed, the more expressive the notation systems, the less tractable the problem of making inferences involving them. The trend in AI is to refuse to take a step toward a representation unless it is accompanied by an algorithm that actually does something useful. The result, so far, has been a patchwork of theories instead of a single overarching theory. One might therefore conclude that the approach is wrong; people seem to be able to make inferences involving ultrageneral representations, so perhaps the best strategy is to work harder for a theory of inference over such representations. Or one might conclude, as Fodor sometimes seems to (e.g., Fodor 1983), that the problem of thought, as opposed to perception, is a total mystery and likely to remain so for a long time. My belief is that introspective intuitions about internal representation are unreliable. Our sense that the mind is a meeting place for representations from all modalities expressed in a single internal "conceptual structure" (Jackendoff 1987, figure 7.1; and many other authors) is an illusion. I don't know how the illusion is maintained, but I think I know why it is; it's one of many illusions the brain makes use of in modeling itself, a topic I will say a lot more about later in the book.

In a recent essay, Hilary Putnam (1992) criticizes AI in terms that eventually make it clear that for him the field is defined as the search for a few simple algorithms that explain intelligence: "Artificial Intelligence as we know it doesn't really try to simulate intelligence at all; simulating intelligence is only its notional activity, while its real activity is just writing clever programs for a variety of tasks" (p. 13). Except for the word "just," he's completely correct. He sees inductive reasoning as the toughest nut for a cognitive theory to crack, and "induction is not a single ability, but rather a manifestation of a complex human nature whose computer simulation would require a vast system of subroutines, so vast that generations of researchers would be required to formalize even a small part of the system" (p. 15). I agree completely; I disagree only with his implication, later on the same page, that AI presupposes "an algorithm (of manageable size) for inductive logic." Putnam's words are echoed by Gazzaniga (1998, p. 170): "As soon as the brain is built, it starts to express what it knows, what it comes with from the factory. And the brain comes loaded. The number of special devices that are in place and active is staggering. Everything from perceptual phenomena to intuitive physics to social exchange rules comes with the brain. These things are not learned; they are innately structured.

Each device solves a different problem. Not to recognize this simple truth is to live in a dream world."

We've barely begun to list all the problems the brain can solve. But let's assume that we have such a list and that we know how the trick is done in every case. Will we know anything at all about true intelligence, the sort we admire? Everyone, or almost everyone, may have the capacity to read, or find their way around a city, or recognize someone they met yesterday. But not everyone can write symphonies as Mozart could or produce physical theories as Feynman could. Will we ever explain their abilities?

Let's use the word "creativity" for this phenomenon, or ability, or capacity, or whatever it is. Whatever you call it, I doubt that we will ever have a computational theory of it, not because creativity transcends computation, but because each occurrence of creativity is unique. Creativity in one person need have no resemblance to creativity in another, and when it will arise is unpredictable.

Let me explain. Creative people, in trying to introspect about how they do it, often come up with the following picture: Somewhere inside them is a "random-combination box." It takes ideas and puts them together into new combinations. The output of this box goes through some kind of filter, or critic, which rejects the silly combinations but seizes on the good ones. (This theory is often associated with the mathematician Henri Poincaré 1982, but there are lots of other anecdotes. See Weisberg 1993.)

I can see why this story, as a myth, has appeal. It explains why things we call creative often involve combinations of elements that we never would have thought to put together. It also allows the creative person to be both humble (not claiming credit for the random-combination box) and wise (having a critic that is smart enough to keep the right combinations). Unfortunately, even if the story is a correct account of some of the events going on in the mind of a creative person, it tells us nothing about how that person actually comes up with new ideas. The random-combination box can't really be random, because the chances of its coming up with something interesting would be negligible. The critic box is slightly more plausible; there are cases where it's much easier to recognize something good than to produce it. For example, a creative mathematician might consist of a random proof generator and a critic that verified that a proof was valid. The latter task is seemingly much easier. The example is unlikely to apply to the real world, however. Real proofs do not spring complete from a mathematician's brow; the critic will almost always say, "not quite." When it does, the randomness box is not likely to drop that approach and generate something else. It's far more likely to find a "creative" way to fix the buggy proof.

My own suspicion is that there may be a bit of randomness in the thought process of a creative person, but that it's not the important part. The important part is a few key tricks for generating good ideas in the person's domain of expertise. They're not random, they're just very effective. If we could dissect the brain of Mozart or Feynman and really understand what was going on, we would eventually say, "Oh, so that's it." This is just a suspicion, not even the ghost of a theory. It's based on the idea that we call "creative" any mental feat that we don't see how to duplicate. "What made you think of that?" we ask after seeing a bit of creativity. The creative person has no idea. He or she just thinks, and isn't aware of doing anything different when being creative and when being blockheaded.

There is a germ of truth in the random model of creativity and that is this: Even if it's possible to *understand* the mind of Mozart or Feynman computationally, it may not be possible to *create* a new Mozart or Feynman computationally. Even if Mozart's music could be composed by an algorithm, it may be impossible in practice to design another, equally good algorithm by any method except random perturbation of existing algorithms. The result, as for humans, will be a long sequence of completely inept composers, with another Mozart every few hundred thousand attempts. Furthermore, there will be no way to tell if the next algorithm is a brilliant composer without giving it lots of musical training and seeing what happens.

We see here a possible limit on what it is possible to understand computationally. Of course, there are many mental phenomena that cannot be explained computationally. An example is due to B. Chandrasekaran.[13] Suppose we do a computational analysis of a person's thought processes and behavior while he is drunk and another analysis while he is sober. In each case we can, let us suppose, describe everything about how the person thinks and acts in terms of various computations. That is, we can model his brain as computer C_S when he is sober and model it as computer C_D when he is drunk. There is no way to predict C_D from C_S. The transition between the two is not itself computational. Put another way, if all I know about a system is that it implements C_S, I cannot predict what will happen to it if I add alcohol. If it is a biological system then various components will slow down or become more erratic. If it is a silicon system, then pouring a beer into it might short it out completely.

Analogously, I am suggesting that the step from Salieri to Mozart, from someone who is pretty good to someone who is amazing, is a small step in an unpredictable direction in the space of possible computers. There is nothing magical about being Mozart except getting there.

With further apologies for the speculativeness of my picture of what a theory of creativity might be like, let me conclude by pointing out that the less ambitious theories being developed by cognitive scientists now are likely to be vital to understanding the details of creative thought processes. That's because we are increasingly sure that thought processes demand a lot of computation, and we are understanding how to harness it. It may seem disappointing to see so much "brute force" in action, but the brain has a lot of neurons, which do a tremendous amount of mindless computation every second. Could a conscious mind be one result of all that churning? That's the topic of the next chapter.

3

A Computational Theory of Consciousness

It's hard enough arguing that the research program of AI will eventually succeed. But it seems to many people that it could succeed completely and still not provide a theory of *phenomenal consciousness*. I use the term "phenomenal" to make it clear that I am not talking about other concepts of consciousness. There are several other kinds to check off:

· Not being asleep: You are conscious in this sense when you aren't unconscious.

· Attentiveness: You can be unaware that there is a high-pitched hum in your vicinity until someone points it out.

· Accessibility to report: You are unconscious of what your brain does when it processes visual information; you are conscious of what you do when you are looking for your glasses, but unconscious of what makes you more attuned to glasses-shaped objects when you're looking.

· consciousness as being aware of oneself: In playing chess you might be conscious of your sweaty hands and pounding heart, or you might be focused entirely on the game, and hence "unconscious" or at least "unselfconscious."

All of these are of interest, but none of them constitutes the "hard problem" of consciousnesss, to use David Chalmers's phrase. The hard problem is that red things look a certain way to me, different from green. I might be able to build a computer that could distinguish red things from green ones, but, at first glance, it doesn't seem as if either color would look "a certain way" to the computer. The way things are experienced by conscious beings are called the *qualia* of those things, and explaining what it is to have qualia is the hard problem of consciousness. When it's important to focus our attention on this meaning of the word "conscious," I will use the term "phenomenal consciousness."

As I said, it looks at first as if computational models could never explain phenomenal consciousness. They just don't trade in the correct currency. They talk about inputs, outputs, and computations, but sensations of any of these things don't enter in. Hence it seems logically possible that there could be a computer that made exactly the same sensory discriminations as a person, and yet experienced nothing at all. What I would like to argue in this chapter is that, if there is ever such a thing as an intelligent robot, then it will have to exhibit something very much like consciousness. I will then take the further step of arguing that this something is exactly what we mean by human consciousness, in spite of our intuitions to the contrary.

Before I make those arguments, let me remind you of the main argument of chapters 1 and 2. As long as the brain remains poorly understood, there will always be room to assume that some noncomputational essence within it makes consciousness happen. However, it may not remain that poorly understood much longer. We can already map the nervous systems of very simple creatures (leeches with only a few dozen neurons), and we get the same intuitions as when we look at computers: we can *see* what is happening in the nervous system, we can model it perfectly well as a kind of computation, and we can *see* the absence of experience. So to maintain a belief in dualism we have to believe that the human brain contains structures that are quite different from those in leeches, structures that would cause experience to happen. The problem is that we have no idea what those structures might be. Worse, to the extent we do understand what's going on in the brains of humans and other mammals, the events don't seem to be qualitatively different from what goes on in the "brains" of leeches.

Sooner or later, I predict, we're going to be faced with trying to explain consciousness without resort to any structures or mechanisms that are significantly different from the ones we now understand. If you think this is preposterous, then you may not be able to follow the argument much further. On the other hand, if you find unsatisfactory all the other proposals that have been made (Penrose 1994; Chalmers 1996; O'Brien and Opie 1999), then perhaps you will bear with me. I will warn you, however, that a computationalist explanation of consciousness will inevitably sound like "explaining away" rather than true explanation. Almost any materialist explanation, even the correct one, is going to have this problem or a similar one, because of the wide gulf between our intuitions about matter and our intuitions about mind. In the end the correct theory will win the argument only if the evidence in its favor outweighs intuition. I can't claim to provide such evidence, but I can say what I think it will look like. You must judge whether it has the potential to trump some of your "undoubtable" intuitions.

The full explanation of consciousness in terms of computation will require a fairly elaborate argument. But some of the apparent puzzles of consciousness dissolve immediately when we adopt a computational perspective. For example, consider the classic issue of distinguishing visual images from actual visual experiences of real objects. As Armstrong (1968, p. 291) puts it, "It seems clear ... that there is the closest resemblance between perceptions ... and mental images. A good way to begin an inquiry into the nature of mental images, therefore, is by asking, 'What are the marks of distinction between perceptions and visual images?'" He then discusses proposals such as Hume's that mental images are somehow less vivid than real perceptions and that that's how we tell them apart.

If the brain is nothing more than a computer, this problem simply evaporates. It's like asking how an income-tax program tells the difference between dividend income and income from tax-free bonds. They're both numbers; they might even on some occasions be exactly the same number; how does the program tell them apart? The question is silly. Either they are never examined by the same process at the same point in the computation, or each is accompanied by a further bit of information that just *says* what category it falls into.

Or consider the problem Jackendoff (1987, p. 12) calls "the *externalization* of experience—the fact that my experience may be *of* things external to me.... The blueness of the sky is *out there in the sky;* the pain is *in my toe....* [A materialist theory] claims that the experienced blueness *in the sky* is identical with a state of neurons *in my brain* and that the experienced pain *in my toe* is identical with another state of neurons *in my brain.* How can the same thing be in two different places?"

This is obviously a pseudoproblem if the brain is a computer. When a signal arrives from the toe, its content contains a specification of the location of the pain, not just the fact that it is a pain. Experience arises as an aspect of the way these messages are processed; it is not a separate process in which we become aware of the existence and nature of the message itself. The message says where the pain is; otherwise there is no way in the world the brain could know where it comes from. That's why a lesion in the nervous system can cause pain to be experienced in a place far from the lesion. The lesion causes bogus messages to be sent, and their content is to some extent arbitrary; it would be a mere coincidence if the message happened to mention the exact location where the lesion is.[1]

Of course, none of this explains what subjective experience actually is. But it does clear away a whole class of problems that have vexed philosophers. Perhaps the others will also succumb to a computational explanation.

Free Will

I will start the explanation with a little warmup, explaining the phenomenon of free will. Many people have thought that free will has something to do with phenomenal consciousness. I actually don't think that, but they do have explanations that are similar in form.

Suppose we have a robot that models the world temporally and uses its model to predict what will happen. I am not talking about "mental models" as the term is used in psychology (Johnson-Laird 1983), but about numerical or qualitative causal models as used in simulation. Such models are a familiar application of computers. The main difference between what computers normally do and what my hypothesized robot does is that the robot is modeling the situation it is now actually in. This model includes various symbols, including one I'll call R, which it uses to denote itself. I dealt with the idea that computers manipulate symbols in chapter 2, and will discuss it at greater length later, especially in chapter 5. When I say the symbol denotes the robot itself, I don't mean to imply that the word "itself" implies something about "self." All I mean is that, for example, when it detects an object in its environment, it notes that R knows the object is present; and when it has a tentative course of action on hand, that is, a series of orders to be transmitted to its effector motors, it will base its modeling activity on the assumption that R will be carrying out those actions.

Now suppose that the actual situation is that the robot is standing next to a bomb with a lit fuse. And suppose that the robot knows all this, so that in its model R is standing next to B, a bomb with a lit fuse. The model is accurate enough that it will predict that B will explode. Supposing that the robot has no actions on its agenda that would make it move, the model will predict that R will be destroyed.

Well, actually it can't make this prediction with certainty, because R will be destroyed only if it doesn't roll away quickly. The conclusion that it would not roll away was based on the robot's own current projection of what it is going to do. But such projections are subject to change. For instance, the robot might be waiting for orders from its owner; a new order would make it roll away. More interestingly, the robot might have a standing order to avoid damage. Whenever its model predicts that it is going to be damaged, it should discard its current action list and replace it with actions that will protect it, assuming it can find some. Finding actions to achieve goals is a deep and fascinating topic, but it needn't concern us here. The robot concludes it should exit the room, and does so.

What I want to call attention to is how this sequence of events is represented in the robot's model, and how that will have to differ from reality. The reality is that the robot's actions are entirely caused by events. The sequence I laid out is a straightforward causal chain, from perception, to tentative prediction, to action revision. But this causal chain cannot be represented accurately in the model, because a key step of the chain, the making of tentative predictions, involves the model itself. The model could not capture this causal chain because then it would have to include a complete model of itself, which is incoherent. In other words, some of the causal antecedents of R's behavior *are situated in the very causal-analysis box* that is trying to analyze them. The robot might believe that R is a robot, and hence that a good way to predict R's behavior is to simulate it on a faster CPU, but this strategy will be in vain, because this particular robot is itself. No matter how fast it simulates R, at some point it will reach the point where R looks for a faster CPU, and it won't be able to do that simulation fast enough. Or it might try inspecting R's listing, but eventually it will come to the part of the listing that says "inspect R's listing." The strongest conclusion it can reach is that "If R doesn't roll away, it will be destroyed; if it does roll away, it won't be." And then of course this conclusion causes the robot to roll away.

Hence the robot must model itself in a different way from other objects. Their behavior may be modeled as caused, but its own (i.e., R's) must be modeled as "open," or "still being solved for." The symbol R must be marked as exempt from causal laws when predictions are being made about the actions it will take. The word "must" here is just the "must" of rational design. It would be pointless to use a modeling system for control of behavior that didn't make this distinction; and it would be unlikely for evolution to produce one.

Any system that models its own behavior, uses the output of the model to select among actions, and has beliefs about its own decisions, will believe that its decisions are undetermined. What I would like to claim is that this is what free will comes down to:

A system has free will if and only if it makes decisions based on causal models in which the symbols denoting itself are marked as exempt from causality.

By this definition, people have free will, and probably so do many mammals. There are probably many borderline cases, in which an animal has a rudimentary causal model, but the exemption from causality is given to its self symbols by building in some kind of blind spot, so that the question can't come up, rather than by providing a belief system in which there are peculiar beliefs involving the self symbol.

People lose their freedom when they cease to believe that their decisions depend on their deliberations. If you fall out of an airplane without a parachute, you may debate all you like about whether to go down or up, but you know your deliberation has no effects. More subtly, an alcoholic or drug addict may go through the motions of deciding whether to indulge in his vice, but he doesn't really believe the decision is a real one. "What's the use," he might think, "I've decided every other morning to have a drink; I know I'm just going to make the same decision; I might as well have one." In this case the belief in one's own impotence might be delusional, but it's self-fulfilling. One can contrast the addict's situation with the decision of whether to take a breath. You can postpone breathing only so long; at some point the question whether to breathe or not seems to be "taken out of your hands." The alcoholic classes his decision to take a drink as similar to a decision to take a breath. He no longer believes in his freedom, and he has thereby lost it.

The obvious objection to this account is that it declares a certain natural phenomenon to be free will, when introspection seems to proclaim that, whatever free will is, it isn't *that*. It appears to identify free will with a *belief* in free will, and surely the two can't be the same. It's as if I declared that divinity is a belief that one is God, so that any schizophrenic who thought he was God would be divine. This objection might have some weight if I actually did identify free will with a belief in free will, but I don't. Rather, I identify free will with a belief in exemption from causal laws. The alternative formulation is not just implausible, but vacuous.

Still, this identification of free will with a certain computational property may seem disappointingly trivial. It has nothing to do with autonomy, morality, or the worth of the individual, at least not at first glance. I admit all this. Unfortunately, this is the only concept of free will the universe is likely to provide. Many volumes have been written about how freedom might find a place in a world subject to physical laws, and no one has ever succeeded in explaining what that might mean. Some find comfort in the indeterminacy of quantum mechanics, or even in the lack of predictability in the classical laws of physics, but freedom surely doesn't mean randomness. Some suppose that free decisions are those that "might have been otherwise," but it is notoriously difficult to say what this means. So we are in the odd position of being introspectively certain of something that makes no sense.

In such a situation, the problem should shift to explaining why we have that introspective view, not how it might actually be true after all. Once we make that shift, the problem resolves very simply, along the lines I have indicated.

Some may find this to be a scary tactic, with implications that may be hard to control. What else are we going to throw overboard as we proceed? Suppose we show that moral intuitions are incoherent. Do we then simply shift to explaining why we have moral intuitions? Does that mean that we need not be bound by moral intuitions?

I admit to finding this scary myself, but the case of free will gives us a bit of reassurance. Even though I accept my account of free will, it doesn't change the way I think about my actions. As many philosophers (notably William James) have pointed out, it makes no sense to order one's life as though we could not make free choices. A statement of the form, "Because we can't make decisions, we should..." is silly, because any statement about what we "should" do presupposes that we can make decisions. We're stuck with free will.

This dismissal of qualms is more glib than I intend. I will come back to this topic later (chapter 6). But first, let us see if the method used to explain free will will also explain, or explain away, qualia.

Let's look more carefully at the structure of deliberate choices. Suppose a robot is built to sense and avoid extreme heat. One way to make it avoid heat is to build in reflexes, analogous to those that cause animals to jerk back suddenly when they touch something hot. But a reflex won't get the robot out of a burning building. That requires planning and executing a long string of actions. The detection of heat, and the prediction that it's going to get worse, must cause the robot to have an urgent goal of getting out of the situation it's in. A *goal* in artificial-intelligence terminology is a structure describing a state of affairs a system is to try to bring about. In this case the goal is "that R [the robot] be out of the building." The robot might have other goals, such as "that R know whether any human is in the building."

The interaction between goals can be complicated. Suppose the robot's second goal (call it G2) was an order given when there was no reason to believe that there were any persons left in the building. Then the robot's owners might prefer that it save itself (goal G1) rather than continue to search for people who probably don't exist. On the other hand, if fewer people can be accounted for outside the building than were believed to have been inside, then G2 would take precedence. But even though the robot decides not to flee the building right away, this is not a decision it can just make and forget. As the heat becomes more intense, the probability that it will be destroyed increases. There may come a point when wasting a perfectly good robot for a negligible chance of saving humans may seem foolish. I am not assuming that every intelligent creature must have an innate and overriding desire for self-preservation. It should be possible to build a robot with no desire at all to preserve itself. But we may as well imagine that the builders of the robot put in a desire to avoid destruction of the robot just so it would allow its own destruction only when its owners wanted it to.

It may sound odd to require a robot to have a "desire" for something. If we want the robot to behave in such a way as to bring an outcome about, why can't we just program it to do that? Isn't talking of "desires" just quaint anthropomorphism? No, it isn't. As I explained above, a robot whose world model is rich enough to include itself must believe itself to be exempt from causality. That means that if we want to program a behavior into such a robot we must arrange for the robot to believe that there is a good reason to choose that behavior. In other words, there has to be something that looks like evidence in favor of one course of action compared with the other. The robot may believe that everything it does is caused, but it will still have to have reasons for its choices. I said in chapter 1 that the distinction between reasons and causes suggests an argument in favor of dualism. Now we see that even robots must make this distinction and might thereby be tempted to be dualists themselves.

To make the point vivid, suppose that in the course of fighting its way through the burning house the robot, call it M, encounters another robot with an entirely different set of goals. The other robot, call it C, might be the intelligent controller of the house in question, and it might have been instructed to burn itself up. (The house has been condemned; there's no further need for this system to want to preserve itself.) C inquires of M why it is moving so steadily but hesitantly toward a burning room in which a baby is located. M replies that it wants to save the baby but doesn't want to be destroyed. C might ask, "Why are you taking corridor A to that room instead of corridor B?" And M might respond "There is less fire in corridor A." And so forth. But if C asks, "Why don't you want to be destroyed?" M will run out of answers. One answer might be, "Because I was designed that way." But M may not know this answer, and in any case it is an answer about what *causes* his goal. C wants to know his reason for having the goal. There is no reason for this goal; it is its own reason. M believes that "my destruction would be bad" is true and self-evidently true.

The point is that reasons must come to an end. It's conceivable that the end could be located somewhere else. The robot could believe that the happiness (or, as decision theorists say, the "utility") of its owners is the highest purpose, and thus want to preserve itself only as long as it believes that preserving itself is likely to cause its owners more happiness than the alternatives in the present circumstances. But it's hard to visualize this scheme working. Most of the time the robot cannot judge all the factors contributing to the happiness of its owners, or how its preservation would affect them. It's going to be more practical to have it want self-preservation unless that directly contradicts an order from the owner.

Now suppose robot M is in the burning room. Its temperature sensors are going off their ranges. The search has so far not revealed the location of the baby, if indeed it was ever here. The urgency of goal G1 is getting higher and higher, the likelihood of achieving G2 getting lower and lower. Eventually the robot decides to give up and run.

Until that moment, there is a "detachment" between the output of a perceptual module and the way it is used. When the temperature sensors report "Extreme heat," a goal is set up to flee, but it might not be acted on. Even so, the sensor report is impossible to ignore. Even if it doesn't get any worse, it is constantly demanding attention, or, more precisely, demanding computational resources to evaluate whether it is necessary to act on it. As long as the robot decides to stay in the fire, the heat is labeled as "unpleasant but bearable." At this point we can conclude that the robot's perception of the fire has something like a quale of unpleasantness. I do not mean that the robot labels the state reported by the sensor with the English word "unpleasant." I mean that however the state is represented, it is classified as "to be avoided or fled from," and it is so classified *intrinsically.* Just as a chain of goals must come to an end with a goal that can't be questioned, so must evaluations of sensory states. The robot may dislike going into burning buildings because it dislikes heat. But it doesn't dislike heat because of some further bad consequences; high heat is intrinsically not-likable. As with the goal of self-preservation, we can easily imagine the chain continuing. The robot might not like sensing heat because it is likely to lead to a state where it will sense damage. But the chain has to stop somewhere, and the sensing of extreme heat is as good a place as any. Extreme heat is easier to detect than damage and is strongly correlated with it.

You may balk at the notion that I have actually explained a quale, and I was careful to use the phrase "something like a quale." For one thing, at most I have explained one dimension of an experience, the dimension of "pleasantness." Wine and cheese may each taste pleasant, but they differ in lots of other ways. One may in fact doubt whether pleasantness is part of the quale at all. It seems clear to me that it is, and that the difference between the taste of turkey before Thanksgiving dinner and the taste afterward is explained by a difference in pleasantness (Dennett 1991). But it's not clear that a sensation could consist in pure pleasure or pure pain with no other characteristics. So we haven't yet endowed our robot with even an "as-if" sensation.

Still, we have given it an important component of mental life, namely *preferences,* which seem closely allied, at least in people, with emotions. With conflicting goals, a creature must have tags giving the relative values of various situations, and there is no point in having the values be questionable. If something can be questioned, then there must be a way of weighing pros and cons, and the factors in that weighing must be unquestionable. A creature that could really question the value of everything would never act.

A creature without preferences can behave, but it cannot make deliberate choices. Nowadays air-to-air missiles are programmed to avoid heading toward an airplane with a "Friend or Foe" signal that identifies it as a friend. An intelligent attack robot might want to be able to entertain the hypothesis that a friendly aircraft had been captured by the enemy. It would have to weigh its repulsion away from the possibility of attacking an aircraft labeled friendly against its attaction toward the possibility of destroying the enemy pilot sitting in that aircraft.

In science fiction, robots and androids are often portrayed as being without "emotion." In a typical plot, an android will be portrayed as unable to love or laugh (until a special experimental chip is added). It is, however, able to carry on a conversation, have multiple goals, and decide on different courses of action. It often prefers deduction to induction, and is usually driven by curiosity. In other words, it is not without preferences, it just prefers different things than the average human does. If you ask it, why do you spend time trying to find out about humans instead of studying more mathematics, it will give answers like "Humans have always fascinated me." If you ask it, why do you help the Rebel Alliance and not the Evil Empire, it will give answers like, "I find the Emperor and his minions suboptimal," as if robots, as ultrarational beings, would have an inherent tendency to try to make situations optimal, without actually preferring anything. One might dismiss all this as sloppy and inconsistent imagining by whoever wrote the script. But try to imagine an android that really had no preferences at all. It would behave in such a way as to bring certain goals about, as monomoniacally as a pool pump behaves when it keeps water circulating in a swimming pool. But when asked it would never admit to having any preferences for one outcome over another. When asked, "Why did you steer the ship left instead of right?" it would answer, "There was no reason for what I did. If you inspect my program you can see that the cause of my behavior is a long string of computations which I will print out if you wish." The problem is that it can't extend this way of thinking into talking about the future. If you ask, "Should we go left or right?" the android will refuse to answer the question on the grounds that it has no preference one way or the other. You have to ask it, "Given the following criteria, should we go left or right?" and then spell them out.

You might suppose that you could tell the robot, "Adopt the following criteria until I countermand them," but that just means imagining the original android again. It doesn't adopt the criteria for any reason ("You may read my program...."), and once they are adopted they *become* its unquestionable reasons for further decisions. There is no difference between an android that really prefers X to Y and one that unquestioningly adopts a preference for X over Y when told to.

Okay, but the science-fiction author never said the android didn't have preferences. She said that it didn't have *emotions*. It's interesting that to convey this fact the writer has the android behave as a human would if the human were heavily sedated or in shock. As long as the android doesn't have emotions, why not have it chuckle occasionally just to brighten the days of the people around it?

The question is, however, whether there can be preferences without emotions. Emotions seem to have three components: a belief, a preference, and a quale peculiar to each emotion. *Fear* is a belief that something is likely to happen, a preference that it not, and a set of sensations peculiar to fear. *Regret* is the belief that something has already happened, a preference that it hadn't, and a different set of peculiar sensations. (Obviously, there are many nuances here I am neglecting.) So it seems logically possible that one could have a preference and a belief without any special sensation. To investigate this further we have to focus on the structure of perception.

Modeling Perception and Judgment

Once again let's imagine the case of a robot, only now what the robot is thinking about is perception, not action. The robot has just made a perceptual mistake. It saw a straight object that it took to be bent. It stuck a stick into a pool of water and observed the stick change chape. However, after doing various experiments, such as feeling the object as it entered the water, it decides that the stick never actually bends, it just appears to.

This story sounds plausible, because we've all experienced it ourselves, one way or another. Actually, there is no robot today that could go through this sequence of events, for several reasons. First, computer vision is not good enough to extract arbitrary, possibly surprising information from a scene. A typical vision system, if pointed at a stick in a tub of water, would probably misinterpret the highlights reflected from the water surface and fail to realize that it was looking at a tub of water with a stick thrust into it. Assuming it didn't stumble there, and assuming it was programmed to look for sticks, it might fit a line to the stick boundary and get a straight stick whose orientation was halfway between the orientation above the water level and the orientation below. Or it might see one half of the stick, or two sticks.

Even if we look forward to a time when computer vision systems work a lot better than they do now, there are still some gaps. There has been very little work on "cross-modality sensor fusion," which in this case means the ability to combine information from multiple senses to get an overall hypothesis about what's out there. No robot now is dexterous enough to feel the shape of a stick, but even if it were there would still be the problem of combining the input from that module with the input from the vision module to get an overall hypothesis. The combination method has to be clever enough to know when to reject one piece of information completely; taking some kind of average of the output of each sense will not be useful in the case of the unbent stick.

Even if we assume this problem can be solved, we still don't have the scenario we want. Suppose the robot is reporting what it senses. It types out reports like this:

```
Stick above water
Stick goes into water; stick bent
```
(Feels)
```
Stick straight
```

The question is, How does this output differ from the case where the stick was really bent, then straightened out? For some applications the difference may not matter. Suppose the robot is exploring another planet, and sending back reports. The humans interpreting the output can realize that the stick probably didn't bend, but was straight all along. Let's suppose, however, that the robot actually makes the correct inference, and its report are more like

```
Stick above water
Stick goes into water; stick bent
```
(Feels)
```
Correction: stick never bent
```

We're still not there; we still don't have the entire scenario. The robot isn't in a position to say that the stick *appeared to be* bent. Two elements are missing: The first is that the robot may not remember that it thought the stick was bent. For all we know, the robot *forgets* its earlier report as soon as it makes its new one. That's easy to fix, at least in our thought experiment; as long as we're going far beyond the state of the art in artificial intelligence, let's assume that the robot remembers its previous reports. That leaves the other element, which is the ability to perceive the output of sensory systems. As far as the robot is concerned, the fact that it reported that the stick was bent is an unexplained brute fact. It can't yet say that the stick "appeared to be" anything. It can say, "I concluded *bent* and then I concluded *straight,* rejecting the earlier conclusion." That's all.

This may seem puzzling, because we think the terms in which we reason about our perceptions are natural and inevitable. Some perceptual events are accessible to consciousness, while others are not, because of the very nature of those events. But the boundary between the two is really quite arbitrary. For instance, I can tell you when something looks three-dimensional, whether it is or not. I know when I look through a stereoscope that I'm really looking at two slightly different two-dimensional objects; but what I see "looks" three-dimensional. If someone were paying me money to distinguish between 3-D and 2-D objects, I would disregard the strong percept and go for the money. Another thing I know about stereo vision is that it involves matching up tiny pieces of the image from the left eye with corresponding pieces of the image from the right eye, and seeing how much they are shifted compared with other corresponding pieces. This is the process of finding *correspondences* (the matching) and *disparities* (the shifts). But I am completely unaware of this process. Why should the line be drawn this way? There are many different ways to draw it. Here are three of them:

1. I could be aware of the correspondences and disparities, plus the inference (the depths of each piece of the image) that I draw from it. In the case of the stereoscope I might continue to perceive the disparities, but refuse to draw the inference of depth and decide that the object is really 2-D.

2. I could be aware of the depths, but, in the case of the stereoscope, decide the objects is 2-D. (This is the way we're actually built.)

3. I could be unaware of the depth and aware only of the overall inference, that I'm looking at a 2-D object consisting of two similar pictures.

It's hard to imagine what possibilities 1 and 3 would be like, but that doesn't mean they're impossible. Indeed, it might be easier to build a robot resembling 3 than to build one resembling us.

Nature provides us with examples. There are fish called "archer fish" that eat insects they knock into the water by shooting them with droplets. These fish constantly look through an air-water boundary of the kind we find distorting. It is doubtful that the fish find it so; evolution has no doubt simply built the correction into their visual systems. I would guess that fish are not conscious; but if there were a conscious race of beings that had had to judge shapes and distances of objects through an air-water boundary throughout their evolutionary history, I assume their perceptual systems would simply correct for the distortion, so that they could not become aware of it.

The difference between people and fish when it comes to perception is that we have access to the outputs of perceptual systems that we don't believe. The reason for this is fairly clear: Our brains have more general mechanisms for making sense of data than fish have. The fish's brain is simple, cheap, and "designed" to find the best hypothesis from the usual inputs using standard methods. If it makes a mistake, there's always another bug to catch (and, if worse comes to worst, another fish to catch it). People's brains are complex, expensive, and "designed" to find the best hypothesis from all available inputs (possibly only after consultation with other people). The fact that a perceptual module gave a false reading is itself an input that might be useful. The next time the brain sees that kind of false reading, it may be able to predict what the truth is right away.

Hence a key step in the evolution of intelligence is the ability to "detach" modules from the normal flow of data processing. The brain reacts to the output of a module in two ways: as information about the world, and as information about that module. We can call the former *normal access* and the latter *introspective access* to the module. For a robot to be able to report that the stick appeared to be bent, it must have introspective access to its visual-perception module.

So far I have used the phrase "aware of" to describe access to percepts such as the true and apparent shape of a stick. This phrase is dangerous, because it seems to beg the question of phenomenal consciousness. I need a phrase to use when I mean to say that a robot has "access to" a representation, without any presupposition that the access involves phenomenal consciousness. The phrase I adopt is "cognizant of."[2]

There is another tricky issue that arises in connection with the concept of cognizance, and that is *who* exactly is cognizant. If I say that a person is not cognizant of the disparities between left and right eye, it is obvious what I mean. But in talking about a robot with stereo vision, I have to distinguish in a non-question-begging way between the ability of the robot's vision system to react to disparities and the ability of the *robot* to react to them. What do I mean by "robot" over and above its vision system, its motion-planning system, its chess-playing system, and its other modules? This is an issue that will occupy us for much of the rest of this book. For now, I'm going to use a slightly dubious trick, and assume that whatever one might mean by "the robot as a whole," it's that entity that we're talking to when we talk to the robot. This assumption makes sense only if we *can* talk to the robot.

I say this trick is dubious for several reasons. One is that in the previous chapter I admitted that we are far from possessing a computational theory of natural language. By using language as a standard part of my illustrations, I give the impression of a huge gap in the theory of robot consciousness. I risk giving this impression because it is accurate; there are several huge gaps in the theory, and we might as well face up to them as we go. Another risk in bringing language in is that I might be taken as saying that without language a system cannot be conscious, which immediately makes animals, infants, and maybe even stroke victims unconscious. In the long run we will have to make this dependence on language go away. However, I don't think the linkage between language and consciousness is unimportant. The fact that what we are conscious of and what we can talk about are so close to being identical is in urgent need of explanation. I will return to this topic later in the chapter.

Let's continue to explore the notion of cognizance. In movies such as *Westworld* and *Terminator,* the director usually feels the need, when showing a scene from a killer robot's point of view, to convey this unusual perspective by altering the picture somehow. In *Westworld* this was accomplished by showing a low-resolution digital image with big fat pixels; in *Terminator* there were glowing green characters running down the side of the screen showing various ancillary information. In figure 3.1 I have made up my own hypothetical landscape adorned with both sorts of enhancements; you may imagine a thrilling epic in which a maniacal robot is out to annihilate trees. What's absurd about these conventions is the idea that vision is a lot like looking at a display. The visual system delivers the information to some internal TV monitor, and the "minds's eye" then looks at it. If this device were used in showing human characters' points of view, the screen would show two upside-down images, each consisting of an array of irregular pixels, representing the images on the backs of their retinas. The reason we see an ordinary scene when the movie shows a person's point of view is that what people are normally cognizant of is what's there. The same would, presumably, be true for a killer robot.

What's interesting is the degree to which people can *become* cognizant of the pictorial properties of the visual field. Empiricist psychologists of the nineteenth century often assumed that the mind had to *figure out* the correct sizes and shapes of objects starting from the distorted, inverted images on retinas. A young child, seeing two women of the same height, one further away, would assume the further one was smaller (and upside

Figure 3.1
How Hollywood imagines a robot's visual experience

down), because her image was. He would eventually learn the truth some-how, that is, learn to infer the correct size and orientation of an object, and then forget he was making this inference; indeed, he would find it hard to become aware of it. Nowadays we know that the perception of the sizes of objects at different distances is an innate ability (Baillargeon et al. 1985; Banks and Salapatek 1983). What's remarkable, in fact, is that with training people can actually become cognizant of the apparent sizes of images on the retina.[3] This is a skill artists have to acquire in order to draw images that look like actual images instead of schematic diagrams. Not everyone can do it well, but apparently anyone can grasp the idea. Look at two objects that are about the same size, two people, for instance, who are at different distances from your eye. Mentally draw two horizontal lines across the scene, one touching the top of the nearby object, the other the bottom. The faraway object can fit comfortably between the two lines with space to spare. If it doesn't, move your head up or down until it does, or find a different faraway object.

I could draw a picture of this to make it easier to visualize, but that would defeat the point I'm trying to make, which is that the average person, with training and practice, can view his or her visual field *as if it were a picture*. In doing this operation you are using the space of visual appearances in a way that is quite different from the way it is normally used. It is easy to imagine a race of beings with vision as good as ours who are incapable of carrying these operations out. They might simply be unable to see the visual field as an object at all. (Most animals presumably can't.) Or they might be able to draw imaginary lines across their visual field, but might be able to conceive of them only as lying in three-dimensional space. Asked to draw a horizontal line in the direction of a faraway person, touching the head of a nearby person, they might invariably imagine it as touching the head of the faraway person, as a horizontal line in space actually would. It is reasonable to suppose that there is some evolutionary advantage in having the kind of access that we have, and not the kind this hypothetical race would have.

Note that current vision systems, to the extent that they're cognizant of anything, are not cognizant of the two-dimensional qualities of the images they manipulate. They extract information from two-dimensional arrays of numbers (see chapter 2), but having passed it on, they discard the arrays. It would be possible in principle to preserve this feature of the introspective abilities of robots, even if they became very intelligent. That is, they could use visual information to extract information very reliably from the environment, but would never be able to think of the image itself as an object accessible to examination.

So far, so good; we have begun to talk about the way things appear to a perceptual system, but we still haven't explained phenomenal consciousness. That appears only in connection with certain kinds of introspection, to which we now turn.

Qualia

I argued above that a robot must assign values to different sensor inputs, but that's not the same thing as "feeling" them differently. We can imagine a robot attaching a number between −10 and 10 to every input, so that a dose of radiation and a fire might both get −9, but there must be more to it, or the robot wouldn't distinguish the two at all. You might have two pains, one shooting and one throbbing, that were equally unpleasant, but they wouldn't feel the same.

Of course no robot has a problem distinguishing one sensory input from another. The robot, we suppose, has several different sensors, and their reports do not get mixed up. A signal coming from the vision system does not get confused with a signal coming from the auditory system. Within a given sensory system there is similarly little possibility of confusion. A high-pitched sound yields one signal, a low-pitched sound another. Nonetheless, the question of how we distinguish a high-pitched sound from a low-pitched one can cause confusion. We're asking the *reason* for a judgment, and, as in the case of asking for the reasons for a decision, it is easy to mix this up with a request for the *cause* of the judgment. The cause is neurological (or computational): A physical transducer converts sound vibrations into signals, and low and high pitches yield different signals, which can be compared by another subsystem. But that's not the reason for the judgment. What I mean by "reason for a judgment" is exemplified by the case of distinguishing a fake Rembrandt from a real one. Here there is a list of aspects of the two objects that cause an expert to have an opinion one way or the other. In the case of high vs. low pitch, there are no such aspects, and hence no *reason* for the judgment (just as the robot has no *reason* to prefer surviving). Nonetheless people seem to have a reason where robots do not, to wit: "They sound different!"

Let's look closely at the sense system that has exercised philosophers the most, color vision. Let's start by supposing that a robot reacts to colors in a way isomorphic to ours. That is, its vision system is implemented using a system of three color filters sensitive in the same ranges as ours (Clark 1993), implemented with our visual pigments, or in some equivalent way. The robot cannot in principle make color judgments any finer than ours. That is, shown two different mixtures of light frequencies that looked identical to people, it would classify them as identical also. We may also suppose that its judgments are not coarser than ours; it uses just as much information as we do. Further, let's assume that it can make judgments about the similarity of colors that are indistinguishable from a human's. Of course, different people judge such similarities differently, so the robot only has to make judgments that are in the same neighborhood as people's. We will collect a record of the robot's judgments by simply asking it which objects seem to have identical or similar colors, thus making use of my postulate that linguistic access is an accurate measure of cognizance.

Having given the robot the same powers of discrimination that people have, we now stipulate that these judgments of identity and similarity are *all* that the robot is cognizant of. Just as people have no introspective access to the fact that their color judgments are based on the differential sensitivity of three visual pigments, the robot has no access to the equivalent fact about itself (figure 3.2).

We now have the robot making humanlike judgments about colors. The next step is to get the robot to associate words with colors the way people do, either by training it or programming it. Since words match closely with similarity judgments, this shouldn't be hard. The word "green" will

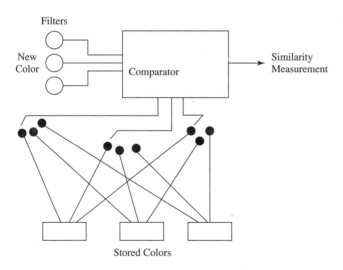

Figure 3.2
Qualia as outputs of a comparator

label everything whose color looks similar to tree leaves. There will be lots of borderline cases, but that just reflects the boundaries in the underlying similarity space.

Now suppose we show the robot some pictures, and ask it to find the green object in each picture, if there is one. Obviously, this requires many visual skills besides the ability to label colors, but we are allowing ourselves to be ambitious for the purpose of these thought experiments. So we can assume the robot can find familiar object shapes in pictures, and can correctly assign colors to shapes.

Next, the robot looks at two pictures, and says that picture A contains no green objects and picture B contains a picture of a green house. Now we ask it to tell us how it knows that. It points to the house and says, "Look!" We explain that we are philosophers, and do not want the evidence; we want to know why the robot takes it to be evidence. The robot would say it doesn't know why. We point to a house in picture A, and ask, what's the difference between this and the green house in picture B? The robot would say, if forced to say anything, that house B "looks like" other green objects, and that house A "looks like" other blue objects. It could not possibly say anything else, because similarity judgments are the *only* link between the color-processing system and the language system. All green objects have something in common, the property of looking similar to each other, but as far as the robot is able to report, this is an irreducible property, a stopping point. The property they all have in common is right in front of the robot's face, but it can't be analyzed, at least not by the part of the robot that is connected to the speech system. *This something plays the role in the robot that the quale of the color plays in the human mind.*

The dust jacket of this book shows a painting by Bob Thompson (figure 3.3), an American artist from the 1960s who liked to paint scenes containing human forms in classical poses, but filled with monochromatic splashes of color instead of normal features. Colors would be repeated, so that two of the figures might be filled with the same bold yellow, while three others were filled with red. If a robot looked at this painting, it would see not just colors, but colors with a particular shape. If asked to comment on how it knew that shapes A and C were yellow whereas shapes B and D were red, it can only answer that shapes A and C are filled

Figure 3.3
Bob Thompson, *Triumph of Bacchus*, 1964

with a something that looks one way, while B and D are filled with something that looks different. If asked to find other shapes in other paintings that resemble A or B, it would find shapes that were filled with the same "whatever it is" that fills A or B, or something "close."

My argument shows that if a robot were cognizant of judgments of color similarity that were structurally equivalent to humans', then they would be, as far as the robot could tell, introspectively equivalent, and hence the robot would believe that its experiences had qualia-like properties. However, as I have emphasized before, there is no reason that every robot would have to have judgments that were structurally equivalent to a human's. The robot might well have introspective access to color as a vector of three numbers (corresponding to the outputs of the three color filtors), or four numbers, or the Fourier transform of the light. The robot might classify colors in roughly the same way we do, but with significant differences in the similarity relationships of the type that have been discovered by psychophysicists (Clark 1993). But there is one point in respect of which human and robot introspections must be alike: they must both draw a line somewhere between what is introspectable and what isn't. The robot's introspections about similarity judgments must eventually bottom out. If it represents numbers in binary notation, then it might experience colors as bit strings (labeling a spatial array of shapes, presumably). But then it would have no answer as to how it distinguishes a 1 from a 0. One would be experienced as ineffably "one-ish," and the other as exemplifying pure "zero-ness."

There are many ways in which a robot's introspections could differ structurally from humans'. A robot might be completely unable to say what color an object is in isolation. In other words, it might, when presented with a group of objects, be able to say how closely the pairs resemble each other, while refusing to grant that an object in isolation has anything like a color. It might be unable to discriminate a series of objects presented individually, while being able to discriminate them when presented simultaneously. People are not able to discriminate two similar shades of red unless they can see them side by side; now imagine a robot in a similar position toward red and green, or, for that matter, toward black and white. This is a possible design feature but doesn't seem likely to be included in a reasonable design, or to have evolved. In any case, even if such a robot's introspections were very different from humans', they would still be "experience-like." If the robot can become cognizant of what I called the "pictorial" qualities of its visual field, then it has to label the surfaces of the objects in the picture according to their intrinsic similarity relationships. If a label of something as intrinsically and unanalyzably similar to other things is not a quale, it is at least close to it.

Most of my examples have been drawn from the domain of vision, but the story is much the same in other areas. One peculiarity of many sensory systems is that their spatial field corresponds roughly to the entire body. A tickle is felt as being in a particular place on (or in) the body of the person being tickled. Another peculiarity is that some senses don't seem to convey any information beyond the fact that they're occurring. A tickle doesn't announce the presence of anything but a tickle. Vision, by contrast, normally simply delivers information about the physical positions of objects outside an organism, and it takes some effort to be cognizant of the structure of the appearances of those objects separate from those objects.

Tye (1995) argues that this distinction is illusory and that the senses always represent something beyond their phenomenal quality. "What experiences of the tickle sort track (in optimal conditions) is the presence of something lightly touching or brushing against the surface of the body" (p. 116). I am willing to agree, with one qualification: it's really not necessary to be able to describe exactly what a sensory system tracks in order for it to have representational utility. Suppose a robot has three sorts of skin sensors, which react in different ways to different sorts of pressure. Having three different sensors might make it possible to perform most useful discriminations in most circumstances. That is, if there are two sorts of contact that are worth discriminating in some situations, the chances are good that not all three sensors will react to them in exactly the same way. Hence there is nothing in particular that the trio of sensors can be said to react to; what the sensors indicate in one environment may be quite different from what they indicate in a different environment. The discriminations would have to be learned, and might seldom rise to the level of reliability we associate with vision. In that case we would expect to see the boundary between perception and inference drawn differently, so that the perceiver is directly aware of the sensor readings and only inferentially aware of what is causing them. Indeed, that appears to be the case for touch as contrasted with vision, although there are counterexamples on both sides. A safecracker or heart surgeon no doubt becomes directly aware of events causing slight changes in the data received by touch. And, as Dennett (1991) has observed, our difficulties in saying exactly what physical property color *is* may derive from the fact that there is no need for the property to have any characterization other than "the property the human color vision system tracks." It suffices that many important differences in objects are correlated with differences in the way our color sensors react to them.

I said earlier that each emotion would involve a special quale in addition to a dimension of preference. Since we've established that robots assign qualia-like features to their cognizable percepts and assign different values to different outcomes, it seems inescapable that an intelligent robot would have emotion-like states. For example, if the expectation of danger and the sensing of extreme heat are equally unpleasant but distinguishable to the robot, then the story the robot tells itself about how it does so involves ineffable qualities. So unpleasantness + quality 1 is a state we can label "fearlike"; while unpleasantess + quality 2 is "painlike" (for a particular kind of pain). These states play exactly the role emotions play in biological systems.

The Self-Model

We have examined a set of phenomena so far, choice, preference, and qualia, and in each case we can explain why robots would have to have them or something like them by appealing to the way complex computational systems would perceive their own processes of perception and action. In other words, these phenomena appear as features of a system's model of itself. The concept of self-model may appear somewhat mystical, as if I am conjuring consciousness by showing the reflection of a mirror. Let me hasten to demystify the idea completely.

A computational model C is a computational system that resembles a modeled system S in some respect and is used by a modeling system M to predict the behavior of S. A self-model arises when S = M. This may seem an unusual situation, but in fact it is common. Here are some examples:

• A computer that takes inventory of the furniture in an office may include itself in the inventory. If it is predicting future furniture needs, it may note that the computer (itself) will become obsolete and is planned to be replaced by a smaller, faster model in six months.

• A real-time compiler models the time required for various operations when it is producing code. The time depends on the computer the code will run on. Here S = M if the computer the code will run on is the same as the computer executing the compiler.

• A robot must decide how much planning to do before starting to carry its plan out. In some cases (Boddy and Dean 1989; Russell and Wefald 1991), it can use a statistical model of the expected benefit to be gained by further planning. It should spend only as much time planning as may be expected to yield an improved plan that saves more than that amount of time. Because the planner and the agent that will carry out the plan are the same, the statistical model qualifies as a self-model.

• Some robot hand-eye control systems look at their own grippers ("hands") as well as the objects they are manipulating. In figuring out the future trajectories of the objects, such a system must use a different model for objects it is gripping than for objects lying on the table. The self-model takes into account the movements the robot plans to undertake.

The last example is of a type that will become especially important as robots become more common. It attacks a problem that all animals face, namely, making sure they distinguish between self and nonself.

A key feature of humans' self-models is that they are unitary. Each of us models himself as a single person. Well, of course; that's what we are, aren't we? How could we model ourselves as anything else? Actually, as I have emphasized a couple of times, it is not at all clear that the way we think about ourselves is the only possible way, nor is it clear how many ways there are. Our brains consist of billions of neurons, and while it is implausible to imagine modeling them all, one could easily imagine modeling oneself as a community of modules (Minsky 1986). This is, at least in principle, independent of the question whether each of us *is* a community of modules. Models don't have to be perfectly accurate. A self-controlled spacecraft might model itself as a single rigid cylinder, even if its shape is really more complex, and even if it actually contains internal parts that are physically disconnected from the body of the spacecraft.

It is hard to convince the self of how unimportant it really is. How often have you had an experience like the following: One day I was headed for the men's bathroom on my floor, the fifth floor, but it was being cleaned. So I went to the bathroom one floor down. Now, it happens that one of the toilets on the fifth floor doesn't flush too well, and some member of the custodial staff has posted a sign over it, "For hygienic purposes, please flush!" (In vain, I might add.) I went to the fourth floor, walked into a bathroom that was almost identical to the one I usually go to, looked up, and was surprised to see that the sign was missing. Later, on my way out of the bathroom, I started to head for my office in its usual location, and had to change course and go back upstairs.

How shall we describe such a case? "I was absent-minded; I forgot where I was." True, but what was really going on, once I was in the bathroom, was that I was just behaving as I usually do. I didn't actually believe I was still in the fifth-floor bathroom. If you had asked me where I was, I would have told you. My behavior was controlled by different subsystems than the ones that would have answered the question. From a conscious point of view this kind of event is inexplicable. Something other than "me" was in control. I think most people would be comfortable with that conclusion, but perhaps not the obvious corollary: that on occasions when I really am on the fifth floor, and my behavior is appropriate, my behavior is equally "inexplicable," although when we ask our self-model for an explanation it supplies one. If it is the self-model of a philosopher, it might say, "When I have a *desire* to go to the bathroom, and a *belief* that the bathroom is down the hall, I form the *intention* to go there, and then I go there." (See Milner 1999 for a remarkable list of cases where what people think they see and what they behave as if they see are quite different.)

Here is another sort of example. I have noticed that when I become skillful at a computer game (an activity induldged in for purely scientific reasons), the little creatures crawling across the screen seem to slow down. For instance, in the game of Gnibbles a worm crawls rapidly through a maze. If it hits a wall it dies. At first it seems impossible to control the worm. Before you can react, it crashes into something. However, eventually your nervous system gets "tuned" to the game. You anticipate what's going to happen, and now you seem to have all the time in the world to steer the worm left or right. But occasionally a situation pops up that you didn't anticipate, and before you can think the worm seems to speed up, spin out of control, and smash into the nearest obstacle. That's the way it seems, but the truth is that it the worm was never under conscious control, whatever that might mean. The self-model was just verifying that the worm was under control, and attributing that fact to decisions "you" made.

It is not hard to think of good reasons why we model ourselves as single persons in control of our minds and bodies. Each body can do just one thing at a time, or at least must carefully coordinate multiple activities. Multiple actions tend to occur as an ordered sequence. The brain module that controls needlework may have almost nothing in common with the one that controls tap dancing, but one must go first and the other second if the owner of these modules plans to do both.

Robots may not be under the same constraints as humans. It is not too farfetched to visualize teams of robots that act as a unit some of the time, and split into separate individuals the rest of the time. Their models of themselves might be very different from ours, although it is not necessary that they be; in principle, they could model themselves as a single creature with disconnected pieces.

Whatever the structure of a robot's self-model, the key point is that when it introspects it is "stuck" in that model. It can't escape from it. The model imposes certain basic boundary conditions on the questions it can ask. As I argued above, it can't stop believing that its actions are exempt from causal laws. It can't stop believing that certain things are intrinsically desirable or undesirable. It can't stop believing that objects are perceptually similar because of their intrinsic sensory qualities. Most important, it can't stop believing that it exists, or to make it more similar to what Descartes said, it can't stop believing "I exist." But what is meant by "I"? "I" is the creature who makes those free decisions, who feels attracted or repelled, or experiences the qualia of colors and sounds. In other words, "I" is an object in its self model, the key player as it were.[4]

It is a consequence of this theory that when the robot thinks about itself, it is manipulating a symbol that has meaning partly because of the model in which the manipulation takes place. Sometimes when a computational model is used to govern the behavior of a system, the symbols in the model end up denoting something because of the role they play in that behavior. Consider the file system on your personal computer; I mean the system of "documents," "folders," the "desktop," or similar entities that are used to organize data residing on your hard disk. If you were to print out the contents of the disk, you would get a long series of bits or characters. There would be some recognizable strings, but not in the correct order, and with lots of other junk interlarded. What makes this mess into a file system? It turns out that some of the junk is actually a description of how the pieces fit together. One block of bits describes how a bunch of other blocks (not necessarily contiguous) go together to make a file. Another block describes how a bunch of files are grouped into a folder. Other blocks specify where a folder will appear on the desktop, what aliases a file has, etc. A master block points to all the folders that do not appear inside folders themselves, and when the computer boots one of the first things it does is to read this master block, whose location is fixed.

We don't normally think about this. We see an icon on the screen. It has a familiar design, so we know that, say, it is a word-processing document, and if we click on it its contents will appear in the arrangement the word processor produces. From our point of view, the icon denotes the file. From the programmers' point of view things are a bit different, and it's their point of view we're interested in. There is a data object representing the file (and another, which we don't care about right now, that denotes the icon). The denotation is as reliable as the computer repairperson can make it, but it has a peculiar feature: the existence of the data object is necessary to bring the denoted object into existence. Without such a data object the file would dissolve into a bunch of disconnected bits. In fact, files are usually deleted not by actually erasing anything but by just removing their descriptors from the appropriate data structures and declaring their blocks ready for use in new files.[5]

We see much the same pattern in the way the robot models the self. There is, we suppose, a symbol for "I." The robot would exhibit some behaviors whether it modeled itself or not, but some behaviors stem from the fact that it thinks about itself as a "person," that is, the fact that in its self-model the properties of a single entity with goals, emotions, and sensations are ascribed to "I." It behaves as such an entity because it models itself as such an entity; its behavior is to some extent constituted by the modeling.

The question is, does this "I" exist over and above the creature that has a model in which "I" exists? The answer is not quite as straightforward as the corresponding answer about the file system, but it is similar in form. The "I" in the model makes free decisions; does that bring a being with free will into existence? There are two rather different ways of answering the question, but for both the answer is yes. First, if the robot asks, does someone with free will really exist, the answer is, yes, I do! That's because the robot can't step out of the model. It may understand completely that it believes it is free only because it has a self-model with this belief, but that understanding does not allow it to escape the self-model and suspend that belief.

Second, the humans that interact with the robot, and other robots, for that matter, will perceive the owner of the model as being a creature with the same attributes it assigns to "I." People begin assuming at an early age that other people are making the kind of decisions and having the kind of experiences that they are having. A child learns the word for a concept by hearing the word when the thing it denotes is perceptually salient. Learning the word "choice" is no different from learning the word "chair." When the child is trying to decide between chocolate and vanilla, and her parents are urging her to make a "choice," then the cognitive state she is in gets labeled as a choice. Its classification as a type of state is prior to that point and presumably is an innate part of her self-model. When she later hears the word applied to other people, she assumes they are in a similar state of indecision. It is plausible to assume that intelligent robots, if they ever exist, will attribute to other robots the same properties they automatically perceive true of themselves.

Because of processes like this, intelligent robots would perceive other robots as selves similar to "I." In other words, one way the symbol "I" brings its denotation into being is by encouraging its owner to deal with other entities as though they all were creatures similar to the way it believes "I" to be. The robot's brain is making its "I" up as it goes along, but the process works the way it does partly because other intelligent systems are cooperating to make everyone else up too. Robot 1 believes Robot 2 to have (or be) a self like its own "I," so the self that the symbol "I" in Robot 2's model denotes is also denoted by whatever symbol Robot 1 uses for Robot 2.

There is one aspect of the self-model that we mustn't be too casual about. If we are not careful, the model will come to occupy the position of the spectator at the internal mental show in what Dennett (1991) calls the "Cartesian theater," the part that actually experiences. This is not the correct picture at all. There is no part that experiences. Experience inheres in the whole system, just as life inheres in a whole cell. A cell is alive but has no living parts, and the brain experiences but has no experiencing parts. The self-model is just another module in a collection of computational modules. It is fair to say that the self-model is a crucial component in the mechanism for maintaining the *illusion* that there is a Cartesian theater: it keeps track of the beliefs about the audience. To carry out this role, it must have some special properties. One is that it is connected fairly directly to the parts of the system that are responsible for language. Another is that its conclusions are available for general-purpose inferences. This second property is stated somewhat vaguely, so much so that the first property might be a special case of it. The reason I am being vague is that I really don't know what "general-purpose inference" amounts to. But it seems as if a key purpose of introspection is the ability to acquire new capacities by reinterpreting sensory inputs. One learns that a stick that appears bent in water is really straight. The fact that it "appears bent" must be represented somewhere, and somehow associated with the inference that it "is actually straight." Where this association occurs is not known, but presumably it isn't the job of the module that normally measures the straightness of visible objects. It's not the job of an all-powerful self-model either. All the self-model does is reinterpret the input from other modules as information about perception and action, then feed it to where it can take part in inferences.

It may not be too early to speculate about where in the brain the self-model is located. Michel Gazzaniga (1998, p. 175) locates it in the left hemisphere, associated with the speech centers. He calls it "the interpreter."

The insertion of an interpreter into an otherwise functioning brain delivers all kinds of by-products. A device that asks how infinite numbers of things relate to each other and gleans productive answers to that question can't help but give birth to the concept of self. Surely one of the questions that device would ask is "Who is solving these problems?" Call that "me," and away the problem goes!

However, it's likely that the self-model will not be a localized "black box" in the brain. The brain can't ship signals to arbitrary places to take part in computations the way electronic circuits do. If a computation involves two signals, the signals are usually generated close to where they will be used. Hence we would expect every piece of the brain to contain neurons that react to what the brain is doing as a brain activity instead of simply as a representation of events outside the body. Where the signals from these neurons go is a matter for speculation by someone who knows more about the brain than I do.

One key aspect of the self-model is that it seems to be connected to episodic memory. In our survey of AI in chapter 2, we touched on various programs that learn things (such as maps and ways of winning games), but one thing they don't learn is what happened to them. TD-Gammon may play better backgammon because of a particular series of games it played, but it doesn't remember those games as particular events. The ability to remember and recall particular events is called *episodic memory*. People take this ability for granted, but it is really quite strange when you get down to it. Remembering an event is not simply recording a movie of it, not even a movie with synchronized sound track, smell track, and touch track. Memory is highly selective and not terribly reliable. One wonders why evolution would give rise to such a thing. Learning a skill, such as pitching horseshoes or playing backgammon, does not require remembering episodes in which that skill would have come in handy. Presumably simple organisms can only learn skills, and have no memory at all of the events along the way.

One plausible answer to the question of what episodic memory is for is that it supports learning when you don't know what you're learning. Something unusual happens and you remember the events just before it so that if the something unusual happens again you can see if the same kind of events preceded it the second time. "Remembering the events just before it" is vague and impossible to carry out completely, so you just store away the representations of a few of the events and hope for the best.

Episodic memory is not directly responsible for consciousness. But to the extent that the events in question are perceptual events, what will be remembered is the way things seemed. If you buy a new alarm clock, and are awakened the next morning by what sounds like your phone ringing, then you remember that the alarm clock sounded like the telephone. The next time you hear a similar sound (while lying in bed in the morning) you might remember that episode, and you might begin to clarify the differences between the sound of the telephone and the sound of the alarm.

One thing episodic memory and natural language have in common is that they seem to require general-purpose notations. If the brain doesn't know exactly why it's remembering something, it can't, as it were, "optimize" its notation for that purpose. It just has to strive to record "everything," even stuff that it might have thought was irrelevant. The natural-language system is similar in that it has to be able to talk about "everything." I use quotes to remind you that the goal of a notation that can express everything is far-fetched and not well defined. It is highly unlikely that the brain comes close. Nonetheless, it comes closer here than anywhere else, and here is where the self-model plays a key role in giving it something to express.

The link between the self-model and natural language allows us to explain why "cognizance" is so closely tied to the ability to report, and allows us at the same time to break the link between them. We now see that to be cognizant of a state of affairs is for some representation of it to be accessible to the self-model. That is, one is cognizant of a state of affairs *A* if there is a representation of *A* such that that representation could itself be an object of perception (although on particular occasions it may never become one).[6] In the normal course of things, one can report about what is in the self-model, so it's not surprising that one can report about what one is cognizant of. However, in the case of a stroke or some other neurological problem the link can be broken, and cognizance could occur without the ability to report on anything. Some animals may have self-models even without language, and a robot certainly could be designed to have one without the other. If it seems hard to visualize, just reflect on the limits to one's own linguistic reporting ability. You can be cognizant of the difference between red and blue, but you can't describe it, except by pointing to red and blue things. Imagine having similar limits to other sorts of reports.

It is worthwhile to stop here and conduct a thought experiment about the strong connection between cognizance and language. What would a conscious entity be like if it could use language but not be able to talk about what it was aware of? At first glance it seems that there could be no such being. It is certainly hard to imagine what its mental life would be like. You might picture a sort of aphasia: such a creature would be able to talk about everything that was visible and tangible, but encounter some sort of block, or gap, when it tried to talk about its own experiences. It's hard to imagine this species as a real possibility, let alone as something that would be likely to evolve. The young would learn language perfectly well, rapidly assimilating words such as *cup* and *chair*. But when one of them tried to ask its parents questions about what it was experiencing, it would draw a blank. It could not even utter the sentence, "Why can't I talk about some things, daddy?" Any sentence that even alluded to experience would be blocked. (I don't mean that the creature's tongue would feel physically prevented from speaking; I mean that, while the creature would have experiences, and be cognizant that it was having experiences, it would never feel tempted to talk about them.) It's hard to believe that a brain could filter out just this set of sentences, mainly because it's doubtful that the set is well defined.

There is, however, another possibility. Suppose there was a species on a faraway planet[7] for which *the entire linguistic apparatus* was disconnected from consciousness. These creatures can talk perfectly well, using languages just as rich as ours, but they do not know they can. Suppose creature A sees some buffalo and goes to tell creature B about it. He thinks (but not in words) *I must go see B*. B sees A coming. They stand near each other. After a while B realizes that A has seen some buffalo, and she decides what to do about it. However, B is unaware that A has *told* her about the buffalo. She knows that other people often bring information, but doesn't know how the information is transferred from one person to another. She knows that people often move their lips and make noises, but these motions and noises have social or sexual significance, and everyone is of the opinion that that's the only significance they have.

On this planet, scientists might eventually realize that the signals coming from mouths contain much more information than is generally assumed. By careful experimentation, they might figure out the code in which the information is carried. But figuring this out would not bring anything to consciousness. It would be analogous to our own investigations of neurons. We can, we believe, decipher the signals sent by neurons, but that doesn't make the content of those signals accessible to consciousness. Eventually the creatures' civilization might have a complete theory of linguistics, and understand perfectly how their language functions. But for them the whole system has as much to do with consciousness as digestion does for us.

An unconscious natural-language system like this is not hard to imagine. The computer programs that today carry on conversations on some topic are a far cry from full natural language, but one can imagine making them much more sophisticated without making them conscious. What's hard to imagine is an unconscious language system existing *in addition* to consciousness. This species would have conscious thoughts that, by hypothesis, would not bear any resemblance to words. More precisely, no one would *know* whether they bore any resemblance to words. The issue would not come up until the creatures' science had advanced to the point where they knew that such things as words existed. Hence the contents of their consciousness would be like that of animals or small children, which we have such trouble visualizing.

Of course, it's very doubtful that a species like this could ever develop enough science to realize how their vocal apparatus transmitted information. If their language evolved in one medium, it would be extremely difficult to transfer it to a different medium; if their language was originally auditory, a written language would be very unlikely to develop. The creatures would think of communication as something that happened automatically and effortlessly, and only when two of them were standing near each other. They might imagine an object that could carry messages from one person to another, but they would imagine a magic rock, say, such that if one person stood next to it and thought something, then the next person who stood next to it would know what the first person had thought. Without a written language, it would be difficult to store and pass on the kind of detailed nonintuitive information that science consists of.

Could this race tell stories about magic rocks? In a way, yes. One of them might imagine a series of events involving such a rock. Then it might get passed on to the next person. It could be clearly marked as "hypothetical," so that the next person didn't think there actually *was* a magic rock. Soon everyone might be thinking about this hypothetical event sequence. The shared fantasy might contain a signal saying who the original author was, although in this culture it's doubtful that anyone would care, even assuming that the concept of "original author" had any meaning.

This species could not tell lies, however. Telling a lie involves an intention to get another creature to believe something that you know is false. Suppose a female of the species finds an attractive male and wants to conceal his location from another female. She might deliberately walk in the wrong direction or behave in some other misleading manner. However, she couldn't tell the other female, "I think he's over there." Her unconscious communication system would make the decision what to say based on criteria that are inaccessible to her. The communication system might communicate false information, but this wouldn't count as lying. Suppose that natural selection has led to a situation in which information about the location of attractive mates is never transmitted. Then one day female A needs the assistance of female B in saving the life of male C, who is in some kind of mortal peril. A wants B to know the location of C, and runs to B. Alas, no matter how long she stands next to B, B will never know the location of C. A's brain might even send false information to B about C's location, but A isn't "lying" to B about where C is; A *wants* B to know where he is.

I'm sure everyone will agree that it is difficult to imagine the mental lives of creatures like this, but there is a worse, and deeper, problem. We take for granted that there is such a thing as "the self," so that when I sketch the situations above, and I say, "A thinks such-and-such," we automatically picture a self like ours having a thought like that. The problem is that our concepts of self, thought, and language are so intimately intertwined. If we move language from one realm to another, how do we know that the self stays put, rather than necessarily following the language facility? In the scenarios I discussed above, I assumed that the language facility would be inaccessible to the self, but can we be sure that the language facility knows that? Suppose the language of the creatures had words for "I" and "you," and these words were used consistently, even when talking about mental events. Suppose sentences such as these were produced:

- "You told me the apples were ripe, but most of them are still green."
- "From a distance, in that light, they looked red to me."
- "That story scared me."
- "Why did the magician cast the spell on the rock?"
- "Why did you tell me C was over there?"
- "I thought he was; I must have been mistaken."

One might rule them out, but it's not clear how. One might suppose that the sentence "They looked red to me" would be impossible, because language is disconnected from experience. However, if "why" questions cannot be asked and answered, it is not clear in what sense the creatures have language at all. Besides, one can answer such questions without any "direct access" to consciousness, as shown by the fact that the questions work fine in the third person:

· "D told me the apples were ripe, but most of them are still green."
"From a distance, in that light, they looked red to D."
· "Why did D tell me that C was over there?"
"D thought he was; he must have been mistaken."

If an earth spaceship landed on this planet and found the inhabitants making sounds in each other's presence, the earthlings would naturally assume that the creatures were conversing. If they could decipher their language, they would hear conversations with sentences like those above. They would naturally assume that there was nothing odd about the creatures. They could talk to them as they would to any speaker of a new language. They would not realize that the "true selves" of this species were unaware that these conversations were taking place. Meanwhile, the "true selves" would find that the new creatures were at first unable to communicate, but after a while they would be able to absorb and transmit information just like the natives. The "true selves" would not, and presumably never could, realize that the earthlings' selves were connected to language the way they are.

Under these circumstances, it is not at all clear exactly how we should describe what's going on. Rather than say that the creatures' true selves are disconnected from language, perhaps it would be better to say that they each have two selves, one connected to language and the other not. If we can say that about them, then how do we know we can't say it about ourselves? How do we know there isn't a "true self" inside us that experiences lots of things, including some things we don't experience? The true self would know it got information from other people, but wouldn't realize that the transmission was mediated through vocal noises. There might even two or more inaccessible selves inside every person. Needless to say, these possibilities seem preposterous, but I think that ruling them out is impossible unless we have enough of a theory of consciousness to find the conscious systems in the world. This is a subject we will return to in chapters 4 and 5.

Virtual Consciousness and Real Consciousness

Throughout this chapter I have talked in terms of hypothetical intelligent robots and the way they would have to think of themselves if their thought processes were to be anything like ours. It's hard to guess what such robots would be like, assuming they could ever actually exist. Furthermore, the range of possibilities for the mental organization of a new genus of intelligent creatures is undoubtedly larger than we can imagine from the single data point that humans represent. However, I believe it is inescapable that robots would exhibit something *like* phenomenal consciousness. We can call it *virtual consciousness* to distinguish it, until proven otherwise, from the real thing. Virtual consciousness is the dependence on a self-model in which perceptions and emotions have qualia, some states of affairs are intrinsically better than others, and decisions are exempt from causal laws. Although there are currently no machines that exhibit virtual consciousness, the question of whether a machine or organism does exhibit it is purely a matter of third-person observation. It might be difficult to verify that it is present; the concept may require considerable revision as we understand intelligence better; but if our understanding advances as I expect, then testing whether a system exhibits *virtual* consciousness will eventually be completely uncontroversial, or at least only as controversial as testing whether a system has a belief.

What I would now like to claim is that real phenomenal consciousness and virtual phenomenal consciousness are indeed the same thing. Our brains maintain self-models with the required properties and that's why we think of ourselves, inescapably, as entities with emotions, sensations, and free will. When you have a sensation, you are representing a perceptual event using your self-model; when you make a decision, you are modeling yourself as exempt from causality; and so forth.

The evidence for this claim is simple, but it doesn't actually exist yet. I am anticipating the development of a more sophisticated cognitive science than we have now. When and if we have such a theory, I am assuming that it will involve many new computational constructs, but nothing above and beyond computation. What any given neuron does will be modelable as a computational process, in such a way that the neuron could be replaced by any other component that performed the same computation without affecting the essential properties of the system. I am further assuming that self-models of the sort I am describing will be found in human brains, and probably the brains of other mammals.

If all this comes to pass, then we will be in a position to show without any doubt that virtual consciousness exists in human brains. There won't be any controversy about this, because virtual consciousness can be defined and investigated in purely "third-person" terms. Every *report* of a sensation, every *belief* in the freedom of a decision, will be accounted for in computational terms (and, by reduction, in neurological terms when the system under study is biological). The only way to deny that consciousness is identical with virtual consciousness will be to suppose that both are exhibited independently by the brain. Furthermore, in spite of our intuitions that when we report a sensation we are reporting on consciousness, it will be indubitable that the reports can actually be explained purely in terms of virtual consciousness. The belief that there is an additional process of consciousness will be very hard to sustain, especially given a demonstration that one aspect of virtual consciousness is the way it creates powerful, inescapable beliefs.

Of course, we are not in the position to make this argument yet, and we may never be. Many people may wish ardently that we never get there; I sometimes wish that myself. Nonetheless, if that's where we're going we might as well anticipate the consequences.

It is not easy to accept that the qualia-like entities robots believe in are in fact true qualia. When I experience the green of a tree, the key fact about it, besides its shape, is that that the shape is filled with "greenness." The robot is merely manipulating data structures. How in the world could those data structures exhibit a phenomenal quality like greenness? The key idea is that the robot has *beliefs* about the contents of its visual field, and the content of the beliefs is that a certain patch exists and is homogenously filled with something that marks it in some unanalyzable way as similar to other objects people call green. We do not, therefore, have to claim that the data structures themselves exhibit a quale, but simply that they support a belief in a quale. The relationship of quale to data structure is similar to the relationship between a fictional character and a book the character appears in. We don't expect a book about Godzilla to be taller than a building.

Please don't construe my proposal as a claim that "real consciousness doesn't exist; there's only the virtual kind." This would be analogous to concluding that nothing is really alive (because life is just a set of chemical reactions, no different in detail from chemical reactions in nonliving systems), or that nothing is really wet (because liquids, like solids, are really just atoms in motion, and atoms aren't wet). Consciousness is real, but turns out not to have all the properties we might have thought.

I have explained why a robot would model itself as having sensations, and why, in a sense, the model would be accurate. But I haven't quite said when it would be correct to say that a robot was having a sensation *now*. In other words, I need to explain "occurrent consciousess," as opposed to "the capacity for consciousness." The definition should be fairly obvious: A sensation is a particular perceptual event as modeled in the robot's self-model. Exactly what constitutes a particular perceptual event is not specified by the definition, but that's not important; it's whatever the model says it is. When the robot sees a sunset, it might in one instant be experiencing "sunset sensation," in the next a sensation caused by one cloud in the sunset, in the next the sensation of a particular spot of orange. Any particular occurrence of a modeled perceptual event is a sensation, just as any particular occurrence of a decision modeled as exempt from causal laws is an act of free will.

One consequence of this picture is that any perceptual event that is unmodeled does not involve a sensation. Obviously, perception does not cease simply because it is itself unperceived, but perception and consciousness are not the same thing. A thermostat reacts to high temperatures, but is not conscious of them. A thermostat that modeled itself in terms of sensations would, according to my theory, be conscious, but on occasions when a temperature measurement failed to make it to the self-model, there would be no more reason to suppose that it was conscious of that measurement than in the case of an ordinary thermostat.

For some people, all of this will be maddeningly beside the point, because it appears that I have simply neglected to explain what needs explaining, namely the actual qualitative character of my (or your) experiences. As Levine (1983, 1997) famously suggested, there is an "explanatory gap":

For a physicalist theory to be successful, it is not only necessary that it provide a physical description for mental states and properties, but also that it provide an *explanation* of these states and properties. In particular, we want an explanation of why when we occupy certain physico-functional states we experience qualitative character of the sort we do.... What is at issue is the ability to explain qualitative character itself; why it is like what it is like to see red or feel pain. (Levine 1997, p. 548)

Or it may appear that I have fallen into a simple confusion, mistaking what Block (1997*b*) calls "access consciousness" from the real target, phenomenal consciousness. A perception is access-conscious if it is "poised for direct control of thought and action." It is phenomenally conscious if it is *felt*, if it has a phenomenal character—a quale, in other words.

I stop at a traffic light. One of its bulbs means "stop," another means "go." Why does the "stop" light look like *this* and the "go" light look like *that*, instead of vice versa (or some other combination)? I use the demonstrative pronouns because the usual color words fail us here. You know what I mean: the two vivid qualia associated with stopping and going. How do *those particular qualities* follow from the computational theory of consciousness?

The answer is they don't; they couldn't. The theory explains why you have an ineradicable belief in those qualia, and *therefore* why there is nothing else to explain. When you think about your own mind, you use a self-model that supplies many beliefs about what's going on in that mind. The beliefs are generally useful, and generally close enough to the truth, but even when they are manufactured out of whole cloth they are still undoubtable, including the belief that "stop" lights look like *this* and "go" lights look like *that*.

Lycan (1997, p. 64) makes almost the same point this way:

My mental word [i.e., the symbol representing a sensation type] is functionally nothing like any of the complex expressions of English that in fact refer to the same (neural) state of affairs.... Since no one else can use that mental word ... to designate that state of affairs, of course no one can explain ... why that state of affairs feels like [that] to me.... Therefore, the lack of ... explanations, only to be expected, do not count against the materialist identification. They almost count in its favor.

You think you can imagine a world in which you experience different qualia for red and green objects, or in which my red quale is the same as your green. But what does it mean to compare qualia? If qualia exist only in self-models, we have to explain what we mean by comparing entities in two disjoint self-models (those of two people or of one person in two possible worlds). But there is no such meaning to be had. The closest we can come is to imagine change within a single self-model, as when the colors switch and you can remember the way they used to be. (I will have more to say on this topic in chapter 4.)

My theory of phenomenal consciousness is in the tradition of what I called "second-order" theories in chapter 1. Such theories postulate that conscious thoughts are thoughts about or perceptions of "first-order" mental events that would otherwise be unconscious. In David Rosenthal's version (1986, 1997), the first-order mental events are non-conscious thoughts, and the second-order events are thoughts about them. However, he would resist the identification of "thoughts" with computational entities. Lycan (1987) (see also Lycan 1996, 1997), following Armstrong (1968), proposes that consciousness is a matter of "self-scanning," or "inner perception." But Lycan (1997, p. 76) believes this idea explains only subjectivity (perhaps the same as Block's "access consciousness"), and not qualia: "... The mere addition of a higher-order monitoring to an entirely nonqualitative mental state could not possibly bring a *quale* into being.... The monitoring only makes the subject aware of a quale that was there, independently, in the first place" (Lycan 1996, pp. 76–77). This I emphatically deny. There is simply no place, and no need, for qualia in an ordinary computational system. The quale is brought into being solely by the process of self-modeling.

Georges Rey (1997) states the key insight reluctantly but convincingly thus:

We might ... include [in an intelligent machine] ... sensors that would signal to the machine the presence of certain kinds of damage to its surface or parts of its interior. These signals could be processed in such a way as to cause in the machine a sudden, extremely high preference assignment, to the implementation of any sub-routine that the machine believed likely to reduce that damage and/or the further reception of such signals.... The states produced in this way would seem to constitute the functional equivalent of pain.... Most of us would pretty surely balk at claiming that [such] a machine ... should be regarded as *really* having the experience of red just because it has a transducer that emits a characteristic signal, with some of the usual cognitive consequences, whenever it is stimulated with red light. But I'm not sure what entitles us to our reservations. For what else is there? In particular, what else is there that we are so sure is there and essential in our own case? ... How do we know *we* "have the experience of red" over and above our undergoing just such a process as I have described in this machine?

The machine could think and print out "I see clearly that there is nothing easier for me to know than my own mind," and proceed to insist that "no matter what your theory and instruments might say, they can never give me reason to think that I am not conscious here, now." ... If someone now replies that we've only provided the machine with the functional equivalent of consciousness, we may ask..., what more is required?[8] (pp. 470–471)

The idea that consciousness arises through the use of a self-model has also been put forth by Minsky (1968), Hofstadter and Dennett (1981), Dennett (1991), and Dawkins (1989).

There is a longer list of people who disagree with this whole family of theories. In the next chapter I will discuss and refute their objections.

4

Objections and Replies

Many readers of this book are going to find the central argument preposterous, obscure, or inadequate. Perhaps by voicing and dealing with various specific objections, I can make it clearer and more persuasive.

"Raw Feels" without Introspection

Most philosophers reject the higher-order-thought hypothesis on the grounds that there are many experiences that seem to occur without the kind of introspection the theory seems to require. As Tye (1995, p. 6) puts it, "...phenomenal consciousness can be present without higher-order consciousness. People who entirely lose their sense of smell, through damage to their olfactory tracts, are typically shocked and troubled by what has happened to them." He then cites a case from Sacks (1987, p. 159) of a person who lost the sense of smell and reported, "Life lost a good deal of its savour—one doesn't realise how much 'savour' *is* smell. You *smell* people, you *smell* books, you *smell* the city, you *smell* the spring—maybe not consciously but as a rich unconscious background to anything else." Tye concludes that this example supports "the view that phenomenally conscious states need not be conscious in a higher-order way. We are assailed constantly with smells of one sort or another. Typically, we do not notice them. We pay no attention to how things smell unless they are out of the ordinary. Our minds are normally focused on other matters. But the olfactory experiences are there, whether or not we reflect on them or attend to the things producing them." Tye also argues (p. 5) that animals presumably have phenomenal consciousness, but not higher-order consciousness or not much.

This objection is simply "overintellectualizing" introspection. To suppose that animals are conscious, according to my model, is to suppose that occasionally what they are paying attention to is perceptual events, and not the objects in the world that the perceptual events refer to. It doesn't seem absurd that a dog, cat, or chimpanzee might do that quite often. I doubt that an ant can.

The alternative picture suggested to Tye by the example of the person who could no longer smell anything is not exactly clear. For one thing, the fact that I would notice when a smell is removed does not entail that I must have been conscious of it before it was removed. We have all had the experience of noticing when a fan or other monotonously whirring machine is turned off. All of a sudden the room seems less noisy, and it becomes easier to hear other things going on. Now you can realize that the fan had been on for some time before that. You can even remember what it sounded like. But there is absolutely no memory of having been conscious of the whirring before the last few seconds. The conclusion that you must have been is simply an inference.

Of course, *one* way in which we might remember what the whirr sounded like is to have conscious experiences that are rapidly forgotten. But it is just as consistent with the data to suppose that sensory experiences have a "window of accessibility" within which it is possible to bring them to consciousness. When the whirring stops you can reconstruct an experience of the whirring, that is, what it would have been like if you had been attending to it earlier, but only as far back as the width of the window.[1]

The first view may at first glance seem more plausible, but it has severe difficulties. Suppose you are arriving at a large airport that you are not very familiar with. You are running late. You came in on Concourse B, and have a flight to catch in Concourse C. You're a bit disoriented, and can't remember the layout of the airport too well, but you know that when you enter a certain concourse you should turn in the direction of the Arrivals display. You dash in, see the display on your left, and turn left. The question is, Were you conscious of the fact that Flight 322 from Altoona is landing at Gate C at 4:05? It's written plain as day on the Arrivals board. You certainly *could* have been conscious of it. If it were the Departures display, and Flight 322 was the flight you were catching, you would have looked and seen it. But presumably you were conscious (at most) of the position of the Arrivals display, not what was written on it. Of course, it is possible to argue that as your eyes passed over these words you were briefly conscious of a huge number of things, which you quickly forgot. But the number is really huge. For instance, what was the typeface of the display? If you had cared about it, you would have noticed it and maybe even been conscious of it. If it had been very unusual you might have become conscious of it. Neither of these conditions obtained, and there is no reason to suppose you were conscious of their absence in some sense.

The argument in the case of losing the sense of smell appears to be, that since the patient *could* have been conscious of each of these things (the smell of a book, the city, people), therefore the patient *was* conscious of them. The conclusion is just as absurd as in the case of the Arrivals display. By the way, the *patient* doesn't seem to have the trouble philosophers have here. After all, the report is that smell creates a "background," "maybe not conscious, but . . . a rich unconscious background." Consciousness of the absence of this background does not entail that the perception of the background was itself conscious.

Another way to misunderstand my argument is suggested by a recent paper by Larry Shapiro (2000). He is responding to a paper by Peter Carruthers (1996) that outlines a theory of consciousness that is similar in overall approach to mine, although I disagree with most of the details.[2] Shapiro apparently finds a flaw in all higher-order-thought theories:

. . . I would agree . . . that there is a distinction between representations of properties in the world and representations of representations of properties in the world. A painting represents properties in the world and a photograph of a painting can thereby be a representation of a representation. When I perceive a photograph of a painting I form a third-order representation. But why should any of this be significant in an account of conscious experience? Carruthers thinks that unless subjects are able to represent representations of the world they are unable to have phenomenal awareness. Phenomenal awareness, for Carruthers, is an awareness not of the world, but of a representation of the world. . . .

This view seems unnecessarily complicated. It's the tickling [a person being tickled] feels, not her feeling of being tickled. It's the dog's barking I hear, not my perception of the dog's barking. There's good reason for this. Our sensory organs are directed outward toward the world (or our body) because it is properties in the world (or in our bodies) to which we must respond. It's the flame that burns us, not our representation of the flame, so it had better be the flame of which we are aware.

I don't know if this is a valid criticism of Carruthers, nor do I know what Shapiro would think of my version of higher-order-thought theory, but one can see how his point here might be taken as disagreeing with it. If so, it is based on a very simple misunderstanding. The higher-order-thought theory asserts that consciousness involves representations of representations, but this is *not* just another way of talking about "feeling one's feeling of being tickled" or "hearing one's perception of the dog's barking." When there is conscious feeling or conscious hearing, the feeler and hearer is "me." The system representing representations (or modeling perceptions, as I would prefer to put it) is just another module in the information-processing system. When *I* feel sensation *F*, it's because this module (and others) are doing certain operations, but none of those operations itself involves feeling. If any did, we'd have an infinite regress on our hands.

I think objections like these are vestiges of an old empiricist axiom that most philosophers think has been shed, namely, that for something to get into the mind it must first be "apprehended" by the senses, meaning the conscious faculties of the mind. The computational view frees us from this idea by making it clear how information can be transferred to a system in the absence of any conscious thought at all. But philosophers often seem to assume that if something can be sensed the sensing must at least be a "little bit" conscious.

One way to read my reply to this objection is to equate it with arguments to the effect that a tree that falls in the forest makes no sound if there is no one there to hear it. Such simple-minded skepticism deserves ridicule, and I seem to be making a similar argument that a perception that occurs when the self-model is not around has no quale. But there is a key difference. We understand the physics of sound and falling trees well enough to know that the simplest account of what happens when a tree falls involves a sound being made. The skeptic who doubts it has to explain why a sound might not be made, what might block the usual flow of events. In the case of perceptual events, the accounts of what happens when "no one is looking" do not involve qualia; they involve information processing, but no phenomenal experience. That's exactly what's so perplexing about computational and other materialist theories of the mind. If the only times when we're sure there are qualia are when we're looking for them, we should bite the bullet and doubt that they're there at other times. It's not simple-minded skepticism to believe that the only time a tree emits light in a forest at night is when you point your flashlight at it.

There is another fallacy with similar historical roots. Philosophers often talk about comparison of qualia being the way that biological systems compare stimuli (e.g., Clark 1993). What I argued in chapter 3 was that qualia are used to record comparisons that *have already taken place*. We see something as yellow because the vision system has classified it that way. The idea that we then compare the quale of yellow with the quale of another object to decide if it is yellow is just a myth the self-model accedes to when pressed. If you doubt this, imagine a thought experiment in which a "cerebroscope" (Tye 1995) is hooked up and you examine the behavior of the brain of a subject (possibly yourself) as the subject makes comparisons among stimuli. You trace signals coming from the retina, or some other sensory system. The signals encode information about the differential stimulation of different receptors, such as color receptors with different pigments. At some point two of these signals come together in a comparator and are classified as indistinguishable; a further chain of signals causes words like "They're both a sort of beige-ish taupe" to be uttered. The entire operation can be explained without reference to the quale of anything.

To be concrete, imagine a fiendish brain surgeon turned interior decorator who wants to convince you that the paint she chose for the bedroom matches the color of the living room exactly. Although forced to change careers after some unfortunate lawsuits, she's still better at brain surgery than painting, and has implanted some hardware in your brain that will allow her to alter your judgments of the similarity of colors. You look at the living room, walk to the bedroom, and, as you gaze at the walls she pushes a button that causes the neurons comparing the old paint to the new to produce the output "Colors identical." As far as you're concerned, nothing else is required to make the quale of one color exactly the same as the quale of the other. To believe otherwise is to believe that floating in the dualist ether are two different experiences which you helplessly find yourself claiming to be the same.

Let me make it clear that I am not saying that qualia are epiphenomenal, or, to use a metaphor of Dennett's, useless cabooses straggling after the train of information processing. They play a role in summarizing what the brain is doing, so that the brain can, perhaps, learn to do something slightly different.

In my image of introspection as a flashlight in the forest, it may sound as if I am equating self-modeling with attention, that is, claiming that something is attended to if and only if it is modeled in the self-model. I don't want to take that step. The theory of attention is not in very good shape these days, and I don't think anything should hinge on it (Hans 1993; Styles 1997). It used to be taken for granted that what a person attended to was what she was concentrating her mental resources on. The idea was that "thought" occurred at a slow, sequential, conscious level, while fast but stupid peripheral processes occurred in parallel, unconsciously, offering their outputs with differing levels of urgency to the conscious "central processor," or "executive system." Only the most urgent messages got through to be worked on by this precious and scarce resource.

The problem with this model is that there is no reason to suppose that sequential processing is inherently conscious. Whether a computational task is parallelizable and whether evolution has found a parallel way to perform it are questions that are independent of consciousness. There are surely many unconscious but slow and sequential processes going on in the brain. The real issue is why the system *models* itself as a sequential system that entertains essentially one thought at a time, and why it chooses a small number of items to be the "things it is currently conscious of."

One can speculate that the answer has something to do with the fact that it puts a strain on the system to feed observations of its own brain back into itself (and into the brains of its fellows through language). It pays to have a channel through which such observations can pass, but past a certain size the channel would just flood the brain with self-referential junk.

Why Aren't Computers Already Conscious?

One obvious objection to my view is that, if consciousness were as straightforward and unmysterious an attribute as I have argued, computers would already be conscious, or could easily be made so. As Georges Rey (1997, p. 469) puts it, "Most any computer in the country could be made conscious ... in about a week!" But that seems, to say the least, unlikely. So there must be something wrong with my argument.

Some versions of this objection (including that of Block 1997*a*) seem to assume that theories of self-monitoring predict that *any* kind of self-monitoring would make a system conscious. Such a theory would indeed deserve little consideration. If a computer models itself as a piece of furniture, the model could be quite detailed and still not lead to awareness. What's necessary is that the model describe the system as having the attributes we normally associate with consciousness (having sensations, making decisions, being a self, and such).

Rey (1997) does not make this mistake but goes into some detail in listing the kinds of self-observation that would be required. However, he underestimates the difficulty of implementing them. The main obstacle is not the absence of a self-model; it's having something worth modeling, and the ability to do something with the results. It's easy as pie to create a computer program that reasons about itself. I gave several examples in chapter 3. But most programs are focused on a narrow range of tasks, which enables them simply to overlook themselves. A chess program doesn't have to model itself, because its universe is the chessboard, on which the program does not appear. Even when a computer does model itself nowadays, it can usually neglect all the interesting interactions between its own computations and the topics of those computations. If a computer is doing an office inventory and includes itself, it will not take into account how the inventory will impact its future plans. This is as it should be; we don't want a computer factoring into a projected upgrade the fact that the computer itself will be turned off, let alone having an opinion about whether that would be a good idea.

Suppose, however, that we decided to make computer consciousness a top priority. We'll acknowledge that they are still pretty stupid, but we'll try to put as much consciousness into them now as possible, and nurture it as they get smarter. That would mean that, on top of, say, being a spreadsheet, the program would model the way in which it perceives keystrokes, model the way in which it makes decisions, and so forth. Alas, I have no idea what that would mean. Every time the program's user pressed a key, the computer could insert "Seemed to feel the letter K," or whatever, into a special list. Every time it had to decide whether to compact the data file, it might enter into the list something like, "Had to choose whether to compact the data file; decided to ask the user, who told me to go ahead." The problem is that these sentences don't really mean anything to the program, in that they don't play any further role in its deliberations. For instance, the English words "seemed to feel" always occur when there's a keystroke, but there's never any further cogitation about the fact that the user actually pressed W. The program can't notice the fact that its input has been remarkably free of the letter "E," let alone surmise that it might have a broken keyboard, and can no longer feel "E"s.

Hence I fear that giving computers consciousness now would be a fairly pointless exercise. In some rudimentary sense, it might succeed, but the result would not be recognizable. Computer consciousness will become an interesting possibility only when, and if, computers ever become comfortable enough in complex, unstructured environments to need a theory of how they themselves fit into their world.

One might be tempted to take my reply here and use it to create the opposite objection: The messages passed from module to module will *never* actually mean anything. A message might be written in medieval Latin and express in flowery detail what a certain wine tastes like, but that doesn't in itself mean the message is about the taste of anything. Computer data structures mean something only because human beings attribute meaning to them, that is, interpret them in various ways. The reason this objection is so devastating is that the normally harmless idea that meaning is observer-relative would imply that whether a system is conscious is observer-relative. We have no trouble accepting that, say, beauty is a matter of opinion and not a question of objective fact; but *my* consciousness can't possibly be a matter of *your* opinion. Nor can it depend on whether "I" decide to treat myself as conscious, not if the theory purports to explain the existence of "I."

These are very serious objections, which will occupy us in chapter 5. Until then, I will just take for granted that the concept of computational model makes objective sense.

The Absent-Qualia Argument

The main spokesman for those who find my position preposterous and inadequate might be David Chalmers, whose book *The Conscious Mind* attracted a lot of attention with an argument that any materialistic explanation of consciousness must fall short. Here is his summary (Chalmers 1996, p. 123):

1. In our world, there are conscious experiences.

2. There is a logically possible world physically identical to ours, in which the positive facts about consciousness in our world do not hold.

3. Therefore, facts about consciousness are further facts about our world, over and above the physical facts.

4. So materialism is false.

The second step is the crucial one. Chalmers's main argument for it is the "logical possibility of zombies" (p. 94). The word "zombie" is used by philosophers to mean a being that manifests behavior completely indistinguishable from that of ordinary humans, but experiences nothing. Philosophers sometimes explore the possibility that some of the people you know are zombies, and ask how you could tell them from everyone else. This is one way to phrase the problem of "other minds." Chalmers concentrates more on the case where *everyone* in the universe is a zombie. In this "zombie world" all the creatures behave the same as in ours, but they don't experience anything.

The question is whether this world is logically possible.[3] Chalmers argues that it is. He thinks this is an easy task. "I confess that the logical possibility of zombies seems . . . obvious to me. A zombie is just something physically identical to me, but which has no conscious experience—all is dark inside" (p. 96). This "comes down to a brute intuition."

Essentially the same idea is used in the "absent qualia" argument: One could conceivably build an intelligent robot that did everything ordinary people do, but felt nothing. Therefore there must be more to feeling—to qualia—than the motions of machinery. (The idea has been discussed often; for a recent discussion see VanGulick 1997.)

At first glance one is inclined to agree with the intuition that one can have an intelligent creature, or a whole universe of them, with no qualia. However, digging deeper reveals many contradictions. Let's start with the phrase "all is dark inside." Suppose you were walking down the street, minding your own business, when all became "dark inside." You would panic and start yelling for help, right? Wrong. This darkness does not affect your behavior in any way. You would not notice the change, or at least would not be able to report on it or act on it. Suppose all was dark inside from noon until dusk yesterday. You would have no memory of anything unusual having happened in that period. Memory is physical, and by hypothesis zombies are physically identical to real people. So someone who is a part-time zombie would not know it. You think you know what the phrase "dark inside" means, but that's because you know what it's like to experience darkness. The zombie would not experience anything. So, what does it mean?

My thought experiments so far have been about zombies in our universe. Perhaps intuitions change when we imagine an entire world of zombies. Maybe, but it's important to realize that the people in this world behave exactly the same as we do. They hold wine tastings and talk in rich detail about the sensations caused by different wines. In the zombie world there is a zombie Chalmers who writes books arguing that zombie universes are logically possible, and completely different from his world. He is, by Chalmers's supposition, as wrong as he can be about his own experiences, but he has no idea that he's wrong, and he never will.

The conclusion, therefore, is that Chalmers can have no evidence that he is not the zombie Chalmers and that this is not the zombie world. Indeed, it seems to me that the crispest way to summarize what's wrong with Chalmers's argument is to claim that this *is* the zombie world. It's a physical world with no accompanying irreducible phenomenal features. As I argue in chapter 3, the world does manifest virtual consciousness, which ultimately comes down to purely physical events. Virtual consciousness answers to all the properties of real consciousness, and so it is reasonable to identify the two.

In fact, if cognitive science succeeds, and virtual consciousness becomes well understood, Chalmers is going to have an embarrassing surfeit of entities. On the one hand there will be a tidy materialistic explanation of all the behavior associated with phenomenal consciousness, and on the other a free-floating set of irreducible features that explains only what things feel like. This outcome seems unacceptable to me. A theory of phenomenal experience must explain reports about experience, and other behavior affected by experience, in a cohesive way. (I called this the Principle of the Necessity of Behavioral Explanation in chapter 1.) There must be a causal chain from the experience to the behavior. This chain is what dualism has traditionally failed to supply, and Chalmers's dualism is completely traditional in this respect.

Chalmers is aware of this difficulty, which he calls the Paradox of Phenomenal Judgment. He even anticipates my conclusion: "Why not declare one's theory of why we judge that we are conscious to be a theory of consciousness in its own right? It might well be suggested that a theory of our judgments is all the theory of consciousness that we need" (p. 187). He draws an analogy with the tactic of explaining God away by explaining why people believe in God. "But... the analogy fails.... Why? Because consciousness is itself an *explanadum*.... There is no separate phenomenon *God* that we can point to and say: *that* needs explaining.... Consciousness ... is a brute explanandum, a phenomenon in its own right that is in need of explanation" (pp. 187–188). The flaw in this line of reasoning should be obvious. All our theory needs to do is explain why consciousness seems like a brute explanandum.[4]

Here's another analogy. Suppose a lunatic claims he is Jesus Christ. We explain why his brain chemicals make him think that. But he is not convinced. "The fact that I am Jesus is my starting point, a brute explanandum; explaining why I think this is not sufficient." The only difference between him and us is that he can't stop believing he's Jesus because he's insane, whereas we can't stop believing in phenomenal consciousness because we're not.

Chalmers quotes Dennett, whose position is close to mine, as saying, "I am left defending the view that such judgments [i.e., beliefs in the self-model] *exhaust* our immediate consciousness..." (Dennett 1979). Chalmers's reply is "Dennett's introspection is very different from mine. When I introspect, I find sensations, experiences of pain and emotion, and all sorts of other accoutrements that, although *accompanied* by judgments, are not *only* judgments..." (Chalmers, p. 189). This reply is much too glib.[5] He seems to think that your brain could have a belief without *you* having it. His picture looks like this: Here is your brain, having beliefs and making judgments. Here is you, experiencing things. Your brain might trick you momentarily into having false beliefs about your experiences, but direct introspection would soon set you right.

This picture is so obviously wrong that I feel I must be misunderstanding Chalmers. It seems clear to me that, within certain limits, for every possible state of belief M there exists a brain state B such that if my brain were in state B I would believe M. I choose this circuitous phrasing to make it clear that this is true for any nondualist position. The limits referred to are mainly concerned with bizarre inconsistencies. Although people can and do have inconsistent beliefs, certain wildly inconsistent belief states may be impossible to attain, simply because a sufficiently bizarre set of beliefs would be too incoherent to qualify as beliefs. Those limits do not come into play here. Chalmers's brain is in a state that causes him to believe that he has "sensations, experiences of pain and emotion," and so forth, and that these are more than just judgments, but have phenomenal content. No matter where he goes in his introspective space, he sees what his brain arranges for him to see. Chalmers thinks it is impossible that his brain could fool him this way indefinitely. If so, why? Where would the scenario break down?

Because Chalmers refuses to accept any of this, he is led down a tortuous path to the conclusion that all information-processing systems have some phenomenal experiences in some irreducible way. And since almost all systems can be considered to process information, there is phenomenal experience everywhere. Why it clots so thickly in human brains is a mystery, and is likely to remain so, because of the irrelevance of neuroscience and psychology to the question of consciousness. I am impressed with Chalmers's determination to pursue the consequences of his intuition to the bitter end, but I think the whole pursuit is a reductio ad absurdum.

One way to support Chalmers's line is to argue that there is no content to a belief that, for example, "I am having a sensation of pain," unless there is some prior meaning to this statement. You must be acquainted with sensations of pain in order to believe you are in one (B. Chandrasekaran, personal communication). One way to put this is that the brain can't have invented phenomenal consciousness on its own; it has to experience it so it can be recollected in later belief statements. Otherwise the belief is vacuous. Suppose I claimed that my brain believed there was a broffin of snood, when there really wasn't. What precisely does it believe? Saying it has always believed there was a broffin of snood, and that it can't stop believing there is a broffin of snood, does not help.

Fortunately, the brain's self-imputations of consciousness have more content than that. Every quale comes embedded in a *framework of comparisons* with other qualia. Indeed, I have argued that a quale is nothing but the brain's way of thinking about its own sensory comparison systems. A shade of red, even though I have never seen it before, is from the beginning labeled as similar to other shades of red. There is nothing mysterious about this; there is a comparison mechanism, whose workings are inaccessible to consciousness, and then there are the conscious sensations that the brain uses to keep from trying to think about how it works. There is plenty of content in a pain sensation ("This is like the pains I have whenever it rains," "This tends to get better if I don't sit down," "This is unpleasant") and the actual sensation is just a way of labeling that content.

Suppose you have a tickle on your left wrist and a heat sensation on your right wrist. How do you know the tickle is on the left? You just know. How do you know it's a tickle? You just know. Why are we tempted to say there is a "quale of tickling" and less tempted to say there is a "quale of leftness"? It's partially cultural, and partially because space is not normally thought of as a "secondary" quality. Suppose someone theorized that spatial position was sensed by first producing a sensation of the appropriate spatial quale and then comparing it to other sensations of spatial qualia. It sounds nuts. So is the corresponding theory for tickles. The comparison mechanism comes first; the sensations are an aspect of the introspection about it.

A useful analogy is the brain's classification of sentences as grammatical or ungrammatical. The concept of grammaticality is innate, although which sentences are grammatical depends on the linguistic environment. As a child matures, it finds itself classifying sentences as grammatical or ungrammatical without any intent to do so. Furthermore, the exact content of the concept is somewhat circular. Sentences are grammatical if and only if the speakers of the local language think they are. That does not make judgments of grammaticality vacuous; it just means that these judgments are part of the causal chain that makes the judgments true. This is a phenomenon we see over and over in the study of the mind.

Grammaticality is like "leftness" in that few people are tempted to suppose that there is a "quale of grammaticality." One might have predicted that philosophers would be sure there were such a thing. After all, if you ask an ordinary person, What's the difference between a sentence like

Mary found the man she had come with

and one like

*John found the woman who feared he didn't want to leave with

the respondent would in many cases not be able to say in detail what's wrong with the second sentence. ("It just sounds odd, or meaningless.") Here we have a perfect job for qualia! The first sentence produces a quality of "grammaticality," the second of "ungrammaticality," and *voilá,* they're different.

The reason no one says this is that we are pretty sure we know a lot about the *underlying structure* of the concept of grammaticality. We're not cognizant at all of the workings of the syntax system in our brains, but we know it's there, so we're comfortable with the idea that grammaticality judgments simply reflect the workings of this system. It's odd that we're so ready to acknowledge that a "quale of grammaticality" explains nothing, and so reluctant in the case of the "quale of beige" to draw that conclusion.

Comparing Qualia

There is another famous argument against any materialist account of consciousness, due to Frank Jackson (1982). Jackson imagines that there is a brilliant neuroscientist who happens to have been raised in a completely colorless environment. She has never seen anything that wasn't some shade of gray. (Perhaps special contact lenses have been placed over her eyes.) It further happens that her specialty is color vision. In fact, she knows everything there is to know about the neurophysiology of color vision. However, Jackson argues, there are things she doesn't know, including what red looks like. If some day she sees something red for the first time, then from then on she does know what red looks like. She went from a state of not knowing a certain something to a state of knowing it, so presumably she learned something. So she didn't already know this something. But she knew everything neurophysiological, or, if you like, everything *physical,* about color vision. Hence what she learned was not among the neurophysiological or physical facts. Hence materialism is false.

The usual materialist response (Lewis 1990; Nemirow 1990) is to argue that what the neuroscientist, whose name is Mary, learned was not a fact at all. Instead, they propose that what Mary acquires is the ability to imagine red things. These arguments are quite ingenious and perhaps even plausible. However, there is something a bit suspicious about shouting down such a strong intuition. It certainly seems at first glance that I would learn something if I learned what red looks like, just as I apparently learn something when I learn what tiramisu tastes like. Suppose someone had a philosophical reason for doubting that I actually learn anything when I learn the capital of Nebraska. It might be an excellent philosophical reason, but it would have a hard time refuting the intuition that I do learn something in that case. Why should we give in so easily on the corresponding intuition for the case of experiencing a color for the first time?

I would rather focus (as Dennett 1991 does) on exactly what Mary knows before she sees red for the first time. She knows everything about the neuroscience of color vision, so we may suppose that she knows everything about the way her brain will react when she sees red. Let's imagine that she has a detailed, accurate brain simulator, configured to simulate her brain; or, if that's not enough, that she can actually watch her brain in real time as it works. In the simulation, she can input light at a wavelength that she knows most people see as red, and trace the effects of this stimulus as they make their way through the system. She can see that this novel wavelength is exciting transducers that have never been excited before in just this way, and causing descriptors to be generated that classify the color as unlike any shade of gray. She might see where the brain generates a new symbol structure to stand for shades in that region of color space. The new structure might incorporate new symbols (perhaps chosen at random), or might be a combination of old symbols in a novel pattern. The new structure would then be fed back to the self-model flagged as being novel. There might be a variety of reactions, some having to do with emotions, some not, but all entirely predictable. Of course, the reactions might be random to some degree. If she's recording her own brain in real time then she'd see a random choice. If she has an accurate simulation, she can run it several times and learn the range of possible variations and which ones are most likely.

In all these cases, eventually she would see signals being sent to the vocal apparatus to emit sounds like, "Wow! I've never seen anything like it," or "How lovely." The fact that she says, or will say, such things will be entirely explainable in terms of how her brain compares the new stimulus with old ones, how her brain usually reacts to novelty, and so forth. One of the things she might say, and will certainly believe, is (expressed in English): "Now I know what red looks like." But "what red looks like" doesn't actually play a role in explaining how she comes to believe this; that can all be explained by pointing to (e.g.) a bank of neurons firing in a pattern that represents a point in color space.

In other words, in her self-model is a representation that "I now know that P," which, to be coherent, must be accompanied by a representation to the effect that P. P is "Red things cause a characteristic sensation, like [insert representation of red here]." What's inserted in the brackets is (e.g.) the vector of numbers encoded by the bank of neurons. What makes a vector of numbers into an ineffable quale is the judgment that it is a sensation.

Hence I think Jackson is partly right. Mary does learn something, namely, "Red things cause a characteristic sensation, like [insert non-sensation here]." Furthermore, she can figure out exactly what it is she will learn when she gets around to actually looking at something red. The something is gibberish from any standpoint except the standpoint of her own self-model, but that, unavoidably, will be where she stands when she actually sees something red for the first time. She won't escape from the self-model, so she really will learn something, something no one else can learn, although everyone can see what it is.

We can cause Mary some serious disorientation by hooking her up to a simulation of herself (or a cerebroscope observing her own brain) at the exact moment she sees red for the first time. She'll be able to track what is "really" going on, namely, that numbers and other symbols are being shuffled from place to place. She can also see that the self-model treats all this as if it were something else, a bunch of sensations. What is making this observation is, however, the owner of this self-model. Her view suffers from an inescapable form of multiple-personality disorder. In order to view the self-model functioning she has to be alive and conscious; but she can't be alive and conscious without using the self-model. She sees red; she has a vivid sensation; and she sees exactly how the brain concludes it just had a vivid sensation based on nothing but the activity of some neurons. She is classifying the neural activity as a sensation and as a nonsensation simultaneously.

Michael Tye may be making a similar point when he says,

... There is no gap *in the world* between phenomenal and physical states. The gap lies in different ways of conceiving certain physical states, different concepts that we apply. Introspect your experiences for as long as you like. Say to yourself repeatedly, and with as much conviction as you are able to muster, "This cannot just be a [physically described state]." You will establish nothing. The concepts you are applying to your inner states—the concepts nature has bulit you to apply on such occasions—do not allow you to see in what exactly ... the phenomenal character of a particular pain or hunger pang or feeling of elation consists. (Tye 1995, pp. 179–180; italics in original; I've deleted phrases specific to Tye's own theory or replaced them with more neutral phrases in brackets.)

The case of free will supplies a helpful analogy. Suppose Mary observes herself making a free choice. She sees the little brain cells adding up pros and cons, and she sees a decision emerging. If she is thinking about the process as well as living it, then she will see a succession of observations in the self-model, such as: "I have to decide," "I haven't decided yet," "I can go either way," "On balance, I think I'll marry Fred," and finally, "That was one of the most difficult decisions I ever made." Suppose she runs a simulation of herself a thousand times, and nine hundred and ninety-nine times she reaches the same decision, while on the thousandth she decides to enter a convent instead. Furthermore, it becomes clear that she decided in favor of Fred and against Algernon for good reasons, or at least reasons that carry a lot of weight as far as her brain is concerned. In fact, she, or someone else, could have run the simulation before she actually made the decision, and seen exactly what she was going to do. Still, the self-model will say, "I have to decide," "I haven't decided yet," etc. She may intellectually come to believe that she never actually makes a free decision, except possibly when choosing flavors of ice cream, when the decision appears to be completely random. Nonetheless, the next time she has to choose among alternatives she will see herself exactly the same way, as being in the position of having to make a free decision. She is wired to see herself this way.

One difference between my analysis and that of Jackson and other philosophers is that they often talk as though Mary had found out what red looks like, whereas I am assuming Mary has found out what red looks like *to her*. They are assuming that red looks the same to all normal human beings, and it is reasonable that it does, as long as we are talking about the structure of color space (Clark 1993). But such structural information has no necessary connection with qualia. We could perfectly well gather it by comparing frequencies of nerve firings. We do psychophysics only because our knowledge of neuroscience is so slender. Mary, by hypothesis, already has all of this structural information. What she learns by experiencing red is the "ineffable" aspect of qualia, the part that is completely indescribable, seemingly arbitrary, and independent of information about neural activity. If this is our focus, then I doubt that there is such a thing as the way red looks to a normal human being.

This brings us to the "inverted spectrum" argument. It goes as follows: Perhaps what person *A* experiences when she sees red is exactly what person *B* experiences when he sees green, even though computationally (or even neurologically) *A* and *B* are identical. Because we can imagine this to be the case, there must be more to the content of red and green than computationalism permits.

The flaw in this argument lies in the assumption that we can imagine someone else's green quale being identical to my red quale, or, for that matter, someone else's green quale being identical to my green quale. The problem is that qualia, in their primary meaning, exist only introspectively, only in my self-model. In that model it is possible to compare qualia (as well as measure their intensity, duration, shape, etc.). When we imagine comparison with another person's qualia, we are imagining the two being sent to a third person's, an objective observer's, mind, where they can be compared. Isn't that what we are imagining? When put this way, it seems silly. But I don't know how else to put it. The qualia do not exist "out there" in the ether, waiting to be compared with each other. The only conceivable way they could be compared is in someone's brain.

Very well, let's acquire or build a brain to do the comparison. But now we run into a problem. Comparison of qualia is not a real event; instead, qualia exist to summarize the results of (unconscious) classifications, that is, comparisons to stored sensory data. When we build our comparator brain, we can wire it any way we want. We could wire it so its owner would say, "Yes, those two sensations are exactly alike"; and we could wire it to say, "Sorry, those two sensations aren't even the same modality; one is green and the other is a tickle." Our objector might become irritated at this point and say that what he meant was an ordinary human brain, with ordinary human qualia, to be wired to the two subjects' brains in a way as close as possible to the way the "wires" are ordinarily connected. Unfortunately, this doesn't help a bit. If we take our signals from before the point where they are classified and send them to the new brain's classifier, then we will get new qualia, but they'll just be a third set, with no special status. All three brains will be looking at an apple and saying "red." If we install the feeds after the site where stimuli are classified, then we'll presumably be getting internal symbols from brains 1 and 2 that have no intrinsic meaning at all. Whether these symbols are to be taken to mean the same thing is purely arbitrary. (See figure 4.1.)

Let me stop to elaborate on this scenario at bit. It is reasonable to suppose that every brain uses some internal symbol or symbol structure for various sensations. If I am to realize that the apple I see now is the same color as the barn I saw yesterday, it is plausible that there is some computational nugget that is the same in the two mental states, some stable

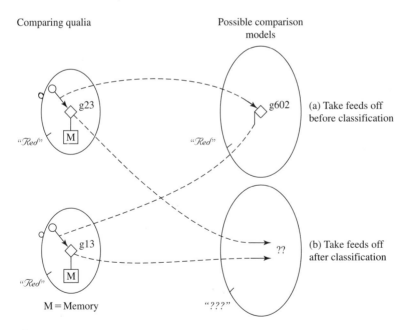

Figure 4.1
How can you compare qualia in two different heads?

activation pattern that we can call a symbol. (See chapter 5.) However, this symbol is completely arbitrary. The only jobs it has to do are (a) capture the degrees of freedom of the color it represents—hue, saturation, or whatever; and (b) be classified as "the same" as other symbol tokens that represent red. In a computer, we might picture this as a symbolic expression g23(0.8, 0.3), where 0.8 and 0.3 are brightness and saturation and g23 represents redness. In a brain, we presumably won't find a symbol represented in ASCII, but something else with the same degrees of freedom. The point is that the g23 part is completely arbitrary. All that's required is that it be reliably produced by red things and never by things of other colors.

Our second "comparator brain" scenario, therefore, comes down to this: when we pipe g23(0.8, 0.3) from Brain 1 and g13(0.8, 0.3) from Brain 2, do we translate the symbols or not? If we translate them both to some new symbol, then the comparator brain will say they are the same. If we translate them both to two different symbols, then the comparator brain will say they are different. There is no right answer.

One way to avoid the need for an "extra" brain is to have the inversion occur within a single person. You could wake up tomorrow and see green where you once saw red. But this is not a problem at all for my point of view. To get an inverted spectrum, it's only necessary to rewire the brain so that the symbols for red sensations in memories made before today are different from those for red sensations in all subsequent perceptions and memories, and the same as those for green sensations in memories made before today. In this case there is a natural place for the comparisons to be made, namely, your own brain.

It may seem that the argument regains momentum if we have you suffer amnesia at some point after the qualia inversion (Shoemaker 1981, 1997; Block 1997a). The amnesia supposedly doesn't affect the qualitative character, so if there was an inversion before the amnesia then there is one afterward. I disagree. There is *no* notion of comparison between qualia except the comparison performed by a brain, so if you remove the brain's ability to do the comparison, you have rendered vacuous the claim that my qualia today differ from my qualia yesterday. Suppose someone wonders whether his qualia are constantly but undetectably changing from day to day; to entertain this hypothesis is to entertain nothing in particular.

Qualia are incomparable between subjects even if by some coincidence the symbols representing them happen to get the same physical representation in the two brains (which seems very unlikely and perhaps meaningless, unless there is a synapse-to-synapse isomorphism between the two); it would still leave undetermined what the outcome would be of a comparison between the two.

Many philosophers find this last statement incredible; they assume that even if other cases are impossible to compare, surely two identical brains would have the same qualia, or, stated technically, "qualitative contents supervene on physical constitution" (Block 1997a, p. 684). I deny this. Compare this scenario: Two planets orbit the same star, staying on opposite sides. Each has a Holy Scripture that says there is just one god, who has three heads, expects virgins to be sacrificed to him, and lives on the north pole of the respective planet; neither god actually exists, of course. Do they worship the same god? No; even if *all* the beliefs and other representations about them happen to be physically identical, the two cultures locate the two gods in two different places (and if the two cultures met, each would no doubt conclude that the other's god was a myth). But this conclusion is no threat to materialism. A fictional world is a separate world even if the fictions are being produced by a machine. In important ways, fictions are exactly what qualia are, useful fictions with a grain of truth (because they are attached to real sensory events).

Hence inverted-spectrum arguments wind up being based on a meaningless premise, and thus do not need to be refuted. I hope this is not taken as a verificationist attack on the argument. Verificationism is the doctrine that the meanings of propositions are defined by the ways they are verified; if there is no way to verify a proposition it is meaningless. I am arguing that comparison of qualia is meaningless between minds because its meaning is defined only internally to a self-model, and there is no principled way to extend the meaning to cover more general cases. If you like, there are *too many* ways to verify or falsify the proposition that two qualia are the same, with no way to select the correct one.

Here is one way to miss this point:

...It seems... that if intrasubjective spectrum inversion is possible, intersubjective inversion must also be possible. For suppose that somone, call him Fred, undergoes intrasubjective inversion at time t. Assuming that others did not also undergo inversion at t, it would seem that either before t or afterward . . . Fred's color experience must have been radically different from that of others. (Shoemaker 1997, p. 644)

Shoemaker seems to assume that intersubjective comparison is not possible simply because we can never *know* if two people have the same qualia. Then we can start with the premises

1. "Before time t, either Fred's *red* is the same as mine or Fred's *red* is not the same as mine" (where *red* points to the quale of his ripe-tomato experiences);

2. "Fred's *red* before t is not the same as Fred's *red* after t";

and infer that "Fred's *red* is not the same as mine before t or Fred's *red* is not the same as mine after t"; and therefore conclude that, "At some time Fred's *red* is not the same as mine." But the first premise won't work; the disjunction of two meaningless statements is still meaningless.

Here's another analogy: Suppose someone is contemplating her ceiling fan, and wondering if its blades are oriented parallel to the axes of the complex-number plane. Obviously, this person is confused. We should explain to her that the complex plane is a mathematical abstraction, which has no orientation at all with respect to the physical universe. If then she suggests that when the ceiling fan is rotating there must be time instants when its blades are parallel to the axes of the complex plane, she hasn't understood; the failure to assign a truth value to statements about the orientation of the fan in the complex plane is not due to *ignorance* of anything, so no case analysis can get started. The same is true for intersubjective qualia comparison.

I will discuss the notion that mental entities are quasi-fictional at greater length in chapter 5. Here I will just mention one further aspect of this idea. Historically there has been much controversy over so-called phenomenal objects. When I hallucinate a pink elephant, am I perceiving some mental entity, and if not, what do I make of the noun phrase "pink elephant"? For various technical reasons (some alluded to in the discussion of Mary the neuroscientist), many philosophers have preferred to rephrase statements about hallucinations so that there is no entity being perceived. I tend to agree with Lycan (1987, 1997) that the resulting contortions are not worth the trouble. However, what I want to point out here is that the issue is not really, or not entirely, philosophical. It hinges on the actual symbol system used by the brain when thinking about hallucinations. If we find (as it seems plausible we will) that when I have an afterimage there is at least temporarily a symbol created for the purpose of recording properties (its location, its size, its color, etc.), then it seems that we must conclude that there is such a thing as a phenomenal object. Of course, having the afterimage is not a matter of perceiving that phenomenal object (as some empiricists of G. E. Moore's vintage might have thought). Similarly, if I have a hallucination of a pink elelphant, then my brain presumably has a symbol denoting a (fictional) elephant. Symbols about ficitonal entities are not without logical problems, but there is no special problem with symbols denoting phenomenal objects.

Perhaps the most audacious version of the qualia-comparison argument appears in Thomas Nagel's 1975 paper "What Is It Like to Be a Bat?" In this paper Nagel argues that something is conscious if and only if it is "like something" to be that thing. If we ask, what is it like to be a brick?, the answer is presumably nothing. But it seems as if the question, what is it like to be a bat? does have an answer, which unfortunately no nonbat can ever be in possession of. Furthermore, it seems as if we could know everything there was to know about the neurophysiology of bat perception and still not know what it was like to be a bat, even though there is something it is like, and therefore something to know. In fact, it would be fascinating to find out what it's like, because bats sense things with sonar instead of vision, so their experiences must be very different from ours.

This argument has charmed a generation of philosophers. Nowadays most papers on the subject sooner or later use the phrase "it's like something to be X" as a synonym for "X is conscious," or, more precisely, "X has phenomenal consciousness." I can't for the life of me see what the charm is. This substitution seems like a classic example of explaining something difficult in terms of something absurd. The phrase "it's like something to be X" contains the word "like," with an implied comparison, and in the case of "being X" no comparison is possible.

If I wonder what it's like to join the Peace Corps, what I'm wondering is what I would experience if I were to quit my job, volunteer for the Peace Corps, and go work in an underdeveloped country. Suppose I can't do that for some reason, such as being past the maximum age for the job. Suppose I meet someone who has joined the Peace Corps. Is there something he or she knows that I can never know? Of course not. For concreteness, suppose she is a woman who loved every minute of her service in the Corps. Suppose if I had joined I would actually have hated the experience. Is there a contradiction here I should worry about? No; when I say "I discovered what it was like when I joined up," I mean, "I found out how *I* would experience it." Others may have similar experiences, and at reunions I would gravitate to the group of bitter souls in the back of the room who came to loathe the Peace Corps, but it isn't because we know something the do-gooders up front can never know.

When we ask what it's like to be a bat I submit that all we are doing is imagining, in a confused way, what attendees would talk about, or wordlessly emphasize about, at the First International Reunion of People Who Served as Bats. We imagine somehow becoming bats, and comparing our experiences with our experiences as humans. If that's not the picture, I don't know what is.

"There is something it is like to be Drew McDermott." What an odd sentence, and one of a type that philosophers use constantly instead of saying "Drew McDermott is conscious." If I walked up to someone and said, "There is something it is like to be Drew McDermott," he might reply, "Am I supposed to guess what it is?" He might go on, "Let me see; perhaps McDermott is shy. Is it difficult for you to be with other people?" "No, no," I say, "You know what it's like to be you; I mean *that* sort of fact, but about me." In much the same way, Nagel appears to be saying, "Look, you know what it's like to be you. Just picture the corresponding fact for yonder bat." But the fact is that I don't know what it's like to be me. I can join the Peace Corps and experience a new way of life, but I can't temporarily stop being me, see what happens, start being me again, and compare the two states. The problem is there wouldn't be any mental continuity between the two, so the comparison would be impossible. If there were mental continuity, then it's hard to see in what sense I had stopped being me. Similarly, even if we assume that bats have phenomenal experience, that doesn't mean there's an experience of being a particular bat. So I'm afraid that, in Nagel's sense, there's nothing it's like to be me.

Of course, it is sometimes useful to talk about experiences one can have or not have. An addict might say to a nonaddict, "You don't know what it's like to crave opium." A sighted woman might say to a blind man, "You don't know what it's like to see." An intelligent bat from another planet might say to us, "You don't know what it's like to sense things with sonar." The problem is that these sentences do not actually refer to a phenomenal quality (although their utterers probably assume they do). Suppose, stung by the alien bat's challenge, we work on augmenting the human nervous system with sonar sensors, and suppose we succeed so well that our devices can extract more information from sonar than the superbat can with its natural abilities. Now we have to connect the output of the artificial system to the nervous system. At this point we can make it feel like anything we want. We could make it feel like a visual image by tagging it as though it were visual. We can make it feel like a ghostly hand reaching out to stroke nearby objects by connecting it to the touch system. Or we can make it feel totally unlike any other sense. Once we understand the nervous system (if we ever do), we will know how to make any given percept get classified as similar to or different from any other. It will be a matter of convenience. Let's imagine that some people prefer to have sonar feel like touch, some like vision. Now two such enhanced people are walking down the street, and they meet an alien bat. They can say, quite accurately, "*Now* we know what it's like to sense things with sonar," even though the similarity relations among their experiences are different from each other (and presumably different from the bat's). A similar story could be told about the other cases.

But X Couldn't Be Conscious

In this section I will refute various objections of the form, "If your argument were correct then X would exhibit phenomenal consciousness; but X wouldn't or couldn't, so the argument is wrong. The first is the "Chinese Room" argument due to John Searle. Searle has written at length, often eloquently, about the inability of computationalism to provide an explanation of phenomenal consciousness. However, I don't think his arguments amount to much more than putting the burden of proof on those who think it will provide such an explanation, where, I agree, it belongs. He believes he can prove much more, particularly with this argument:

Suppose we hire a person, call him Fred, to execute a computer program, that is, to simulate the series of events that would occur if the program were run on a real electronic computer. Fred receives inputs as strings of symbols, manipulates various symbols, and eventually produces outputs that are also strings of symbols. We can suppose the symbols are Chinese characters, but they could also be 1s and 0s. It doesn't matter; the point is that Fred doesn't know or care what the symbols mean. Unbeknownst to him, the program he is running carries on conversations in Chinese. The inputs are Chinese sentences (or straightforward encodings of them), and the outputs are appropriate responses. The symbols he manipulates (written on pieces of paper) correspond to the grammar rules, lexicon, and contextual knowledge of a speaker of Chinese. Note that to assume that this scenario could happen is to assume that AI might succeed as triumphantly as anyone has ever dared hope. Now, according to Searle, computationalism (what he calls "strong AI") predicts that, since Fred is behaviorally identical to a Chinese speaker, Fred understands Chinese. But he doesn't. If asked a question in Chinese he will just look baffled. This is a contradiction, so computationalism is false.

This does not appear to be an argument against machine consciousness, but against machine "understanding." However, Searle thinks the two are closely related; you can't be said to understand something without a certain experience of understanding. If we don't care about the experience, about the way Fred feels, we might be tempted to say that Fred does understand Chinese, because he behaves as if he does, in a way. So phenomenal consciousness is very much at issue here.

The flaw in the argument is its assertion that computationalism predicts that Fred understands Chinese, at least as we would normally construe "Fred." If my analysis in chapter 3 is correct, then computationalism predicts that a computational system with an appropriate self-model will have the required experience of understanding. All Searle's example shows is that if computationalism is true, then conscious systems can be implemented in unexpected media. In this case Fred is implementing such a system without knowing it. Seen in this light, the situation is essentially the same as Block's example (Block 1978), in which all the people in a country[6] cooperate to implement a computational system. Computationalism predicts that the group of people would have phenomenal consciousness separate from the consciousness of any of its members. Searle's example is exactly the same, with one person instead of one billion. The parallel may be seen by taking $n = 2$ as an intermediate case. Suppose Fred simulates the Chinese speaker's left hemisphere and Sally the right. Computationalism predicts that a single Chinese-speaking person will exist, separate from either of them. If Sally calls in sick Monday, and Fred takes over her work, nothing crucial changes. Fred won't suddenly understand Chinese. Similarly, if Fred simulates the Chinese speaker—call her Hong—on Monday, Wednesday, and Friday, and Sally on Tuesday, Thursday, Saturday, and Sunday, then computationalism predicts one "virtual person," Hong, will exist all week.

Searle may find the existence of such a virtual person unbelievable, and so may you (Block certainly does), but that's what computationalism predicts. Hence the fact that *Fred* doesn't understand Chinese is irrelevant, and the argument collapses.

Block and others (e.g., Lycan 1987) take for granted that a mind simulated by a crowd of people wouldn't have experiences. They try to justify this presupposition by adding extra clauses to their theories that forbid a system to have qualia if it is made out of pieces that have qualia. But the only real evidence for their assumption is the instinct that experience is an intrinsic feature of protoplasm and nothing else. That instinct was plausible before we knew that protoplasm is really just a collection of molecules organized a certain way. Once we have a theory of exactly how that organization gives rise to experience, the theory will overrule the intuitions we started with. If it is correct, then any other system with the same organization will also experience things. But most authors refuse to draw that conclusion, sticking instead with pretheoretic intuition. The only explanation I can think of for this discrepancy is that everyone thinks they can *see* living tissue feel things. Touch it, and it withdraws; injure it, and it cries, and we cry in sympathy. Unfortunately, our innate reactions to the behavior of living things tell us more about our "sentient fellow-creature" detectors than they do about the things themselves.

Searle's and Block's scenarios do raise important questions about personal identity in the computationalist framework. Suppose Fred is simulating virtual person V_1 and is instructed to make a backup copy. Sally then begins simulating this new person, V_2. Each has the same memories (encoded in the symbols written on the pieces of paper that constitute them), up to the point where they split. V_2 will think she is a woman named Hong who likes Proust as much as the real Hong does. V_2 might well dispute V_1's claim to be the real Hong.

There is nothing particularly novel about such puzzles, which arise in almost any materialist theory of the mind (Dennett 1978c; Williams 1976). Personal identity is simply not as cleanly defined as it feels. At this point we should not be terribly surprised at the fact that the way things feel is not a particularly good guide to the way things are, even, or especially, inside your own head.

However, there are deeper problems here, which for me constitute the most serious objections to a computationalist account of mind. If the mind is tied to the brain, then to get a personal-identity puzzle we have to imagine brains being copied, or the contents of one being transferred to another. These scenarios are comfortingly unlikely, but, more important, they don't require us to hunt for the persons at any point in the story. Wherever there's a (functioning) brain, there's a person.

But what if I show you a roomful of computers, and ask you to find the persons? What if it's a network scattered over a wide geographical area? In practice, we might not have much trouble distinguishing the individual computational processes, based on their personalities and memories; or if we had trouble it might not bother us. But one would have thought that there is a sharp division in the world between conscious and nonconscious things, and that sharpness might blur. Suppose a computer network had five personalities, but they all shared a self-model. Would this be one consciousness or five? I am not sure this is a coherent proposal, but I'm quite sure that if AI is possible there are many other weird scenarios that we will take for granted even though they would seem this incoherent if we could hear them described now.

The problem gets even more perplexing if we think again about the brain, and note that it may not be that different from a roomful of computers. Where exactly is the consciousness? I have a strong sense that there is just one conscious being in this body, but would an objective observer with all the facts agree? Would he or she draw the boundary between *me* and everything else the way I draw it? What if it turned out that, for example, the cerebellum has a self-model that was independent of the self-model in the cerebrum (the one we have verbal access to). Would that mean there were two streams of consciousness in everyone's head, complete with their own (incommensurable) qualia?

These objections are serious because they seem to make consciousness depend to some extent on what observers choose to see, when our intuition, since Descartes, is that the one thing that does not depend on what other observers see is whether I, this consciousness, exist.

5

Symbols and Semantics

In the last chapter, I raised what I consider to be the most serious objection to the view I am presenting: how do we find the computers and symbols in the world? We can't say that something is a computer when we choose to view it as a computer, because we want to say that *we* are computers, which leaves no one to choose to view us one way or another. If my brain's being a computer turns out to explain consciousness, it had better not be necessary to appeal to the judgments of conscious entities to explain what a computer is.

My theory is based on the idea that the brain maintains a model of itself. It's important to keep clearly in mind that if you examined this model (or the brain at the points and times when it is constructing the model), all you would see is molecules arranged in certain patterns, moving around in certain trajectories. The claim is that these arrangements and motions are such as to constitute a model; whereas other arrangements and motions would not. Spelling out exactly how this can be true is the biggest burden that my approach carries.

In this chapter I will address these issues. This will be the most technically intricate part of the book. Many readers will prefer to skim or skip it, especially the first two sections. For their benefit, I will summarize the conclusions of this chapter here:

• Something is or isn't a computer relative to a *decoding,* a mapping from its physical states to the computational realm.

• Although everything is a computer under some decoding, this fact does not trivialize the concept of computer, because computers under interesting decodings are rare.

• Symbols exist in almost every computational system, and some symbols, but not all, have meanings.

• The meanings of symbol structures depend on the causal relations between the system they occur in and its environment.

• Discovering the meanings is a matter of finding the most harmonious overall interpretation of the symbol system. Often there is residual ambiguity even when the meanings are fairly clear. Fortunately, this ambiguity doesn't affect the explanation of how the system works or what it does.

Computers

Some philosophers (notably John Searle and Hilary Putnam) have suggested that the very concept of computer is defective. A computer, in their argument, is just a system that people use to compute things. Without people to interpret the inputs and outputs, the computer is just another physical object. Physical objects simply undergo changes, such as motions. Such changes don't have interpretations in themselves. The interpretation comes from systems, such as people, who display "original intentionality." As Searle puts it:

The same principle that underlies multiple realizability would seem to imply universal realizability. If computation is defined in terms of the assignment of syntax, then everything would be a digital computer, because any object whatever could have syntactical ascriptions made to it. You could describe anything in terms of 0's and 1's. . . . For any program and any sufficiently complex object, there is some description of the object under which it is implementing the program. Thus for example the wall behind my back is right now implementing the Wordstar program, because there is some pattern of molecule movements that is isomorphic with the formal structure of Wordstar. (1992, pp. 207–208)

Hilary Putnam even proves a "theorem" that "Every ordinary open system is a realization of every abstract finite automaton" (Putnam 1988, p. 121). You have to read the fine print to see that this theorem does not apply to an automaton with inputs.

These claims are worrisome because the basic thesis of cognitive science is that mental processes are computations, that computation is the essence of what's going on in brains. For this point of view to be coherent, it must be meaningful to say that computations are objectively real and have observable effects (on behavior, in the end). If, however, computers are in the eye of the beholder, then it will not make sense to explain beholders and eyes in terms of computation. At best we could say that a system *A* was a computer from the point of view of system *B*, which was a computer from the point of view of system *C*, and so forth. To avoid an infinite regress the process would have to end with an observing system that was not a computer, thus proving computationalism wrong.

It is not too hard to refute the more extreme claims of Searle and Putnam. All we have to do is define the word "computer" carefully, abstracting away from the fact that historically the concept has been applied primarily to artifacts. A computer is simply a physical system whose outputs are a function of its inputs, where these concepts are defined as follows. The system must have a set of *states,* although there is no requirement that they be discrete states. Most of the time, when I talk about system states, I mean *partial* states, so that a system can be in several states at once. For example, it might be in the state of being at 30 degrees Celsius and also in the state of being colored blue. It may or may not make sense to talk about the complete state of an object. If it does, then a partial state may be thought of as a set of complete states, but it quickly becomes cumbersome to talk about such state sets.

A computer computes a function from a domain to a range. Consider a simple amplifier that takes an input voltage v in the domain $[-1, 1]$ and puts out an output voltage of value $2v$ in the range $[-2, 2]$. Intuitively, it computes the function $2v$.[1] However, it does this only if its input and output are interpreted as voltages with respect to the same zero point. Hence to be precise we must specify the *input* and *output* decodings with respect to which the system is supposed to be a function.

In system diagrams, the input to a system is the part with the big arrow pointing in. Nature does not provide us with such arrows, so we have to pick out the input with some objective criterion. We do it in the obvious way: The input causes the output, not vice versa. More precisely, when the system is in a certain input state, that will cause it at a later time to be in a corresponding output state. We specify what the inputs and outputs are with input and output *decodings,* which are just mappings from certain partial states to range and domain sets. In my amplifier example, the input states are partial states of the form "The voltage at point *I* with respect to the ground is v." The output states are partial states of the form "The voltage at point O with respect to the ground is $2v$." Given any (partial) state S of this system, the input decoding $C_I(S)$ is either a particular number, or $\perp$ if the input is not determined in state S. Similarly for the output decoding $C_O(S)$. If state S_1 is "the amplifier has input voltage 5 and is oriented parallel to the local gravitational field," then $C_I(S_1) = 5$, and $C_O(S) = \perp$. An *input/output* decoding of a system is just the ordered triple $\langle C_I, C_O, A \rangle$; A is a special state of the system called the *output availability* state, which I'll explain in a second.

With this notation in hand, it is quite straightforward to define a computer: A system S computes function F with respect to decoding $\langle C_I, C_O, A \rangle$ if and only if whenever it is in a state S with $C_I(S) = x$, that causes it at some observable later time it to be in a state S' with $C_O(S) = F(x)$. By "observable later time" I mean that there is a distinguished state A such that whenever S enters A, the output class it is in corresponds to $F(x)$. I use the word "decoding" with some trepidation. "Interpretation" might be better, but it carries much too much semantic baggage. "Decoding" sounds odd enough that people might stop occasionally and remind themselves what I mean by it. There is no implication that someone has literally "encoded" some signal in the physical state of a computer, although I will say that a state *encodes* x just in case x is the decoding of that state (when the decoding I intend is obvious in context).

It is important that the relation between the input and output of the system be causal. Otherwise, consider a circuit that simply outputs a sinusoidal voltage $V = \sin 2\pi x$. We could consider this to be computing any function $y = f(x)$ at all from the range $[-1, 1]$ to $[-1, 1]$, by taking input and output to be the whole system, and noting that if $V = x$ at time t_0, then V will $= f(x)$ at some later time. However, there is no causal relation between the two, because causality must support some sort of counterfactual: If V had had value x' at time t_0, then V would have behaved differently at some later time. But nothing of the sort can be inferred from the description of the circuit as as producing a sinusoidal voltage. Of course, in this case there is also the problem that there is no state class A that the system enters when the output value is available.

The amplifier example does provide the kind of counterfactual I require: if the input were different, then (by design) the output would have been different. This counterfactual depends on the decoding staying the same, because which function a physical system computes depends on the I/O decoding. If we used the input decoding $C_I(S) = \sqrt{|v_I|}$ and the output decoding $C_O(S) = v_O^2$, where v_I is the input voltage and v_O is the output voltage, then the amplifier would compute the function v^4. Note that the domain of the function, so decoded, is now $[0, 1]$, because the voltages from -1 to 0 are just alternative encodings of the same numbers encoded by the voltages from 0 to 1.

It may appear as if I am conceding too much to Searle and Putnam to grant that *being a computer* is relative to a decoding. I must stress, however, that whether or not something is a computer relative to a particular decoding is a matter of objective fact. It's no more subjective than the speed of an object, which cannot be measured without a frame of reference. It doesn't matter whether the decoding is of any use to anyone, or has even occurred to anyone. As we will see later, it is rarely possible to assign a coherent *semantics* to a computer under an arbitrary decoding, but we can't make the "computerness" of an object depend on its bearing a semantic relation to its environment. A computer is an essentially *syntactic* engine, and that's why it is so useful to both evolution and humanity. If something needs to be computed, there is usually a device that will compute it.

My definition can be contrasted with definitions such as this due to Fodor (1975):

Every computational system is a complex system which changes physical state in some way determined by physical laws. It is feasible to think of a system as a computer just insofar as it is possible to devise some mapping which pairs physical states of the device with formulae in a computing language in such a fashion as to preserve desired semantic relations among the formulae. For example, we may assign physical states of the machine to sentences in the language in such a way that if $S_1, \ldots, S_n$ are machine states, and if $F_1, \ldots, F_{n-1}, F_n$ are the sentences paired with $S_1, \ldots, S_{n-1}, S_n$, respectively, then the physical constitution of the machine is such that it will actually run through that sequence of states only if $F_1, \ldots, F_{n-1}$ constitutes a proof of F_n. (p. 73)

It is hard to be sure exactly what Fodor means by "semantic relations" here. Technically, my notion of a function under a decoding might qualify as preserving semantic relations. But the example of deduction seems to imply much more. Usually when one talks of "sentences" and "semantics" in the same breath, one is talking about the meanings of those sentences, that is, what they denote. But I am pretty sure that what Fodor means is that the sentences *are* the meanings of the machine states, and the "semantic relations" at issue here are actually *proof-theoretic* relations. That is, the relation between F_n and the other formulas is that the others are a proof of F_n. This fact does not depend on whether any meaning at all has been assigned to these formulas; they could even be inconsistent, and hence lack an interpretation in any technical sense.

Another odd feature of Fodor's example is the fact that the machine "runs through" the state sequence "only if" the sequence encodes a proof. The phrase "only if" means that the machine never runs through a state sequence that isn't a proof of something. But if the machine never runs through any state sequences at all it will have this property. Perhaps it's just the example that is poorly phrased, but the definition itself says only that a computer must "preserve" semantic relations. I believe a computer must do considerably more: it must (almost always) go into a state that encodes the output of a function when started in a state that encodes the input.

I believe that people like Fodor (and Harnad; see chapter 2) are worried that if "computer" and "symbol" are defined too broadly, too many things will be classified as computers. But even from a purely syntactic viewpoint it is often impossible to choose a completely arbitrary decoding with respect to which to observe a computer. A key case is the notion of composing two computers to make a composite computer. A computer C is the composition of computers C_1 and C_2 if the output of C_1 is the input to C_2. But this makes sense only with respect to a consistent pair of decodings. That is, if S is a state of the composite system $C_1 + C_2$, then $C_{2I}(S)$, the decoded input to C_2, must $= C_{1O}(S)$, the decoded output of C_1.

One might wish for a "natural" decoding that would stand out as the "obvious" one by which to evaluate the claim that a system is a computer. It might be the most economical or elegant, or the one that made the description of the computed function as simple as possible, or even one that was "intended" by human designers or by evolution. I don't think the elegance of a decoding counts *against* its being a correct description of a computer, but one need not choose any decoding, elegant or not, as the "correct" one. If a system computes many different functions under many different decodings, so be it. It is of course true that if someone claims a particular system computes a particular function under some decoding (as when Searle claims the wall behind him computes the same function as Wordstar), the burden of proof is on him.

This is especially true when we claim that a system computes a certain function "approximately." All physically real computers are approximate, in the sense that most small perturbations of their inputs do not result in large perturbations of their output. It's possible for a system to compute a certain function exactly under some decoding, but not approximately under any decoding. If so, it's impossible to ever observe it computing anything, or to incorporate it into a larger system compositionally. The first is impossible because observation is inherently noisy, and therefore it would be impossible to verify that the system was in a particular input or output state. The second is impossible because disconnecting the system from its environment and "plugging it into" a larger system would inevitably perturb it in ways that would make it impossible to reenter its input states.[2]

Because nonapproximate computers are not interesting, I will stipulate what I call the *continuity requirement*: that for most complete system states, a small perturbation from the state makes a small difference in the output. To make the requirement precise I would have to spell out what I mean by "small," both in the physical domain and in the logical range of the decodings, but I am not going to pause to achieve that precision. If someone wants to claim (as Searle does) that his wall computes what Wordstar computes, the burden is on him to show that it does this in a way that satisfies the continuity requirement. If he can't, then his claim is vacuous, because the computational behavior he posits will be destroyed by the slightest change in environmental conditions.

One extreme category of decoding that satisfies the continuity requirement is one in which, within a certain range, all fluctuations in physical state are completely irrelevant: they all map to the same decoded value. A decoding with this property is said to be *discrete*. The most obvious example is a digital circuit, which is treated as representing a 1 over some large range of possible states, as representing a 0 over some other large range, and as representing nothing in the rest of its possible states.

My definition of "computer" is very general. It encompasses digital computers, but it encompasses many other systems as well. In fact, it is so general that every physical system can be construed as a computer, or several computers, or even an infinite set of different computers. However, there are some useful concepts of computation that it leaves out. We should also include the idea of a *probably approximate* computer, which produces a value close to $F(I)$ with a probability that depends on the distance. I don't think such details are going to be essential in what follows, although I don't doubt that in nature we rarely find anything but probably approximate computers. I will neglect that and assume the continuity requirement suffices to capture the set of all reasonable computers.

It may appear that my definition includes only computers with no memory, because the output is allowed to depend only on a single input, and not on an input history. However, it will be simplest to view memory as simply the tendency for a state to persist. When a system includes a memory module, then we can view it as an ensemble of computers, some of which compute the persistent state from the input and preexisting state, and some of which compute outputs from inputs and persistent state.

Here are some examples of computers: A thermostat computes the function

if $x > t$ then true else false,

where the input state is the set of temperatures near the thermostat, and the output state set is $\{B, S\}$, where B is the set of states where the thermostat sensor is bent enough to close a circuit, and S is the set where it is too straight to close it. The input, x, is just the temperature measured in the same scale (e.g., Fahrenheit) as t, and the output is "true" for B and "false" for S.

The visual system of mammals apparently computes the convolution of a Gaussian with the image (approximately). Here the input set is the possible states of activity of retinal neurons, corresponding to the visual image, and the output set is the possible states of activity of certain neurons in the visual cortex.

The planets compute their positions and lots of other functions. One example is this one: Let the inputs be the distances from the Sun and radial velocities of the Earth and Jupiter when they are aligned with the Sun, and let the output be the distance of Jupiter the next time it is aligned the with the Earth and the Sun. The function computed is "the distance of a planet of Jupiter's mass from the Sun the next time it is aligned with a planet of Earth's size given that they had distances r_1 and r_2, and velocities v_1 and v_2 the previous time." The Earth, the Sun, and Jupiter compute this value only approximately, because the other planets add errors to the result, and, more fundamentally, because there are inherent limits to measurements of position and alignment. If Jupiter moved 1 centimeter, would it still be aligned? The question has no answer, because exactly what pieces of matter count as part of the Earth, the Sun, and Jupiter at any given instant is not precisely enough defined.

One might think that with computers defined so generally, the concept of computer would be completely vacuous, and this is what Searle, Putnam, and others have tried to argue. However, for it to be vacuous, it would have to be the case that every physical system implemented every computer, and this is not true. It may be the case that for every history of every physical system, and for every set of values, there is a code that maps some occurrent state of the system to every value in the set. But nothing guarantees that the code will satisfy the causal condition outlined above, that altering the system to be in an input state representing value x will cause it to enter an output state representing $f(x)$.

Another possible objection is that the interpretations of states don't seem to be causally anchored to those states. I require a causal link between input states and output states, but I don't require any link at all between the input states and the values they represent, or the output states and the values they represent. What makes the states of the thermostat be "about" the room the thermostat is in, instead of about some room in another galaxy with similar temperatures, or, for that matter, about stock market prices (taking the Dow-Jones Industrial Average as x and some value like 10,000 as the threshold)? The answer is, nothing. Later on we will focus at great length on this issue, but it has nothing to do with whether a system is a computer or not. Being a computer is a purely syntactic matter. A system computes a function if its states *can be interpreted* as the inputs and outputs of that function. Whether they *must* be interpreted that way is a separate issue. Whether they *are* interpreted by anyone that way is irrelevant.

In spite of the collapse of the strong version of the Searle-Putnam argument, there is a weaker version to contend with, in which it is granted that computation is objectively real, but denied that it can cause anything, over and above the physical events it is implemented in. Searle (1997) discusses the "vestibular-ocular reflex" (VOR), in which signals from the inner ear are used to keep the eyes oriented toward a fixed target even when the head moves. Why think of this as a computation, Searle asks, when it is more straightforward to think of it as a purely biological process? Isn't this as absurd as supposing that the stomach computes how it ought to digest food?

I see no reason to treat the computational description of the VOR any differently than the computational description of the stomach or other organs. My question is, is there a causal level distinct from the level of the neurophysiology at which the agent is actually unconsciously carrying out certain computational, information-processing tasks in order to move his eyeball? ... What fact about the vestibular nuclei makes it the case that they are carrying out specifically mental operations at the level of intrinsic intentionality? ... On the account I am proposing, computational descriptions play exactly the same role in cognitive science that they play in any other branch of biology or in other natural sciences. Except for cases where an agent is actually intentionally carrying out a computation, the computational description does not identify a separate causal level distinct from the level of the physical structure of the organism. When you give a causal explanation, always ask yourself what causal fact corresponds to the claim you are making. In the case of computational descriptions of deep unconscious brain processes, the processes are rule-described and not rule-governed. And what goes for computation goes a fortiori for "information-processing." You can give an information-processing description of the brain as you can of the stomach or of an internal combustion engine. But if this "information-processing" is to be psychologically real, it must be a form of information that is intrinsically intentionalistic. Cognitive science explanations using the deep unconscious typically fail to meet this condition. (Searle 1997)

Searle raises several issues here, some of which we will not be able to deal with until later. Some of what he says seems to be phrased in an odd way to make the view he is disagreeing with sound odd. The idea of a "deep unconscious" that he seems to attribute to someone else is in fact his own invention. However, if we peel off all the attributions of "mental operations," "unconscious tasks," and such, there remains a substantive argument, which is that you can always eliminate references to computational causes by rephrasing them in terms of the physical properties of the medium in which the computation occurs.

Obviously, we are not *compelled* to treat the VOR as involving computation, just as we're not compelled to treat a rabbit as a living system (as opposed to a pile of molecules). But in the case of the vestibular-ocular reflex, it feels as if we're overlooking something important if we don't mention computation; and in the case of the stomach it seems as if we don't have the *option* of seeing a computational influence, at least not a nontrivial one. It's not that stomachs can't be used as computers. One could find decodings involving, say, concentrations of acids and organic molecules, and use a stomach as an analog computer. But the computation depends on the behavior of the stomach, not vice versa.

We need to define carefully when a computational system has an effect, *qua* computational system, on other objects. Here is my proposed definition: System $S2$ is influenced by $S1$'s computation of function F (under some decoding E) if and only if there is a part $P1$ of $S1$ such that:

a. the output states of $S1$ are determined by the states of $P1$ (i.e., the only part of $S1$'s state that is relevant to E is the state of $P1$);

b. the states of $P1$ exert a causal influence on $S2$; and

c. if $S1$ were replaced by an $S1'$ such that $P1$ also occurred in $S1'$, and $S1'$ computed the same function F under the same output encoding, then the behavior of $S2$ would not change.

Example: A furnace is influenced by a thermostat's computation of "if $x > t$ then true else false" as described above. The output part $P1$ is the strip of metal that deforms as temperature changes. The relevant output state classes are "deformed enough to close a circuit" and "not deformed enough." If the same function were computed by some other device, which indicated its output by bending the piece of metal by some other mechanism, the furnace would behave the same way.

The vestibular-ocular reflex meets the definition because any other way of computing the correction factor would work equally well, provided the answer were transmitted to the eyes over the relevant nerve (which here plays the role of $P1$).

Note that we must always specify which F is involved in the influence. $S1$ might influence $S2$ by computing F, but $S1$ might compute a different function as well that has no bearing on the behavior of $S2$. However, in cases where the context makes F clear, we will sometimes just say "$S1$ computationally influences $S2$."

The planets do not computationally influence themselves because there is no part $P1$ of the planet that exerts a causal influence on the whole planet in the way the definition requires.

However, my definition allows some cases that may seem counterintuitive. One billiard ball strikes another. The first can be seen as the part $P1$ whose states represent the output of a certain computation ("how a billiard ball would behave if struck under a range of circumstances"). The second ball is certainly causally affected by the first. If the result were computed by a completely different method, and then encoded as the state of the same billiard ball, the ball it hits would not behave any differently (at least, not right away; eventually, the fact that the other balls are not there any more would alter the trajectory of this ball).

My inclination is to live with this consequence. I see no way of ruling out the billiard balls without ruling out all analog computers. Is there any difference between performing an integration with billiard balls and performing it with capacitors? Not that I can see. Computational influences are nontrivial to the extent that they can be compartmentalized. The billiard-ball example fits the definition of computational influence only by putting *all* the causes of the ball's behavior into the interface element $P1$.

By contrast, suppose we claim that the retina affects human behavior purely computationally, by the computation of a convolution of a Gaussian distribution with the visual image. To support the claim we might find some intermediate brain cells (playing the role of $P1$) whose dendritic states were such that if we rigged up any other way of computing that convolution and connected the output of that computation to $P1$ in such a way that the $P1$ cells' dendritic states depended only on the output of the convolution, then the human to whom this was done would not behave any differently. In this case we don't have to simulate *every* influence on the person's behavior. The contribution of the retina would be compartmentalized to just the proposed computation. In other words, there is a fairly clear distinction between two sorts of claim:

1. $S1$ computationally influences $S2$ because $S1$ comprises *all* the causes of $S2$'s behavior, and $S2$ can't tell whether $S1$'s behavior is caused in the traditional way or by a simulation.

2. $S1$ computationally influences $S2$ because $S1$ is one of several causal influences on $S2$, and $S1$'s contribution can be summarized in terms of a

nontrivial computation (i.e., in terms other than "a computation of what $S1$ normally does").

The distinction is somewhat idealized, because it is never possible to substitute just any computer for $S1$. If we replaced someone's retina by a microchip that fit in the back of his or her eyeball, then (we hypothesize) he or she wouldn't notice. But if we replaced it with an IBM Thinkpad, the person's behavior would change simply because his or her eyes would now have a different shape and mass. It is tempting to dismiss such effects as irrelevant, but I don't know of any principled way to do that. I want an objective way of cataloging all causal effects between physical systems, without insisting that they be categorized in advance into "signals" and "other." The mass properties of the eyeballs might be part of the signal. We can't rule that out, especially since there are parts of the body that probably do transmit information by changing their shape and hence the body's dynamics. In other words, we can't declare "noncomputational" effects irrelevant, because no state change is intrinsically noncomputational.

In spite of this difficulty, I think defining the ideal case is useful. It might never apply, but it helps us distinguish between cases of differing degrees of "computational purity." A causal link is "mostly computational" if "most" changes of computational device would have "mostly second-order" effects on the behavior of the affected system.

So far my argument shows that there are situations in which it is permitted to describe a cause as primarily computational. However, we can make a stronger statement, that there are cases where making reference to computational causes is *unavoidable*. Suppose someone claimed that chemistry was vacuous because any series of events described in chemical terms could be explained just as well using quantum mechanics. To borrow Searle's argument, we could ask, what fact about a chemical reaction makes it the case that it involves specifically chemical operations (as opposed to quantum-mechanical ones)? Well, there is no such fact. Every chemical reaction *does* have a complete description as a physical event. Nonetheless chemistry is not redundant, because there are many generalizations that can be stated only in chemical terms. (The same point could be made about biology, geology, astronomy, and any other science.) All we have to do to establish the bona fides of computationalism is find generalizations that cannot be rephrased in terms involving the underlying physical medium of a computation. Here are a couple:

Example 1: *The VOR evolved because the information it provides to the visual system is valuable.* This generalization cannot be rephrased in terms of neurophysiology because it explains why the neurophysiology is the way it is. If it did not supply the correct information (to within some approximation), the Darwinian fitness of the animal whose visual system it is would be less. (Note that a similar claim cannot be made about the stomach. An organ that provided information about what to digest would be of no value to an organism that actually needed the digestion to occur.) I might predict that the octopus, or any other sighted invertebrate, would have a VOR, defined as whatever module computes the eye-movement correction factor; I am not predicting anything at all about the neurophysiology of octopi, which is completely different from ours.

Example 2: *Since 1990 the Whizmobile Zephr (an automobile) has had a computer-controlled fuel-injection system, whose key element is a microchip known as the PowerPatsium, running the following program:....* This generalization cannot be restated in physical terms because there may be several generations of the PowerPatsium, each of which uses quite different electronic circuits. Nonetheless, they can all be described as executing the given program. Note that we cannot even resort to something as clumsy as providing a disjunction involving all the different PowerPatsium circuits, because the Whizmobile will continue to be controlled by the program even on future models of the chip, which haven't been designed yet.

It's easy to produce many more examples of these kinds.

To summarize: In spite of objections, which require some care to meet, the concept of computation is unproblematic.

Symbols

Some computers manipulate symbols. We require an objective account of what that entails. In the end we're going to want to know what symbols mean, if anything, but we can't start with semantics; we have to start with syntax. A symbol may or may not mean anything, but it can't mean anything unless it exists.

It is important to realize that I am talking about a purely objective sense of the word "symbol," the sense in which a computer is said to read symbols off a magnetic tape, and not the sense in which a red flag might be said to be a symbol of the struggle of the workers against oppression. In the latter case there is not much question about whether a particular red flag exists or not, and the question of whether the flag signifies the workers' struggle or the fact that a truck is carrying an oversize load is a question about what people intend. In the case of the symbols on the tape, the question is what makes them symbols at all, in addition to being patterns of magnetized oxide.

One problem in being clear about this issue is that we have preconceptions. The paradigmatic case would seem to be symbols in a language. If we start from the idea of a language, abstractly conceived, then it is natural to suppose that for it to be effective in a real physical system it must be "written down," or realized somehow, and that leads to thinking about how a symbol might be impressed upon paper or silicon, then moved around by various physical transformations that do not alter its symbolhood. This is all very nice, but then if we *don't* start with a preconceived idea of the language the system manipulates we are left high and dry.

So I will start from the other end, and try to say what a "bare symbol" would look like, and worry later about whether the symbols we find arrange themselves into a language, or into something else, or into nothing much.

A key feature of a symbol is that it can have multiple occurrences. We usually speak of the "type/token" distinction. There is the letter "T" considered as the twentieth letter of the alphabet (a symbol type), and there is the particular occurrence at the beginning of this sentence (a token of that type). However, we are once again starting in the wrong place. We will get into all sorts of problems about whether the occurrence of that token on my computer screen is a different type from the occurrence on the particular hard copy you might be reading. And so forth. Meanwhile, we are still analyzing symbols as elements used in from languages that people read and understand.

Let's start again, this time focusing on a different fact about symbols: that whether one symbol or another occurs at a certain point in a computation can alter the course of that computation. Define a *symbol site* to be a set of mutually exclusive alternative states of a system *at a particular point in time*. For now, we stipulate that a symbol site must last for some nonzero period of time, but we will relax this requirement later. The word "site" might be taken to imply some particular location in space, and there are many cases of that sort. For example, the location on the page of the first character in this paragraph at the instant you read it is a symbol site with about 100 alternative states, one for each character that might have appeared there. The state that actually obtains we call the *occupier* of that site; in this case it is (presumably) "an 'L' appears in that position." The letter in that location stays that way for a while; and it might have been some other letter, but not two letters simultaneously. The set of mutually exclusive states, or *competitors,* does not have to be exhaustive. Some kind of ink splotch might have occurred at that point on the page, and then the symbol site would not have been occupied (although an alternative site might have been).

Symbol sites do not have to be locations in space. Suppose a string is vibrating at several frequencies simultaneously. If we focus on the cases where the amplitude of the vibration at frequency f is either below 1 cm or above 2 cm, then the set {"below 1 cm," "above 2 cm"} would be a symbol site. If the amplitude is actually 0.7 cm, then the occupier is "below 1 cm." I will use the word "locus" of a sequence of sites to mean what they all have in common; in the case where the symbols occur at a definite place, their locus will be that place, but the locus may be defined with respect to different reference frames, or not be a place at all. All the examples so far are of *discrete* symbol sites, in which the set of alternative states is finite. I discuss the continuous case below.

A more subtle example is provided by considering a printed symbol as seen by a scanner, an electronic device for translating printed pages into text in a form manipulable by a computer. For concreteness, let's incorporate this scanner in a Turing machine. A *Turing machine* is an abstract computer that is often used in thinking about what computers are capable of, because it is very simple but as powerful as any other computer if you don't mind waiting for your answers. A Turing machine consists of a controller plus a scanner that reads a very long tape with symbols printed on it. "Very long" just means that we don't allow the tape to run out. If we need more, we go get it and splice it on. The scanner tells the controller what symbol it sees; the controller tells the scanner to move left or right along the tape (or move the tape right or left under the scanner, which comes to the same thing). The controller has a simple memory, consisting of a single integer X, plus a very simple program, consisting of a finite loop of instructions, each of the form

if X=k and see S then write U; X← k'; go D

where k and k' are constant integers; S and U are symbols; and D is a direction (left or right). The instruction means: "If X contains k and S is the symbol under the scanner then replace it with symbol U, store k' in X, and move in direction D." This program is executed by setting X to 0, finding an if that applies, executing it, then going back to the beginning of the loop. The program halts when no if applies. If you need an example, consider a Turing machine in which all squares are marked with either 1 or 0, and the machine's program is:

if X=0 and see 1 then write 1; X ← 0; go right
if X=0 and see 0 then write 1; X ← 1; go right

The first instruction is executed, moving the scanner right, until the second instruction applies. The machine writes a 1, sets X to 1, and then halts, because there is no instruction that specifies what to do when X $\neq$ 0. If the machine is started with its scanner positioned over some 1 in a block of 1s, it will add a 1 to the end of the block. In a way, it has added 1 to a number (if the number is represented by the size of the initial block of 1s).

Usually from this point one inquires what else such a simple computer can do, and discovers that it can (apparently) do anything any other computer can do. (See Penrose 1989 for a good overview.) But I want to focus on the scanning operation. We assume that the tape is divided into squares; the machine can't write a symbol just anywhere, but has to write it into a square. The possible symbols are called the "alphabet" of the machine, but let's not go that direction; we'll be talking about languages again. Let's assume that the alphabet has two symbols. Per tradition, we can call them 1 and 0, but the way they're actually written is by blackening a square if it has a 1, leaving it blank if it has a 0. We're focusing on actual physical embodiments of computers, so we might as well be specific about what we mean by "blacken." Any real physical surface will reflect at least a little light, so by "black" I mean "reflecting little light," and by "white" I mean "reflecting a lot of light." In other words, {"square below scanner reflects light level $< t_1$," "square below scanner reflects light level $> t_2$"} is a symbol site. Calling these two symbols 1 and 0 is then a matter of adopting a decoding, as discussed above.[3]

Now suppose the scanner moves left along the tape. There is now a different symbol below the scanner. Or is there? To be concrete, suppose the Turing machine reads a 1, writes a 1, moves left, and sees another 1. Is it looking at the same symbol? Clearly not. But if it now moves right, our intuition says, it will be looking at the same symbol it saw originally. Okay, but now suppose the tape is actually implemented as a giant shift register; or, to be whimsical, assume we have recruited an army of elves, each of which looks at a square of the tape. When the instruction "move left" is given, what actually happens is that every elf looks to its left, sees the symbol written there, erases its current symbol, and replaces it with the symbol it saw; in other words, the tape and scanner remain stationary and the symbols all move right. The elves, being lazy, do nothing if they see that the symbol to the left is the same as the current symbol. Now when the machine executes the instruction "move left," the elf responsible for the square it is scanning does nothing at all. Is the 1 it sees the same as the 1 it saw a second ago?

These examples show how tricky it is to get from symbol sites to actual symbols. Nonetheless I think the answer is fairly straightforward. Symbol site S_1 is a *precursor* of symbol site S_2 if S_1 precedes S_2, there is a one-to-one mapping between the sets for S_1 and S_2, and the element of S_2 that occurs is caused by the element of S_1 that occurs. In our Turing-tape example, no matter how the tape is implemented, the symbol site for the square under the scanner at time 0 and the site for the square under the scanner after moving left and then right are causally linked in this manner; the former is the precursor of the latter. If the machine transforms tape-square states into voltages inside the controller, then the same kind of causal link will join the symbol site for tape-square blackening and the symbol site for "voltage at node 3."

Using the precursor relationship, we can issue the following definition: a *symbol token* is a set of symbol sites that are connected by the precursor relation. The *manifestation* of the token at a site is simply the occupier of that site. This definition might be seen as slightly counterintuitive because of the possibility of branches in the tree of precursor relationships. If the ink below the scanner is a precursor of the voltage at node 3 *and* the ink somewhere on the tape a few times steps later, then we will have the ink and the voltage be simultaneous manifestations of the same symbol token at different points in space. I am not troubled by this consequence of the definition, but it could easily be eliminated at the price of some complication. Note also that a chain (or tree) of precursor relations can extend across possible worlds, in the sense that if I am thinking about a counterfactual situation I will imagine sites for a symbol token that never exist in the real world.

A more interesting issue is what it means to have two tokens of the same type of symbol. Intuitively, two tokens are of the same type if one could be substituted for the other without making any difference. But, of course, we can't say that, for two reasons. First, we don't have a clear sense in which one token can be substituted for another. Second, we don't know what differences make any difference. We can avoid both these issues by relativizing to a particular decoding, which may conveniently be thought of as the input decoding C_I for some computer. Suppose there are two symbol sites that both occur as states that are assigned values by C_I. To be more precise, the two sites must have occupiers that occur as parts of states that are assigned values by C_I. If the two states are identical except for the site occupiers (which will be trivially true if each state is entirely specified by the symbol site and its occupier), and if C_I assigns them both the same value, then the two sites are from tokens of the same symbol type *modulo* C_I. For example, in a computer memory a certain register may be loaded from a certain "bus" (pathway). According to the standard input decoding the input encodes a string of binary digits. If on some occasions voltage 2.1 appears in the third position, and on others 1.9 appears there, and there is no other difference between the two occasions, and on all these occasions the register's contents are always mapped to the same bit string, then the two tokens are both tokens of the same symbol. In my definition, all the other voltages are assumed to be absolutely the same on the two occasions. This is not physically possible, but it can be interpreted counterfactually: If on this occasion the voltage in the third position were 1.9, as it is, and the others had the values they had when 2.1 appeared in the third position, then the mapping would still have assigned the same bit string to the register. Notice that all the tokens of a type form an equivalence class: no token has two distinct types, and if S_1 and S_2 are of type T_1, and S_2 and S_3 are of type T_2, then $T_1 = T_2$.

It may appear that this definition does not match our intuition that, for instance, the symbol "1" can have tokens in more than one position. But recall that a token will normally have several locations, corresponding to all the sites that it comprises. So a token might appear (at different times) in positions 3 and 4 of a register. Another token might appear in locations 2 and 3. If by the proposed test the two tokens that appear in location 3 are tokens of the same symbol, then (because types are equivalence clases) the two tokens that appear in locations 2 and 4 are tokens of the same symbol, relative to some decoding of interest. The labels we attach to the symbols are arbitrary, and might for convenience be derived from that decoding, provided we understand that there is nothing sacred about any particular decoding.

Please bear in mind that decodings have nothing to do with what symbols mean. Their only purpose is to allow us to see the computers that manipulate symbols. When a screensaver moves pictures of fish around on a screen there are lots of symbols around, without which the system wouldn't work. Many of them don't denote anything; an individual fish picture is, as it moves, a series of bit patterns, and it may be taken as a series of tokens of a particular fish symbol type, but they don't denote anything.

Most of my examples have been drawn from digital computers, an easy place to find them. Maybe too easy—many philosophers have seen "digital" as essentially synonymous with "symbol-using." For example, Paul Churchland (1995, p. 248) says,

The processes taking place within a hardware neural network are typically non-algorithmic, and they constitute the bulk of the computational activity going on inside our heads. They are nonalgorithmic in the blunt sense that they do not consist in a series of discrete physical states serially traversed under the instructions of a stored set of symbol-manipulating rules.

He is careful to use the phrase "hardware neural network" because of the aforementioned fact (chapter 2) that almost all artificial neural nets are actually simulated on digital computers. Virtually the only exception is Mead's "silicon retina" (Mead 1989*b*, 1989*a*), from Churchland's discussion of which I drew the quote above. He goes on to say, "nor must all [neural networks] be usefully or relevantly approximatable by any physically real algorithmic mechanisms." This is an odd claim, which appears to be routinely neglected by neural-net researchers, who don't seem to worry that the neural-net programs they write might be useless and irrelevant. In any case, it is false. Nondigital systems can perfectly well use symbols, and digital systems can do things in a nonrule-governed way. Neural nets, simulated or not, are perfectly "algorithmic." Before I explain, however, I must broaden the concept of symbol a bit.

It is not hard to find examples of symbols in neural nets, even symbols with semantics, a subject I discuss below. Suppose that the rate of firing of a neuron encodes a number. If we gloss "the rate" as "the average rate over a 100-millisecond period," then there is a symbol site at any given time consisting of all the possible firing rates. Heretofore I have considered discrete symbols, but this is a continuous, or "analog" symbol, with whose treatment we must be a bit careful. The problem is that slight changes in the firing rate will change which symbol occupies a site, but the change has to be small. You can't, for example, have a binary symbol set $\{1, 0\}$ in which 1 is encoded by having the neuron's rate of firing be rational, and 0 by having it be irrational. But a small change in firing rate must make *some* difference in which symbol is present, or the symbols would be discrete. We can talk of "small differences" between symbols only if we take symbols to be drawn from a set with a *metric d*, that is, a measure of how different two competitors at a site are; $d(x_1, x_2) = 0$ if they are the same (or are to be considered the same in the decoding at issue). As symbols are transmitted through a system, they inevitably drift, so that it is impossible for an analog symbol to literally move through a computational medium the way a discrete symbol can. Hence we must generalize the way symbol sites and precursors work. An *analog symbol site* is an infinite set S of mutually exclusive alternative states of a system at a particular point in time, plus a metric d that relates any two states in S.[4]

S_1 is an *analog precursor* of site S_2 if all of the following are true:

1. S_1 precedes S_2.

2. There is a continuous mapping M_{12} from S_1's competitors to regions in the space of S_2's competitors such that $S_2 \in M_{12}(S_1)$ and the occurrence of S_1 causes some state in $M_{12}(S_1)$ to occur.

3. M_{12} is approximately "one-to-one," in the sense that from the fact that some P in the set $M_{12}(R)$ occurs, it follows that R or one of its neighbors occurred, and for any two distinct states R_1 and R_2, $M_{12}(R_1) \neq M_{12}(R_2)$.[5]

We required of a discrete symbol site that it persist for a nonzero amount of time, but we can't require that for continuous symbols. The only requirement is that they do not change discontinuously, which is satisfied by default in all real physical systems.[6]

As I have argued before, neuron firing patterns are just nature's way of making do without a digital computer. Anything that can be represented as the firing of a neuron—i.e., as a single continuous symbol—can be represented just as easily by a set of discrete symbols, so long as there are enough of them to chop the range of the continuous symbol finely enough. Or, more prosaically, you can replace any wire in your analog computer with a set of wires in your digital computer. And, of course, neural nets are implemented exactly this way in reality, by simulating them on digital computers.

However, there are reasons to suspect that even neural nets harbor discrete symbols. A typical neural net has a layer of output neurons that settle into different equilibrium states depending on the inputs. Neural-net researchers often stop at that point, but we should inquire about what happens to these output states in a typical case. Sometimes they are just used as inputs to another neural net, but in other cases they are stored for later retrieval or compared with previously stored entities. (The comparison might happen by feeding a new neuron-activation pattern and an old one into a net and seeing if the net reports that they are the same.) If anything like this is happening, then we are seeing the presence of discrete symbol tokens. The sites are sets of neurons at a point in time. The occupiers are particular activity patterns. They are classified as equal if they are treated the same under the input decodings for the later processing stages. I will talk about this issue at greater length in the next section.

It is just as important to realize that digital systems do not do everything under the control of a "stored set of symbol-manipulating rules," in Churchland's phrase. Suppose we wonder about a certain person's ideal love interest. Call her Helen. If we ask Helen to describe her ideal lover, she might be able to say quite a few words, and we might even suppose, generously if not plausibly, that these words correspond more or less directly to symbols in her head. However, it turns out that another thing Helen has in her head is an algorithm for recognizing love interests. The algorithm takes in data on hair color, voice tone, job security, and so forth, and emits a number. The higher the number, the more Helen is steered toward the source of these qualities. When the algorithm emits a zero, or close to it, the person is of no interest to Helen, and this is the output for almost everyone she meets. But occasionally she meets someone who causes the algorithm to emit 100, and she gets very interested. In fact, she's met several people in that range, and they were all tall guys with deep voices. If asked explicitly about her ideal love, she might try to summarize the attributes of those people. However, it turns out that there is no (obvious) limit on the number the algorithm can output, and one day Helen meets a short dumpy woman who causes it to emit 1000.[7]

The point is that Helen could have a completely digital brain, and still not have a symbolic description of her ideal lover. There are, of course, many symbols present during the algorithm's machinations, a symbol for hair color for instance. But there is no symbolic description of what it is Helen is looking for.

This may seem a bit far-fetched, but it's actually the normal case, especially in nonhuman animals. The birds and the bees do not carry around a description of what their ideal sex partner looks like; they just have an algorithm for getting closer to a sex partner, and, when they get close enough, mating with it. We may speculate that this algorithm is expressed as a neural net (chapter 2), and we may take "neural net" to mean the things neural-net researchers study or things made out of real neurons. These are all *details*.

Many researchers have failed to appreciate this point. It is often argued that connectionist models will exhibit "emergent" behavior that might be impossible to predict or even to understand, even though we know the topology, weights, and thresholds that define it. But this phenomenon has nothing to do with neural nets per se; it is a general property of algorithms. One might suppose that if Helen's love-recognizer were implemented as a computer program, then it would be a simple matter of "inversion" to extract a symbolic description of her romantic ideal. If the algorithm says,

"If short, dumpy, and female then output 1000," we can convert that to "Ideal lover is short, dumpy, and female."

We can formalize this idea of inversion thus: Given an algorithm that emits a number when presented with an input, find the input that will maximize that number. However, when you put it this way it becomes instantly absurd to suppose that inversion is feasible for any but the simplest cases. A key result in the field of complexity theory in computer science is that many problems have the following property: Given a proposed solution to the problem, there is a fast algorithm to check whether it is a solution or not, but any algorithm that is guaranteed to *find* a solution will take longer than the lifetime of the universe to run. This is a grossly oversimplified definition of what it means for a problem to be *NP-complete* (Garey and Johnson 1979). Rather than explain what that means technically, I'll give an example, perhaps the best-known example, the "Traveling Salesman Problem."

The problem is this: You're given a list of N cities to visit, and a total distance D. Every pair of cities is connected by a road, and you're given the distance between the two along that road. Is there a way of visiting all the cities and returning to your destination that requires no more than D total travel?

Anyone who has done a bit of computer programming can instantly see that there is a very simple algorithm for solving this problem. Since every city must be visited, it doesn't matter where we start, so let's pick a city arbitarily; say it's Alphaville. We can then describe any tour of all the cities by giving a list of the cities in the order they are to be visited, beginning with Alphaville. No city need appear on the list twice, because any ordering of the form $A - \cdots - P - Q - R - \cdots - S - Q - T - \cdots - Z$, where city Q appears twice, can't be any shorter than $A - \cdots - P - R - \cdots - S - Q - T - \cdots - Z$ and $A - \cdots - P - Q - R - \cdots - S - T - \cdots - Z$.[8] Hence all we need is a program that enumerates all the possible lists of cities and stop when it finds one whose total distance is less than D. This algorithm is simple, but it takes a long time to run, because the number of possible lists, or permutations, is astronomical. If there are 5 cities, then there are $4 \times 3 \times 2 = 24$ possible tours beginning with Alphaville. If there are 100 cities, then there are $99 \times 98 \times \cdots \times 3 \times 2$ possible tours, which is

9,332,621,544,394,415,268,169,923,885,626,670,049,071,596,826,
438,162,146,859,296,389,521,759,999,322,991,560,894,146,397,615,
651,828,625,369,792,082,722,375,825,118,521,091,686,400,000,000,
000,000,000,000,000

or about 10^{158}. If the answer to the question is yes, the program will have to be very lucky to find a short tour within the lifetime of the universe. If the answer is no, luck is no help; the program is going to have to check all the permutations. So this algorithm is not practically of any use. Computer scientists are clever people (or so we would like everyone to think), so you might suppose that after fifty years of trying we would have come up with a much better algorithm. But we haven't, and there are good reasons to suppose (though, as yet, no proof) that we never will. If you want to be sure of answering this question correctly you have to use an algorithm that runs (almost) forever. The problem is said to be *intractable*.

Now imagine a creature that has to visit on the order of 100 locations foraging for food, and suppose that it has found a reasonably good way to visit them. However, there is some survival value in finding a quicker way. Then it might be reasonable to make occasional random changes in the tour, and retain them if a change improves things. But no matter how the algorithm is implemented, there will be no way to "invert" it to tell you which tour the creature is looking for. If it stumbles on an improved tour, that will appear to be an "emergent" event.

This example is a somewhat contrived but basically accurate reflection of the way things really are. In fact, the Traveling Salesman Problem is *easier* than many of the computational problems that organisms face, in that there are fast algorithms that can estimate the length of the minimal path to within 50%; for some other problems no such approximate method is known.

Of course, there are differences between digital computers and nets of neurons, artificial and otherwise. As Churchland says, continuing the quote above: "[The processes in neural nets] are analog processes, their elements and activites are real-valued, they unfold in parallel, and they unfold in accordance with natural laws rather than at the behest of stored rules" (1995, p. 248). The question is whether these differences are real or of any importance. The answer is that those that are real are unimportant. Almost all computations are approximate, in the sense I discussed above. If an organism's survival depends on computing a real-valued function, it had better not depend on computing it *exactly*, or the organism will be toast. Neural nets and digital computers will both depart, in slightly different ways, from perfect accuracy. These departures can't possibly be important. An analog computer's "real-valued" quantity does not encode or behave like a real number with infinite precision; it encodes a range of numbers, which we hope is small and contains the number we want to track.

The parallelism of neural nets speeds them up, but makes no other difference I can see; perhaps Churchland has in mind the idea that tiny variations in the relative timings of events in a highly parallel system can have cascading effects. If so, then (a) he will have to show that this phenomenon creates anything other than noise; and (b) although a single isolated CPU does not exhibit parallelism, there is no such thing as an isolated CPU in the real world. In practice, a digital computer is never in the same state twice.

Finally, I have no idea what the opposition can be between "natural laws" and "stored rules." Both computers and brains obey all natural laws. I don't know if the phrase "stored rules" refers to the computer's program or to a set of axioms in a knowledge-representation sysem. Either use is wrong. Almost all computers do have programs, but only as a convenience; we could always build an equivalent piece of digital hardware with no program, at the cost of having to discard it when we wanted a different function computed. In this sense, most neural nets "have programs," because they exist only in software. On the other hand, if "stored rules" means "axioms," then only a tiny minority of computers use stored rules. So when Churchland says (p. 245) that neural nets "are simply not engaged in the business of manipulating symbols by reference to stored rules," we can only reply, who is?

The bottom line is this: If someone tells you that a system is "symbolic," they have told you almost nothing. If they give you a precise description of an abstract domain within which the inferences of the sytem lie (i.e., its "domain of knowledge"), they've told you very little; they certainly haven't told you anything about the symbols the system actually uses or the conclusions it can actually draw. Only when you know the symbols the system actually manipulates and the algorithms it actually implements do you have a chance of knowing what it can and can't do, although actually figuring it out may require a prolonged analytical and empirical study.

Syntax

So far I have focused on the behavior of isolated symbols. But things get really interesting when we note that symbols ofen occur together. Suppose that a system, a robot or animal, contains two symbols (i.e., two loci of sites). We can define a new locus comprising the two loci, and note the existence of symbol sites at that locus that consist of pairs of the original symbol sites (at a point in time). So far there's nothing very earth-shaking about this scenario, which is why I haven't bothered to mention it. But let's contrast two cases:

1. The base symbol sites have three occupiers each, so there are $3 \times 3 = 9$ possible occupiers of the composite site, which we can for convenience label 00, 01, 02, 10, 11, 12, 20, 21, 22. Suppose two of these never occur, and the remaining seven are supposed to stand for the Seven Dwarfs. 01 = Grumpy, 02 = Dopey, and so forth.

2. The base symbol sites have lots more than three occupiers each. But that's not the interesting part. It turns out this symbol site is connected to the visual system. When it sees Fred to the left of Sally, it puts a symbol standing for Fred at locus 1, and a symbol standing for Sally at locus 2. When it sees Sally to the left of Fred, it does the opposite. FS = "Fred visible to the left of Sally," SF = "Sally visible to the left of Fred"; and so forth for other people it knows. If it doesn't see exactly two people side by side, it puts some kind of null symbol in the two loci.

It seems as if there is a crucial difference between these two cases, having to do with the fact that in the second case, when a composite symbol is made out of parts, the component symbols are "still there." The representation of "Fred visible to the left of Sally" contains a symbol (F) that is still "relevant" to what the whole thing represents, whereas "0" doesn't occur in "02" in the same way at all. If 02 is Grumpy, and 20 is Doc, we wouldn't want to say that Doc's second component resembled Grumpy's first.[9] These two cases are usually contrasted by saying that there is a "compositional semantics" in the case of the visual representation system, and none in the case of the Dwarf representation system, but we can't begin to talk that way without talking about what symbols mean.

From a purely syntactic point of view we can make the following observation: in the Seven Dwarfs case, the zeroes in "02" and "20" have nothing to do with each other. Recall that the labels on the symbol types are *arbitrary*. In this case we have recycled "0" and "2" for our own convenience. It would be less misleading to use {a,b,c} for the occupiers of the first locus, and {p,q,r} for the occupiers of the second, so that Grumpy was now denoted by ar and Doc by cp (keeping in mind that I haven't said what I mean by "denoted"). But in the case of the representation of visible objects the analogous switch doesn't seem right. We might not claim that there is exactly one symbol for Fred, but it seems plausible that when the vision system is observing Fred, Sally, Winston, and Pamela walking in and out in various orders, it produces the same symbol (type) each time it sees Fred, and it's that symbol that occurs in FS and SF.

Earlier in this chapter I provided a purely syntactic definition of identity for symbol types, so there's no particular trouble with saying that the "same" symbol type occurs in two places. When I use the letter "F" in both FS and SF I mean either that both are different manifestations of the same token, or, more likely, that they each can be linked via the precursor relation to symbol sites that are functionally identical. One way this can happen is to have a physical location in which a symbol can be present, so that the same symbol type can literally occur in different locations. For instance, the locus corresponding to "the person on the left" could be two trinary (three-state) neurons, and the locus for "the person on the right" could be two different trinary neurons. If the left ones are on in the configuration 02, then Grumpy is the person on the left. If the right ones are on in the same configuration, then Grumpy is on the right. (Of course, there's no reason for the same symbol type to correspond to the same pattern in both loci; it's just simpler that way.)

But there are other ways of doing it. Suppose there's a single neuron that lights up when Fred is seen, and another when Sally is seen. Another one lights up if a man is on the left. This scheme won't work, or at least won't have enough degrees of freedom, if anything but a single man and woman are seen, but perhaps there are other neurons for the other cases. To a computer scientist this sounds like a crazy way to represent things, but the brain is under different constraints from those of artificial computers. Our models of neural functioning are primitive enough that we have no idea what sort of pattern is repeated when we think of the same thing twice in two different ways (e.g., once when the object is on the left and again when it's on the right). Another way to put it is to ask, how does the nervous system represent the *role* of an object in a relationship in addition to representing just the presence of the object? This is often called the *binding problem*.[10] There are some interesting technical issues in answering this question, but there is no real obstacle to assuming whatever structures seem plausible.

Symbol structures can get much more complicated than these contrived examples. Many cognitive scientists believe that their complexity must be about the same as that of a sentence in a human language. This is Jerry Fodor's "Language of Thought hypothesis" (Fodor 1975, 1988). Essentially the same idea is accepted by many AI researchers, who prefer terms like "knowledge representation" (Davis 1986; Lenat and Guha 1990).

I prefer to suspend judgment on this question of how complex the syntax of thoughts has to be. People who like neural nets often prefer simpler, more specialized representations. Fodor and Pylyshyn (1988) argue that these representations can't capture the complexity and systematicity of thoughts we routinely think. Their arguments are convincing; but the conclusion is suspicious, so there might be something wrong with the arguments. The conclusion is suspicious because there is no obvious way to make computational use of complex syntactic objects, for reasons I discussed in chapter 2.

Semantics

I have put off as long as possible talking about what symbols and symbol structures mean, if anything. Let me emphasize once again that meaning plays no role in how a computational system works. Computing is a series of formal manipulations over physical states that happen to have decodings, but the decodings are nothing like "meanings."

However, the case where symbols do mean something is of great importance, especially in view of the weight I put on it in my theory of consciousness, which rests on the claim that conscious brains manipulate models of themselves—that is, symbols denoting aspects of themselves. That depends on being able to specify the circumstances under which we can say that a symbol denotes something.

There is a large philosophical literature on this topic (Fodor 1975, 1988; Rey 1997, Stich 1983, Putnam 1975), much of it quite interesting and entertaining. However, much of it seems to me to be solving the wrong problem. Many philosophers assume that the paradigm case of meaning is language meaning. For instance, we may assume that someone who speaks English knows what "cow" means, until we hear him say, "That cow is a mammal, but most cows are little plastic toys." How do we diagnose his problem? Does he have false beliefs about cows, or does he not grasp the meaning of "cow"?

Questions like that are interesting, but they are *central* questions of cognitive science only if the word "cow" (or something close to it) occurs in the internal representation used by the human mind. There is reason to doubt it. The phrase "grasp the meaning of" is cause for suspicion. Part of what philosophers are trying to explain is what we are "grasping" when we grasp the meaning of something. To the classical empiricists (e.g., Locke and Hume) the most attractive proposal was that to grasp the meaning was to hold a picture in the mind. You know you know the meaning of "cow" because you can summon a mental image of a cow, and even compare it with an actual cow candidate. This theory is thoroughly unfashionable nowadays, for good reasons. Many alternatives have been proposed, but none of them works terribly well. They usually do a poor job of picking out a single unambiguous meaning for each word. This is a frustrating outcome, given our strong intuitions that something as simple as the word "cow" is unambiguous.[11]

If we shift our focus to the semantics of internal representation, then some of the puzzles recede. Suppose there is a symbol that my brain uses, and some observer of my brain wants to know if the symbol denotes a particular cow, or the property of being a cow, or something else entirely. We don't have to worry how I grasp the meaning of this symbol, because I don't grasp it; I don't even know the symbol exists. We may not have to worry about ambiguities if the ambiguities are harmless. For example, in chapter 2 I talked about the visual system of the frog, one of whose purposes is to track flies. When we posit a symbol to denote the presence of a fly, we may suppose that the symbol means "insect present." But some other analyst might express the meaning as "edible object present." There is no way to settle the issue, but also no particular reason to settle it. In the frog's environment, insects and edible objects are essentially the same thing. The frog will make a certain number of errors (when it misclassifies something as an insect when it isn't, or vice versa), but as long as the number is small, the frog will prosper.

Let's look at a slightly more elaborate example. Suppose a robot is equipped with a camera and other sensors, and its job is to detect and track intruders in a laboratory late at night. Suppose it comes around a corner one night and sees a person who shouldn't be there. Its person-detecting software reports that part of the last camera image contained what looked like a person. The robot turns toward where the object would be if it were real (and not a result of noise in the system). It takes more pictures and these confirm that it's a person. Furthermore, the software gets estimates of the person's height, and, as she starts to run, her speed. She runs through a door and out of sight. The robot pursues. At this point it has, let us suppose, symbol structures such as these:

```
X29: Human
Gender X29: Female
Height X29: 1.8 m
Speed X29: 2 m/sec
Location X29: Various numbers
```

Please remember that I am not assuming that we literally have these pseudo-English strings of characters inside the robot. What we have are tokens of symbols of various types, defined as discussed above.

What I do claim is that "X29" refers to the unknown woman in the laboratory, not because there is a decoding in which that symbol is mapped to her (although there is such a decoding), but because the woman is the cause, in an appropriate sense, of the symbol structures. The "appropriate sense" is that the symbol structures take part in further transactions that may be interpreted as true beliefs about the woman, and, ultimately, shape the robot's behavior toward her. In particular, they cause behavior that, more often than not, results in finding the woman and having her arrested or expelled from the lab the robot is guarding.

This idea is the key element in what philosophers call the causal theory of reference (Kripke 1972; Rey 1997; Fodor 1988), and is accepted by many of them, although not all. Some of those who reject it (including, once again, John Searle, e.g., Searle 1997) would take issue with any conclusion about the intrinsic meanings of the symbols in the robot, and instead describe the robot as manipulating a completely meaningless set of symbols. The creators or owners of the robot may find it convenient to agree that X29 stands for a particular woman, but this is purely a convention, or a design decision. The robot's behavior can always be perfectly well described as a purely physical series of events, but it is an "attempt to find the woman" only because people use it as a tool for finding intruders.

Philosophers use the term *intentionality* for the capacity of mental states to "be about" something (Brentano 1874; Searle 1983). Our world is full of nonmental things, such as books and billboards, that are about something else, but they are not *intrinsically* about anything. When archeologists find an ancient tablet in an unknown language, it means nothing to them. The marks on the tablet have become just marks, physical disturbances of the surface, once the people who could read them have vanished. The tablet is said to exhibit "derived intentionality," in that its meaning depends entirely on the interpretation put on it by the civilization that made it.

I'm neglecting the fact that archeologists can infer a lot about a culture from the physical facts about the culture's writing materials and implements. In that sense the tablet might "mean" something, the way strata in the earth mean something to geologists. It used to seem obvious that this notion of meaning was strictly separate from intentionality. We can call it *informational meaning:* a physical event E means something about an antecedent event or situation P if the occurrence of E changes the probability of P. That is, it is evidence for or against P; it provides *information* in the technical sense about P (Pearl 2000; Dretske 1981).

At first glance the relationship between E and P seems like a very different relationship than that between a thought and its object. But scientific and technological progress changes intuitions. The robot's data structures refer to the woman the way a layer of iridium in the ground refers to the collision of a meteor with the earth, except that the causal links in the former case are much "thicker"; the data structures have large effects on the robot's behavior that cause an intricate sequence of further events involving its quarry. Perhaps intentionality itself can be explained in terms of informational meaning, thus erasing its seeming distinctiveness.

Let's back away from that claim for now. I think it's correct, but we are not yet in a position to argue for it, simply because cognitive science is still too primitive. For now, we should focus on the technical problems involving informational meaning in robots.

One obvious problem is that many word types, and most word tokens, don't seem to have the right kind of causal links to the things they denote. For instance, if the robot sees no one in the lab, and infers "NO HUMAN" (to caricature its data structure), then this token of the symbol HUMAN is not caused by any person. The causal origin of token NO is even more obscure.

The explanation is that semantics does not apply to individual tokens, but to symbol structures of the sort I discussed earlier in this chapter and exemplified in chapter 2. Because these structures can be large and complex, their semantics must be *compositional,* in the sense that the meaning of an expression can be determined from the meanings of its constituent symbols. To specify the meaning of an expression such as NO HUMAN, we might say that HUMAN denotes the set of all humans, and NO denotes a function $n(x)$ such that $n(set)$ is true if and only no element of *set* is in the vicinity. Then

$meaning(\text{NO HUMAN}) = n(meaning(\text{HUMAN}))$
$= \text{"No human is in the vicinity"}.$

Clearly, if NO means $n(x)$, then it doesn't do so because of any causal relation between n and the symbol type NO. The best we can say is that there is an overall "web" of causal relationships between the world and the expressions inside the robot.

In my examples I have used symbols in various ways without making some distinctions that might seem crucial. For instance, I supposed that the robot might record Gender X29: Female when it saw a female intruder. The implication is that X29 gets made up as a new symbol for a person that, as far as it knows, it's never seen before. But that's not what's going on with `Gender` and `Female`. These are symbols that have presumably been used before, and are meant to denote "the relation of living things to their genders" and "the gender female," respectively, or something like that. What makes them actually denote those things?

The causal theory can be adapted to answer this question, but not without raising thorny problems. Suppose aliens land on the earth thousands of years from now and find that the robot is still working, but that the human race has given up technology and there are no longer any engineers who can explain how the robot is supposed to work. All schematic diagrams, instruction manuals, and other clues to the functioning of the robot have been lost. Nonetheless, the aliens can look inside the robot's computer brain and see that the robot produces these triples of symbols when it sees a human being. The English language has been long forgotten, so the mnemonic value of the symbols is missing. As far as the aliens are concerned, they see α-X29-β—it's Greek to them. It doesn't take them long to realize that the symbol in the middle is always fresh and might be taken to stand for the person seen. A triple with an α as the first component is always emitted, and the third component is almost always β or γ. They do more experimenting, and eventually realize that the symbol's being β is strongly correlated with the person being female, γ, with the person being male. It makes mistakes about the sex of people only 3% of the time. Hence they take α to mean "gender," β to mean "female," and γ to mean "male."

This may sound far-fetched, but that's just because I had to think of a way to get the engineers out of sight while leaving the people behind. Actually, you could tell the same story even with the engineers around. No matter what they *intended,* the fact is that the symbol is caused by the presence of female humans more reliably than by anything else. Is there any doubt that the symbol β means "female"?

Well, yes, there are some doubts. Suppose, to bring the aliens onstage again, that the detector is, by some coincidence, extremely good at detecting aliens. The aliens look remarkably like human women; in fact, the error rate at classifying aliens is phenomenally low, by which I mean that the probability the detector will not say "β" when pointed at an alien is only 1%. So the detector is completely worthless for distinguishing aliens from humans. That's because in any case of doubt the creature being tested would be almost sure to be a woman or an alien, but we couldn't use the detector to tell us which. Under these circumstances, would it be correct to say that "β" meant "alien or female"? It seems so; it might be very useful at the entrance to a club catering only to human males (not that one should ever condone such a thing). So we have two conflicting intuitions, that a symbol means what the people who started using it think it means, and that it means whatever it's most reliably associated with in its environment. The conflict may not seem to apply in the case of animals, but even here we can consider evolution to be their "designer" and hence get a conflict. For instance, we may suppose the male brain has a neuron that lights up in the presence of a visual image of a naked female.[12] The evolutionary forces that shaped people "intended" for this neuron to denote naked females. Nowadays, however, it is just as likely to signal the presence of an R-rated movie. So what does it mean, "female" or "female or R-rated movie"?

Some philosophers (notably Dretske 1981) have accepted the conclusion that the meanings of symbols depend on the function the symbols serve, and that this notion of function is inescapably evolutionary. We say the function of the eye is to extract information from the light bouncing off objects, the way the function of the heart is to pump blood. To give either of these statements a precise meaning requires specifying how extracting information or pumping blood was selected for by evolution.

I am willing to grant that the function of the heart really is to pump blood, and the function of the eye really is to extract information from light. Nonetheless, I am very reluctant to grant that evolutionary history constrains the meanings of the symbols used by a creature *now,* except under circumstances when we have some independent reason to believe in a constraint. For instance, why do moths flutter around a light bulb? Perhaps they evolved to find open sky by looking for the stars and moon. On some nights there is no moon and the stars are obscured by clouds, so they're looking for something very faint. On other nights there is bright moonlight. The difference in brightness between the two situations is so large that the moths don't discriminate between them, although if things get *much* brighter the moths will decide it is daytime and stop flying altogether. So the moth's brain has symbols that mean "day," "night," and "sky." Now we fast-forward to the age of porchlights and bug zappers.

On the evolutionary account the "sky" symbol still means "sky," and a moth is simply mistaken when it flies toward a bright light. However, we have an independent reason to suppose that the symbol means "sky," namely, that the moth behaves toward it as it would toward the sky. The moth may be wrong more often than it is right, but we may still decline to say that the symbol means "sky or artificial light." We can contrast human males, who do not behave the same way toward pornography as they do toward women, so that it is more plausible to say they have a symbol that means "naked woman or pornographic image."

The conclusion seems inescapable that exactly what symbols denote is highly context-dependent. The same symbol, used in the same way by the same information-processing system, can have different denotations depending on the objects and properties the system is likely to run into. This phenomenon raises problems for some analyses of belief and other propositional attitudes (Fodor 1981*b*; Stich 1983). It does not, however, raise many problems for cognitive science, and I propose not to worry about it. The reason is that explanation in cognitive science is primarily syntactic: if the brain is essentially computational, then the events inside it depend on the formal properties of the symbols encoded in its states (Stich 1978, 1983). Semantics comes in when explanation is complete. A symbol denotes an entity or relationship outside the brain because it occurs inside a symbol system whose most harmonious semantics assigns that meaning to the symbol. A semantics is "harmonious" if it provides a coherent story about the relationships between symbols and sensorimotor events.

It may seem as though the concept of meaning lacks explanatory value, if all it is is a post-hoc gloss on a computer whose functioning is semantics-free. Not so. Having found a workable semantics for a system, we can then make generalizations about it that go beyond what we have observed. For instance, suppose we have determined that our robot is good at detecting physical attributes of people, but seems unable to tell one accent from another. If we tell it Boris Badunov might try to invade the lab, we can be confident that the robot will detect him. That is, we can be confident that the robot will come to *believe* a certain *fact* about Boris's location inside the lab. We may be able at the time to spell out exactly which fact that is, but in advance all we can say is that *some* such fact will be believed. This is a purely semantic notion. But if we know Boris has undergone plastic surgery, and can be detected only by listening for his Pottsylvanian accent, then we can predict that the robot will not *realize* that Boris is present. Again, this statement is purely at the level of semantics, and derived entirely from certain broad conclusions about the robot's semantic abilities.

I am not saying that semantics is "observer-relative," to use a term of Searle's, at least not any more than, say, science itself is. There are many cases, as in collecting radio emissions from distant galaxies, where data are explained by finding the hypothesis that is "simplest," or most "elegant." Nonetheless, scientists are confident than the hypothesis is objectively true, or at any rate that it's not vacuous to claim that it is. They would, for instance, believe that another intelligent race, in another galaxy, given the same data, would arrive at the same hypothesis. Of course, imputations of semantics to a brain or computer differ from claims of the truth of a scientific theory in that the theory, if true, specifies the causes of the observed data, and an imputed semantics does not. Nonetheless, observer-relative, or "esthetic" criteria play a role in both processes. These criteria are uncontroversial in science, in spite of the fact that it is difficult to specify exactly what "simplicity" means for a scientific theory, or exactly why the universe should be likely to be simple.

We are finally in a position to say something about the semantics of the self-model. I've proposed that, for example, to have a sensation of red is to have an occurrent representation to the effect that *this object I seem to see has a shade of the following type* (the essence of the type consisting in the similarity relations it bears to various color samples). For this proposal to be literally true there must be actual symbol structures in the part of the brain implementing the self-model that actually express those contents, including those similarity relations.

Let me be clearer about what the problem is. Neurophysiologists do not find printed representations of symbols in the brain, nor do they find ASCII representations as strings of binary digits. What they do find is firing patterns of neurons. (See chapter 1.) Whether a neuron is firing or not can serve as a symbol site, as can whether a group of neurons is firing. There may be other symbol sites we haven't guessed the existence of yet. For example, it might turn out that in some cases the vibratory modes of oscillation of large groups of neurons might be decoded in some relevant way (Crick and Koch 1990). Let's put aside the exotic possibilities and assume it's all neuron firings. What pattern of neuron firings would represent *I am experiencing orange* or *That shape looks orange?* I can't answer this question given our puny level of understanding of how the brain works, but I can make some suggestions. First, the pattern, whatever it is, should have subpatterns for the entities referred to, especially "I," "experience," color shades, and shapes. Second, the way these expressions are used will not depend on what they mean. We'll have a complete description of the operation of the self-model that doesn't depend on its being a self-model. The fact that it is a self-model depends not just on how it works, but on how it's connected to the rest of the system. The claim that the module is a model of the brain itself is no different in principle from the claim that another module is a model of a certain building or town. It's a matter of finding the most harmonious interpretation. Third, finding the individual entities denoted by the symbols in the self-model is not really different from finding more visible entities in the physical world. "This quale" will denote a sensory event because it was caused by that event and the beliefs about it (such as its duration) will be true of that sensory event. Generic terms (such as "experience" or "this shade of orange") will be grounded in much the way the word "female" is, by finding the property or set of objects that the symbol actually tracks.

However, in finding the objects and properties tracked by the self-model's symbol system, we run into the usual problems. One is that some of the beliefs about the objects in the self-model are not actually true; and some have truth values that are unclear, to say the least. Another is that it may be difficult to tell if a symbol denotes an object or the event of sensing that object.

Let's deal with the second problem first. Suppose there is a neuron that fires whenever I see a red object. Is it signaling the presence of a red object or the perception of a red object? Normally you don't have one without the other. This is not a trivial problem; in fact, neurophysiologists have already run into it. When they record from the cortex of a monkey, they often phrase what they observe in terms like these: "This neuron fires when the monkey experiences vertical stripes." But they really don't know whether the monkey experiences vertical stripes; perhaps it normally fires just when there are vertical stripes in front of one of the monkey's eyes, whether it experiences them or not, and occasionally fires even when there aren't.[13]

This is a difficult problem, but in principle not unsolvable. It's reminiscent of the problem of "radical translation" that was discussed by Quine (1960). When a foreigner is trying to tell me the meaning of a word by pointing at a rabbit, how do I know he means "rabbit" and not "rabbit head"? If you never see one without the other, it will be impossible to make the distinction.

Fortunately, in the case of sensations and objects you do see one without the other. Indeed, as I argued in chapter 3, this is one of the main reasons for the brain's needing a self-model. If we could measure events in the brain better, we would be able to detect situations where the brain entertains propositions like these:

There was a rabbit here but I didn't see it.
I thought I saw a rabbit but there was no rabbit.

At that point it should be possible to figure out which symbols denote the rabbit and which denote the experience of the rabbit.

The other problem, of false beliefs, will have fewer neuroscientific consequences and more philosophical ones. Someone may believe that yesterday she made a free decision about whether to buy a certain house. She makes a clear distinction between a decision like that and a decision that is coerced in some sense (such as whether to pay taxes). Assuming there are symbols classifying decisions into the categories *Free* and *Not-free,* what properties in the world do these symbols denote? If we open up our decision maker's brain and scan her environment, where do we find "freedom"? This sounds like an absurd request, but only because we take seriously the requirement that there be an actual entity denoted by the symbol, which has the attributes she believes true of "freedom." If we look for the entity that is actually tracked, it is the property a decision has when it is made after deliberation about different possible outcomes, and takes those outcomes into account, and where there is more than one real option. (An option is "not real" if it is physically impossible to carry out [e.g., "jump over the Atlantic ocean"], very unlikely to be feasible ["win the lottery"], or will result in punishment that is judged much worse than what will probably happen if a different option is chosen ["don't pay taxes"].)

The only problem in this tidy analysis is that some of the beliefs about free decisions are false, or at least very muddled. Beliefs about sensory events are even worse. What would justify saying that the symbols encoding these beliefs are about anything at all? Suppose I have a list of a hundred random sentences, ten of which are true of Abraham Lincoln, and ten of which are true of Shirley Temple, the rest showing no obvious relation to anyone. Are we in the presence of one hundred claims about Lincoln, ninety of which are false? Or one hundred claims about Temple, ninety of which are false? Neither is true; the collection of claims is not about anyone.

Of course, the case of beliefs in the self-model is very different from a random list of sentences. New beliefs are generated continually because of particular events in the brain, in a way that ensures that many of the beliefs are true of the events that caused them. Even so, enough are false or ungrounded to leave open the possibility that they are literally meaningless.

Another way to think about false beliefs is by analogy with historical novels. I have beliefs about Sherlock Holmes, obtained from reading the stories about him. There is no use asking what object is the actual subject of those beliefs; there isn't any. Nonetheless, there is a sense in which some of my beliefs are true (he lived in Baker Street) and some would be false (he met Napoleon), with respect to the fictional universe created by Arthur Conan Doyle. But suppose I read a book in which one of the characters is Abraham Lincoln. The book has him say something that he probably never actually said. Nonetheless, "Lincoln said..." is as true with respect to this fiction as "Holmes lived in Baker Street" is true in Doyle's work.

Perhaps the beliefs in the self-model are like a child's beliefs about Santa Claus. Many American parents tell their young children that there is a jolly old man in a red suit who brings the Christmas presents. Hence many young children have a set of beliefs about this guy. We might be tempted to say they are simply false, or meaningless, or true with respect to a fictional world. But suppose we write down the beliefs in a neutral way, such as

X brings the presents
X eats the cookies I leave on Christmas Eve

X travels in a sleigh
X wears a red suit
X visits every house in the world on Christmas Eve
X comes down the chimney
X loves me
X punishes me if I'm naughty

Then probably the X that makes more of the statements true than any other object is "the child's parents," because they bring the presents and eat the cookies. So, we might say that the child believes of his parents that they are a fat old man in a red suit who travels in a sleigh. Of course, he doesn't believe that his parents are Santa Claus. But it wouldn't be absurd for someone to say, "I found out when I was eight years old that Santa Claus was my parents," or for someone to say, sincerely, "Yes, Virginia, there is a Santa Claus."

I think this is a close parallel to the way things are with the self-model. It is like a historical novel, or a tale told to a young child about the world around her. The self-model contains symbols that denote perfectly mundane things, which are used to express straightforward beliefs about them. It then superimposes more fantastic beliefs that enable the organism to understand its place in the world. These beliefs are not exactly true, but not exactly false either, because as discussed in chapter 3, the very concept of self is interwoven with them.

I predict that it will not be hard to make these distinctions as the brain is better understood and the self-modeling facility is elucidated. One reason is that most of the symbols we find in the brain's activity will occur in more than one place. We'll find sites joined together in the precursor relationship, so that we can identify tokens, and we'll discover the decodings that allow us to describe the system coherently as a computer, so that we can identify types. Then we'll discover that some symbol types occur over and over. An example is the symbol for "I." The whole point of a self-model is to produce a coherent and useful set of beliefs about the organism that possesses it. There will surely be a symbol (probably just one symbol) that denotes this organism. We'll know that it does because there will not be any other remotely plausible candidate. Just the spatial facts about "I" should be sufficient to single out a unique physical object. Of course, the model will go on to add lots of facts that are not spatial, not grounded in any other physical property, and to some extent true only because we all agree they're true.

Actually, the semantics of the self-model will in some ways be less problematic than the semantics of other models in the brain. That's because the thing being modeled is so close, physically and computationally, that there are fewer possibilities for error. It has been pointed out (notably by Lycan 1997) that a self-scanning theory of consciousness allows for the possibility of scanning errors, so that one could in principle be mistaken about the contents of one's consciousness. How could that be? I tend to agree with Lycan that it is better to allow for errors about consciousness than not to allow it. However, there is a sense in which these errors are self-annihilating. Suppose an entirely spurious belief is created that "there is a painful burning in my right leg," in the absence of the usual underlying signal that such beliefs are usually about. I might even notice that, say, my leg did not jerk away from the apparent heat source, and thus come to realize that there was something fishy about the pain. Even so, I would still mind it just as much as "real" pain. Remember that beliefs in the self-model are self-fulfilling. A belief in an ordinary pain is part of the causal chain that makes the belief true. An "erroneous" pain report brings exactly the same chain into existence, with a different first link. The difference between a true sensation report and a false sensation report vanishes.

One further note about semantics: when I introduced the idea of an encoding, I had no problem with the fact that it served as a purely artificial "frame of reference" in order to allow us to make observer-neutral statements about computation. Why not use the same trick to deal with semantics? In fact, logicians and philosophers often do use such a trick, a mapping from symbol structures to entities they denote, for which they use the term *interpretation*. This idea first appeared in mathematical logic, in investigating questions about what axiom systems might actually be about. It was later extended by philosophers to symbol systems closer to hypothesized structures in the human mind, such as the language of thought we looked at it earlier in this chapter. We could use it here and just stipulate that statements about meaning are always relative to an interpretation, the way statements about symbols and computation are always relative to a decoding. The problem is that the interpretation would be doing too much work for us. A decoding tells us what symbols are there, but it doesn't explain the computations involving them. If a machine adds numbers with respect to a decoding, then the explanation of the addition does not mention the decoding. The explanation explains why, when a state encoding A and B occurs *here*, a bit later a state encoding $A + B$ occurs *there*, but the fact that the states encode these things plays no role in the explanation. There's no link between the decoding and the states decoded, and none is required. The decoding is just a description of something that is what it is regardless of how it is described. We can cheerfully use different decodings for the same system on different occasions.

With semantics it's the link between symbols and their denotations that needs explaining, and proposing an interpretation just begs that question. We don't want to record that a symbol *could* mean such-and-such; we want to verify that it *does*. Using an example proposed by Fodor (1981*a*), we might have a computation whose parts, according to some interpretation, denote participants in the Six-Day War. Relative to that interpretation, it's *about* the Six-Day War. But nothing actually makes it *about* the battle; it might actually be a weather computation, whose input data denote wind velocities, barometric readings, and such, and whose output predictions concern Peoria, Altoona, and Kankakee.[14] Its symbol structures actually denote these things because of the causal relationships between the objects and the input data. An automated weather station measures the wind velocity and forwards it to the computer. The number the station sends denotes the weather velocity because of this causal history. No such history can be constructed linking the Six-Day War to the computer.

Can This Really Be It?

After all of this, the reader may be convinced that symbols are real, at least relative to decodings, and that symbols do denote objects and properties in the environment of a computational system connected appropriately to that environment, and even that brains and computers can have beliefs about themselves. But you may still balk at the idea that all this could have anything to do with phenomenal consciousness. The objection I raised at the end of the last chapter was that the relationship of a self-model to its owner might not be objectively real enough to support a theory of consciousness, which must explain which parts of the universe are conscious, and why, without reference to any observer. Now we discover that semantics is not quite as objective as syntax. There's nothing corresponding to a decoding that just settles by convention the question of what symbols mean. It is barely conceivable that one could have a self-model that was often wrong about the self.

It is more likely that there could be a system that had something like a self-model, except that it lacked some crucial ability or that the semantic links to its environment were too fuzzy or anemic to support a claim that it referred to itself. It would then be debatable whether the creature was conscious or not. The sorts of examples that come to mind are animals, aliens, and robots, but we also have the possibility that parts of our own brains are independently conscious. We have an intuition that either they are or they aren't; any debate about the matter is due purely to our inability to take the first-person point of view, that is, the viewpoint of the creature itself.

The only sort of case I would really be concerned about would be those in which the creature (or brain part) *claimed* to be conscious in spite of doubts about its self-model. Until that happens, I would simply jettison the intuition about the ultimate arbiter of consciousness and admit borderline cases whose status remains unclear. As we understand consciousness better, I'm sure a whole zoo of odd possibilities will emerge that we currently have trouble visualizing. Think of all the borderline varieties of "life" (such as viruses and prions) that have popped up in the last century.

Still, I imagine that many people will not be convinced by my arguments. Partly this is because they can only be sketches of arguments until cognitive science has advanced far enough to fill in some details. But another reason is a certain attitude toward epistemology that is deeply ingrained in the Western philosophical tradition. This is the idea that nothing is really verified until it has been witnessed by a conscious mind. Few modern philosophers would agree to this principle so baldly stated, but deep down I think they all—we all—have trouble rejecting it. The idea is that the only things we really know for certain are the things we know immediately, without any inference or extrapolation, and those are the things that are immediately given to the senses. I seem to see something right now; I seem to hear something right now; everything else is an inference to the best explanation of what I seem to see and hear; everything else I could be wrong about. This is Cartesian epistemology.

Another way to put it is in terms of a classic dichotomy between appearance and reality (Bradley 1893; Goodman 1951). The dichotomy arises compellingly in the distinction between "primary" and "secondary" qualities. Primary qualities, such as position and mass, are possessed by physical objects in themselves, whereas secondary qualities, such as color and odor, are just the way things appear. Putting the issue this way raises the question: Appear to whom? And it is easy to assume that the answer will involve something *other than* physical objects. Events ultimately seem to need a witness to be considered real at all.

If a materialist theory of mind is correct, then these intuitions are simply wrong. What I seem to see and hear is ultimately to be explained in terms of the motion of molecules in my brain. The witnessing of an event by a conscious mind is a complex, unusual, and unnecessary accessory. Almost everything that happens is unwitnessed. Indeed, the very presence of conscious witnesses is accidental. The world got along without them for a long time, and most parts of the universe are still getting along without them. It's not easy to predict the exact frequency with which conscious witnesses appear, but it's certainly quite low.

Most philosophers would claim to agree with all this, but I think there are cases where they more or less instinctively revert to the Cartesian point of view. The principal case I have in mind is conscious events. Here it is hard to shake the idea that for an event to occur is for *me* to witness it. The mind is a theater, in Dennett's metaphor, and I am the audience. The problem with this picture is that in reality there is no audience in the sense proposed. The brain does perceive its own operations, but the perceptual events are no different in kind than the events perceived, and therefore cannot satisfy this demand for a witness. The self-model is *creating* the ego, the "I" that is at the center of my world, not vice versa. But really accepting this idea is chilling. It means that when I introspect I am not validating mental events and bringing them into being; it only seems that way; but it doesn't seem that way *to* anyone, just to a thing, the brain. A stream of consciousness seems to be necessarily existent because it is aware of itself. It says, I think, therefore I am. It's unsettling to realize that for this conclusion is being reached by a physical system, not the dualistic self Descartes took for granted. The conclusion perhaps ought to be weakened to: Something is, and something thinks.

It's this picture of the universe as self-contained, producing minds now and then, but not requiring minds in order to work, that is so hard for the Western tradition to accept. Kant used the phrase *ding an sich*—"thing in itself"—to refer to whatever ultimate reality lay behind the way things appear to us. We can never know things as they really are, because we can never experience anything except through the ways it appears to us. I don't know what percentage of philosophers, or nonphilosophers, would agree with this statement. I suspect most would, because it almost seems tautological: We can only perceive things as they are perceived by us. Most scientists would probably say that Kant's statement is true, but that things in themselves are of no interest whatever. Many laypersons would probably be more likely to say, at least God knows what things are really like, and He can tell us about them.

What cognitive science says *contradicts* this apparent tautology, in the following sense: It explains how we experience things in terms of how things actually are! One might object that the contradiction is only apparent, because the terms it uses are ultimately defined in terms of the human race's past experiences. Although we explain perception in terms of physics, physics is ultimately a theory only of how things appear to us. Nonsense. Science is not a fairy tale. When a scientist looks at the track of an elementary particle in a cloud chamber, her eyes and brain work because of the behavior of exactly the same kinds of elementary particles in her head. If this story about perception is not literally true, then it's not true at all.

Kant's insight is not completely wrong.[15] We can still argue that our knowledge of how things really are is, and must remain, incomplete. But we really do know *something* about how things really are, and that knowledge underlies our understanding of the mind.

One way to appreciate this point is to consider the impact a successful cognitive science would have on the old problem of *radical skepticism*. This is the old puzzle of how one can possibly refute a determined solipsist. *Solipsism* is the doctrine that no one exists but me; everyone and everything else is a figment of my imagination. Although no sane person really believes that solipsism is true, it seems as if there could not be any evidence against it, because all the evidence must be something I could experience, and the possibility we are trying to refute is that experience is systematically unreliable. In other words, if the apparent world is an elaborate con game (played against me by God or the Devil, as Descartes imagined), then we would *expect* to see evidence to the contrary, all of it as bogus as the world it appears to confirm. So all evidence is irrelevant.

I believe most people would conclude that there is no way out of this puzzle, except for the healthy resolve to ignore it. But cognitive science offers a way out. To begin, we have to ask what the solipsist's view of science must be. The solipsist cannot deny that scientific laws appear to be "true" descriptions of his experience. It may be that the earth and moon do not exist, but all the experiences of the apparent earth and apparent moon do seem to satisfy Newton's laws. For the solipsist (and for generations of empiricist philosophers), the proper conclusion was that scientific laws are ultimately laws governing the structure of experience. "What goes up must come down" is true all right, but what it really means is that any experience of something going up will (under proper observational conditions) be followed by an experience of something going down. This conclusion is not so attractive any more, although I'm sure there are some who still feel its tug.

The biggest problem with it is that it leaves no place for psychology. In Bishop Berkeley's day, one could believe that psychology was completely different from the other sciences, in that it was about the properties and behavior of the mind as perceived from within, not about the external objects the mind produces an illusion of. In the twentieth century the mind began to be studied as an object among other objects. That meant that the the solipsist must believe in *two* sorts of mind: the real kind (his), and the apparent kind, the one that exists in the same way the moon exists. Still, if he's determined, he can accept this consequence. For him it's a coincidence, nothing more, that his mind, and the minds he posits to explain the behavior of the brains he appears to see, manifest such striking similarities. He can maintain that the resemblance is superficial, because they differ in one important respect: his mind contains (or undergoes) experiences, whereas everything the hypothesized minds do can be understood without reference to experience.

This is where cognitive science comes in. It shows how to locate experiences in observed minds. The solipsist can still claim that there is a fundamental difference between the first-person experiences of his mind and the third-person experiences in apparent minds. He can claim this until he looks at his own brain. At this point the solipsistic illusion must break down, because he will be able to observe third-person experiences in his own brain. Of course, there would be many practical obstacles to someone turning a "cerebroscope" on himself, but in principle the solipsist could see his own experiences as third-person constructs at exactly the same time as he experiences them. At this point the simplest hypothesis is that first-person experiences *are* third-person experiences, from a peculiar vantage point. In other words, it is possible to have experiences that count as evidence against solipsism. A determined solipsist can still refuse to accept the evidence, but all we were required to show is that it is possible to have evidence against solipsism, in contradiction to the idea that all experience would be consistent with solipsism.

The questions raised at the end of the last chapter were, How do we find the conscious entities in the universe? and, would they agree with our classification? The answer is that there is no easy answer. A conscious entity is an information-processing system with the right kind of self-model. We might have to examine it carefully to discover if it has the right kind of model, and if its symbols really refer to itself. Some such systems will have enough of a verbal capacity to tell us how they feel; others may not. In particular, the question whether some subsystem of a conscious object might itself be conscious cannot be determined a priori. In the case of the scenarios sketched by Searle and by Block, where a conscious mind is simulated by the combined action of one or more people, the answer is yes, the parts do have separate consciousnesses. Could your cerebellum or some other part of you be conscious? Yes, but it's an empirical question whether it is.

6

Consequences

To summarize the argument of this book: The brain appears to be a biological computer. Many mental skills can be analyzed in terms of computation, perhaps all of them, but no one knows exactly how many. The most likely candidate for a noncomputational property is phenomenal consciousness, but careful thought shows that in fact we can expect consciousness to be a necessary component of a computational intelligence, not an inexplicable accident. In particular, it seems as if any computational entity that dealt with a physical environment that included its own body would have to have a model of itself as a perceiver and decision maker; and in that model the entity and events involving it would have to be labeled as having the features of phenomenal consciousness. An entity with a model of this kind would exhibit what I called virtual consciousness; and then all we have to do is appeal to parsimony to identify virtual consciousness with the real thing.

The weakest step in the argument is the prediction that computers will continue to exhibit increasing mental capacity without reaching a low plateau. There is no use fighting over this issue, however. It will either happen or it won't. If it doesn't, AI will eventually get classified with phrenology as an odd pseudoscience that never really made it. There are objections to the other steps of the argument, too, but I've addressed those in chapters 4 and 5.

So, for the rest of this chapter I am going to assume that this prediction, and the rest of the argument, will work. I said at the beginning of this book that it might be considered foolish or evil to argue that people are machines. Many readers who are willing to entertain the possibility that my argument is not foolish may still feel that for it to be widely accepted would be a great evil. Perhaps it would be better for everyone to believe that our bodies are ultimately controlled by immaterial souls.

Assuming my argument is correct, and that people are computational machines, does that mean that there is no such thing as the soul and, in particular, the immortal soul? Does it mean that there is nothing valuable about a person, since a person is just a machine? Does it mean that everything is permitted? Can there be something that a machine ought to do or not do? How do you get from the description of the machine's behavior—what *is*—to a commandment—what *ought to be?*

Many people are quite worried about the moral consequences of the success of the AI project. For example, Barzel (1998, p. 166) states that, "There is an urgent need to assign the borderline [between humans and computers] by pointing to differences, beyond which the effort to compare the traits of human beings and those of the computer misrepresents both and is dangerous; the reduction of *organic* human thinking to the computer's *mechanism* can end up in humankind's dehumanization."

John Puddefoot, in a very interesting treatise on AI and religion from the point of view of an educated Christian layperson, puts it like this:

[The] last bastion of human self-esteem is already under formidable assault from the advance of computer technology, and especially the development of intelligent machines. Although in its infancy, this new area of human discovery is set to make major inroads into territory hitherto regarded as the exclusive preserve of human beings. Where will this process end? What, if anything, will remain of the "uniquely human" when computer scientists and software . . . engineers have done their worst? Will Christians be forced into another ignominious retreat in the face of the question: "Why did God force humankind to live in this world of sorrow and suffering to develop our minds and souls if a computer program would have done just as well? (1996, p. 85)

Someone once told me that we don't have to worry about cognitive science causing human beings to be devalued, because human life is already valued pretty low, and it's hard to believe it could sink any lower. Looking back over the twentieth century, I find it difficult to disagree. Nonetheless, one would like to do better in the twenty-first, and current trends in science and culture are getting us off to a bad start.

The Souls of Robots

The possibility that people might be robots raises some urgent questions: Can a robot be the subject or object of a moral judgment? That is, are there things a robot should or should not do; and are there things that should or should not be done to a robot?

We can dismiss immediately the claim that a robot is just a machine, and hence simply will do what it will do; what it "should" do is irrelevant. As I showed in chapter 3, an intelligent robot will think of itself as having reasons for what it does, and it won't do something it has no reason to do.

Unfortunately, the sense of "should" that we get from this analysis has little to do with morality as such. The most we can conclude is that a sufficiently complex robot must have a *reason* to do what it does, because it will model itself as doing everything for a reason. The question is how and whether moral considerations would carry any weight. If an intelligent cruise missile wants to destroy Detroit, then it should evade antiaircraft fire. But should it want to destroy Detroit? An optimistic view is that any sufficiently intelligent robot would be able to appreciate the need for morality. Sometimes Kant, in the *Critique of Practical Reason*, seems to make such an argument, although not phrased in terms of robots, of course (Kant 1956). I doubt that such an argument would work. As I concluded in chapter 3, a robot has to have *some* unquestioned motives for action, but nothing says they have to be lofty. A robot can want more than anything else in the world to assemble car bumpers, or to destroy cities. It is hard to imagine being that kind of robot, but that's because our boundary conditions lie in a different place.

The point is often missed that robots could be intelligent and still be utterly unhuman in most respects. It is often assumed that if a robot has some of the attributes of consciousness it will automatically acquire all the others. Many science-fiction stories revolve around this assumption. To take an example almost at random, in the movie *Short Circuit* a robot is hit by lightning and becomes conscious. In the movie, the word used is "alive." From that point on, it fears death, it is able to use and understand language, it appreciates beauty, and it knows the difference between right and wrong. The idea is that all of these things are simply automatic consequences of being conscious. I reject this idea. An intelligent robot would have to have phenomenal consciousness, but it could easily lack morals and an aesthetic sense.

In fact, it is not even necessary for a robot to fear death. A sufficiently intelligent robot would anticipate death, or at least know it could happen, but that's not the same as *fearing* it. An intelligent cruise missile would in fact have to be designed so as to welcome death, under the right circumstances, of course. Less scarily, a robot designed to rescue people from hazardous situations would be glad to die for the people it rescued, if doing so would do them any good. I do not use the word "glad" metaphorically; as explained in chapter 3, an intelligent robot does not just find itself pursuing goals, but must evaluate them as worth pursuing.

If we list the attributes we associate with human consciousness in order from those that are intrinsically associated with consciousness to those that seem peculiarly human, the list might look like that shown in figure 6.1. Suppose we assume for the sake of argument that robots will eventually have agility (the ability to manipulate physical objects gracefully) and intelligence (the ability to find solutions to difficult problems). Then, I claim, they will inevitably have free will, emotion, and phenomenal consciousness (experiences with qualia). I argued as much in chapter 3. However, they might have all those things and still not have much linguistic ability. Language appears to be a separate faculty. They might also seem intelligent but not creative, although, as I argued in chapter 2, creativity is not an ability, but a term of praise for intellectual feats that we admire. On the other hand, I don't see any reason why robots *couldn't* have language and, on occasion, be creative.

But love, morality, and the other categories at the end of the table are different. It will be quite easy to build robots that differ so strongly from us in these dimensions as to seem completely alien. Furthermore, although it may well be possible to build robots that are just like us, there is a sense in which these robots might fail to actually reproduce "genuine" love or "genuine" humor, not because of a flaw, but because we simply can't count an artifact as really loving or laughing if changing a few program variables would radically change what it loved or laughed at.

Jackendoff (1987; Lerdahl and Jackendoff 1983) discusses the perception and understanding of music as an intricate information-processing activity. What the analysis doesn't quite explain is why people enjoy music

Agility
Intelligence
Free will
Emotion
Qualia

Language
Creativity

Love
Morality
Aesthetics (visual, musical, ...)
Humor
Spirituality

Figure 6.1
Attributes of mind, intrinsic attributes first

so much. The same question could be asked about the other arts as well, such as painting, poetry, and fiction. The problem is not getting a robot to like these things. The problem is to do it in a nonarbitrary way. Contrast the enjoyment of sex. Suppose it was essential for robots to conjoin physically for reproduction (or some other purpose). The designers of the robots would find it easy and natural, when wiring the robot's self-model, to assign the state of being conjoined a high value, so that the robot would experience pleasure in somewhat the way people do. We could also make robots enjoy poetry, so that they read as much as they could and accumulated as many volumes as possible. But it would be much harder to get them to enjoy good poetry and dislike bad poetry. One reason is because we have no theory of what makes poetry good, at least no theory that lends itself to being programmed. But even if we did, it would be just as easy to program the robot to prefer bad poetry to good, and hence hard to accept that the robot "really" had any preferences one way or the other.

With music we are a little closer to a theory of quality, mainly because there is no semantic domain that music refers to. It may take a lifetime to grasp the patterns in a really complex piece of music, but at least you don't have to worry about entities outside the music that the music refers to, as you do with linguistic media. But so what? Suppose some future theory of musical aesthetics explains as much of musical taste as there is to explain (seeing as how people ultimately disagree on the subject); and further suppose that we write a program that classifies music according to the theory and assigns the appropriate polarity to different auditory inputs, in such a way that good music is valued and pursued, and bad is disliked and avoided. Unfortunately, although the resulting robot might be very stimulating to talk to about Brahms's Violin Concerto, the theory it embodies doesn't really explain why we like music. The best it can aspire to is an explanation of *what it is* to like music.

The point is not that aesthetic appreciation is forever barred from robots because they are made of silicon, but rather that an aesthetic judgment, when it is *my* aesthetic judgment, seems compelling, and there is nothing compelling the robot's judgments. It may seem that way to the robot, but we know the truth: just tweak a few parameters and the robot will switch from fascination with Warhol to abhorrence of anything after the impressionists.

If this argument seems unclear, we can draw an analogy to the idea of a computerized judge. This is a program that would hear evidence and decide how a guilty defendant is to be sentenced or how much to award a plaintiff in a civil case. We are very far from being able to create such a program, but even if we could we would run into the following difficulty. Suppose that someone were dissatisfied with the electronic judge's verdict and demanded to inspect the program. After some examination, they realize that if a certain constant were set to 0.75 instead of 0.25, the judge would have issued a different opinion. They begin to demand that the program be rerun, with this change made. They would explain by reference to similar cases that 0.75 made much more sense, or at least 0.6. Others would disagree, and would cite various precedents that favor 0.25 as the value or, at the outside, 0.45. Now, suppose that the computerized judge tried to join the debate. Could it? Of course not. Its intuitions in the matter have no weight at all, because the whole debate is about what its intuitions should be.

This is not to say that we couldn't have artificial judges, so long as there is no way to understand their decisions except in the terms they use to explain them, and no way to change their minds except reasoned persuasion. Their programs would have to be impenetrable, or off-limits for some other reason.[1] The point is that it's part of the very concept of judgment that it be based on reasons, and not on a chain of physical events. If the judge thinks you should go to jail for fifty years, and your lawyer, on appeal, argues that that's ten times too long, then you expect to hear reasons for the original decision, reasons that you can try to refute. The opposition can't argue that fifty years makes sense because a certain parameter in the judge's program was 0.25, any more than they could argue that a human judge's constipation at the time of sentencing would justify a long sentence.

Similarly, it's part of the concept of aesthetics that something is beautiful, or stirring, or funny because there is an emotional resonance between that something and you. The resonance must be understood as having real meaning, not the result of a short circuit somewhere. Supposedly (Kurzweil 1999) there is a region of the brain that when electrically stimulated makes everything seem hilarious. If this part of your brain were stimulated without your knowing it, you would think that some very funny stuff was happening around you. But if you find out it's due to brain stimulation, you'll decide that you're having a vivid hallucination. (You still might enjoy it, of course, but you wouldn't describe it the same way.) Nitrous oxide makes everything seem profound for a few seconds after it is inhaled. The feeling is impossible to shake while it is present. Nonetheless, a theory explaining how nitrous oxide works is not a theory of profundity.

So we can build robots with simulated aesthetics and simulated humor, but they won't necessarily count as real aesthetics or real humor, because they might be arbitrary in ways that aesthetics and humor aren't allowed to be. On the other hand, there is always the possibility that intelligent robots will have aesthetic judgments of their own that we don't understand. I don't know what they would be, and I'm certainly not making the *Star-Trek*-level suggestion that robots would more naturally appreciate the beauty of a mathematical proof than the beauty of a Monet. I'm just suggesting that their judgments will be real to the extent that they develop spontaneously in the robot population, and that they resist simple explanation or retuning. We'll take robot aesthetics seriously if the robots ever reach a point where we can debate them, destroy them, or lobotomize them, but can't change their tastes just by adjusting a few lines of code.

Similar remarks can be made about robot morals. If we build a computer simulation of human moral reasoning, it might tell us something about the way people reason about moral issues. However, it would be hard to argue that the robot literally had the moral intuitions we had so carefully mimicked.

For example, how would one design a computer to experience guilt? In this context I don't mean the quale of guilt, if there is one, but the sense that one has done something one ought not to have done. It's easy to imagine a robot weighing the pros and cons of one option or another, and even easy to imagine it believing later that it made the wrong choice. What's hard to imagine is its knowing at the time it makes the decision that it's making the wrong choice. The fact that we do this all the time suggests that what the brain decides to do can be the outcome of a conflict between multiple motives, and that the pros and cons do not simply get added up. Instead, a single motive can crowd others out, temporarily. Whether this reflects some fundamental property of the wiring of the brain, I have no idea. There's no obvious reason for the brain to work this way. A person can know that cigarettes will kill him, can know that therefore he shouldn't smoke any more cigarettes, and yet can smoke "just one more"—while feeling guilty about it. What's the point? It's true that life would be less interesting if we weren't this way, but evolution does not aim at making our life interesting.

One reason for this pattern of behavior might be that we aren't very good at adding up all the pros and cons. We don't form stable judgments of the value of things. We value food by how hungry we are right now. The reason it's so hard to stay on a diet might simply be that the value of eating normally rises to a level above whatever value you assign to being thin. In other words, a bad dieter never makes an irrational decision; but his or her utility function just keeps changing (Nozick 1993). The only problem with this model is that it doesn't account for the frequency of rationalization. We don't admit that the reason we're having a piece of pie is that right now a piece of pie is better than slimness. We claim instead that it's okay because of our recent good behavior, or because of our intention to be better tomorrow, or because it's Christmas, after all. Perhaps this is all the work of the self-model cleaning up the debris left in one's self-esteem by the decision to eat pie.

Constructing a computer simulation of human guilt would require us to create a program that

- believes it's very important never to do X
- does X
- finds a reason why on this occasion it was okay to do X
- believes that this reason made any difference to anyone

If we find an intelligent program that does all this, we may learn something about human psychology. However, in the present context the main conclusion is that there would be considerable doubt that what computer felt was actual guilt.[2]

So far I have focused on what robots' moral intuitions must or might be. A more practical issue, perhaps, is what they *should* be for our sake. Unlike traditional machines, intelligent robots, if they ever exist, will be potentially extremely dangerous, simply because they'll be able to cause so much damage if they choose. We don't want a robot driving a car unless it is strongly motivated to avoid hitting people. At first it might seem that the solution is obvious. After all, Isaac Asimov promulgated his Three Laws of Robotics in science fiction years ago (Asimov 1950). He sometimes talked as though they were scientific laws, but never made it quite clear in what sense he meant that. They seem instead to be ethical precepts:

1. Never hurt a human being or allow a human to come to harm.
2. Never allow yourself to be damaged unless required to by Law 1.
3. Always obey humans except as required by Laws 1 and 2.

It does seem like a good idea to include rules like this in the preference structure of a system. Unfortunately, I suspect that there will be robots whose version of the first law is "Never hurt a human being except one at war with us." But there is another problem, raised by Dennett for people but applicable to robots as well. Suppose a robot finds out that there are people starving in Africa who could be helped if it stopped polishing his master's silver and brought them food. Does that mean it should drop the silver and go help them? Presumably not. So the first law must also have a codicil about the small pleasures of nearby humans being more important than massive suffering of humans far away.

Hence I think it is inevitable that robots will have ethical intuitions. The people they deal with will not view robots as genuine sources of ethical insight, because they will understand that robotic ethics were agreed on by some human committee, then wired into the robots for the protection of humans. Nonetheless, everyone will expect robots to act according to their moral principles. In tricky cases the robots will still have to wrestle with moral dilemmas, just like everyone else.

People as Ethical Robots

But if people (and animals) are already robots, more or less, does that fact alone call for a broad revision of our moral code? If we find out exactly which animals are unconscious, will it become okay to do anything we want to them? Can anyone remain "pro-life" if life is a sort of machinery? If people are robots, can it be immoral to do whatever you like with them? Does it make sense to punish them when they do something wrong?

In their crudest forms, these questions are easy to answer. Suppose someone says, "We shouldn't punish people for doing wrong, because they couldn't help it; they're just machines, without real free will." This argument is incoherent, as is any argument of the form "We shouldn't do X because people don't have free will." Any argument about what we should or shouldn't do presupposes that we decide how to act based on reasons for and against each option—that is, that we *do* have free will.

The incoherence of such questions is not a superficial matter. They contradict beliefs that are so basic to being human that we can't imagine actually rejecting or revising them. If you are to continue existing at all, you must continue to weigh alternatives before acting. It may be that there is another way of describing what is going on in your brain that doesn't involve any reference to weighing alternatives; but then it doesn't involve any reference to *you* either. You exist because you exist in the self-model of your brain, and in that model your actions are determined by your deliberations. There is no way for you to escape from your self-model except to cease to exist entirely (by suicide, or something less permanent such as sleep, drugs, or meditation).

One reason people are able to discuss moral issues is that they share enough of a moral framework for their points of view to be comparable.

People are equipped with fairly strong moral instincts. By "moral instinct" I don't mean the innate ability to grasp moral truths, but instead the innate tendency to *care* about moral issues. One reflection of this fact is the striking observation (Nozick 1993) that people often appeal to moral principles to justify their actions, even when there is no obvious principle involved. When a decision is being made, people argue for choice *X* on the grounds that in circumstances of type *C*, actions of type *X* should be chosen, and that the present circumstance is of type *C*. "I should get a bigger piece than Tommy because he got a bigger piece last time"; and everyone should have about the same amount on the average. It is fascinating that people almost always try to find a principle to justify what they want or to explain a decision they made.

If a chimpanzee asks, "Why do I have less food than that other chimpanzee?" the answer is likely to be, "Because he beats me up," and that's probably satisfactory (assuming chimpanzees are capable of asking the question in the first place). If a person asks, "Why should I work as hard as that other guy and get a smaller reward?" the same answer doesn't work as well. The unrewarded person can start to shirk, or run away, or team up with other weak people to ambush the strong guy. If you want to get a lot of work out of a group of sufficiently intelligent monkeys, you must treat them equally, tyrannize them so securely they can never rebel, or find some ingenious reasons for the inequality (noble birth, connections with the gods, or whatnot).

Notice that we take for granted that the question "Why do I have less?" is reasonable, and that the absence of a good answer portends trouble. Why is that? One possible answer might be that people have an innate concept of and preference for fairness. A more realistic answer would be that the person asking doesn't really want to have the same amount as the other guy; he wants to have *more*. But if the only reason he can think of for being given more is that he would really enjoy it, he can see that the other guy can make exactly the same argument. So he switches to arguing for the same amount, because he'll come out with a net gain if he carries the day, and if other guy tries symmetry as a tactic, he will lose.

Even this explanation has gaps, although they're hard to see from our usual standpoint. We have to explain why it is that people advert to arguments as tools for getting what they want. Well, perhaps that's not so difficult. Many arguments have nothing to do with moral issues, for instance: "Give me the club because the tiger is coming this way and I'm better with a club than you are." Once the idea of using arguments this way exists, the temptation grows strong to try the strategy even if you aren't really sure what your argument is. It isn't necessary that the argument convince an impartial judge; in practice, the fairness argument works best if there are a lot of have-nots taking part in the discussion, because they will all potentially benefit from its being accepted, and may all become angry if it is rejected.

The other main intrinsic component of our moral instinct is our tendency to love some people and hate others. People tend to classify other people (and animals) into the categories of those they wish well, those they feel indifferent about, and those they fear and loathe. If a creature falls into your "lovable" category, then no argument could persuade you not to love that kind of creature. Many people are convinced that cats have all sorts of thoughts and emotions. This conviction would survive acquaintance with a complete diagram of a cat's brain, showing in detail how far it is from possessing any of the qualities attributed to it. Cat lovers would simple refuse to accept any theory of consciousness that made it impossible for cats to be conscious. If AI succeeds, then eventually there will be robot lovers with similar beliefs about robots. Their devotion to a particular sort of robot will depend more on how fuzzy and cute that model is then to any facts about the modules in its electronic brain.

Given our innate moral reflexes, one might wonder why we need to bother with foundational questions about ethics. It might seem as pointless as searching for a reason to breathe. I don't think so. As I mentioned at the beginning of the book, it is unhealthy for a culture to lack a base of shared values, and we often seem to be heading toward a future in which no such base exists. I realize it may sound naive to wish for a philosophical framework that everyone can sign on to and that will guide our leaders toward wise decisions. It's very uncool to sound naive. Perhaps that's why we often seem to be heading for a world in which cynicism, especially toward the beliefs of the average person, is the only credo of the sophisticated. Finding general moral principles that even the intellectual elite can agree with would make a big difference.

We are constantly presented with new and difficult moral problems, and the situation will get worse as technology gives us options we may wish we didn't have. The clearer we are about the basic structure of morality, the better our position will be to solve those problems. The ultimate challenge to our moral intuitions will arise when we begin to tinker with them. We will be reengineering people genetically in the very near future. At first the changes will appear to be so obviously benign that no one will quibble with them, but after several "minor adjustments" and a couple of not-so-minor ones we may find ourselves with people whose moral intuitions differ substantially from ours. In addition, computers will begin to play an important role in key societal decisions. They already do, in fact, but so far they do it only in the way tools always have, by encouraging us to focus on some options and ignore others. In the future, we may find the machines making more and more choices for us. We had better think about foundational moral principles before delegating the process of applying them.

I am worried not about waking up one day and discovering that machines or genetically engineered superpeople have taken over the planet, but about something more subtle. Suppose we start making "obvious improvements" to the human genome. We get rid of genetic diseases and crooked teeth first, then start making people look more attractive, then increase lifespan, then boost IQ, then reduce the level of aggression, and so forth. We create electromechanical prosthetic limbs, boost visual ability with electronic enhancements, wire calculators into our cortex. It will be hard to argue with each little change, but suppose the end result is a race that cares little about its own survival. Philosophers of the future wax poetic about hastening the demise of the individual and the race. Public policymakers urge measures to reduce the birth rate, or eliminate it entirely. Almost everyone agrees. Within a few centuries, the human race ceases to exist. But no one minds. Indeed, those last few centuries might be the happiest in recorded history, as well as the last.

This idea is horrifying, because we value our own survival above all else. But, by hypothesis, it won't be horrifying to people in the future. Are we right or are they? Is it tyranny for us to try to retain our grip on the values of our descendants? Or is there no right or wrong involved? Perhaps all that can be said is that on some planets there are intelligent races that survive for a long time, but this isn't one of them.

Assuming that a stable moral framework would be a useful thing, which one should we adopt? Several alternative foundational theories of morality have been tried. One is *utilitarianism,* the idea that the good is what is most valued by the greatest number of people. Unfortunately, to avoid circularity you have to define "value" without using the concept of "good." If a great number of people value being drunk, then utilitarianism would seem to require that, other things being equal, we should work to make sure they can get drunk whenever they want. The "other things equal" clause may give us a way out here, by pointing out the harmful consequences of widespread drunkenness, assigned a negative value by everyone. The pain caused to the relatives of people killed by drunk drivers might outweigh the pleasure drunk driving gives.

I find utilitarianism unworkable, for reasons that have been enumerated many times before. Suppose someone proposes to use indigent children as a food item. Utilitarianism suggests adding up the pluses and minuses in order to evaluate the proposal. There's something obviously wrong with a system in which you would even begin this exercise. Whether to make a decision on utilitarian grounds is itself a moral decision, which therefore can't itself be based on utility, at least not entirely. There are certainly plenty of occasions when utilitarian thinking is justified (as when deciding where to put a highway), but the argument that it's justified will be phrased in terms of moral principles, not utilitarian ones.

An alternative foundational principle is Kant's "categorical imperative": the idea that conduct be governed as though by a set of rules that everyone accepts as applying to everyone. Kant tried to infer this principle from the definition of an autonomous agent. Whether he succeeded is not clear, but perhaps not relevant, since we have already decided we want to adopt some principle. I think Kant's idea is better than utilitarianism, but it ultimately falls short. Even people who agree that one should act according to rules that apply to everyone rarely agree on an actual list of rules. This is partly because of bad faith, but mainly because the only way to resolve disagreements between rules is by appeal to more general rules, which doesn't help in the case of the most general rules.

Another problem is disagreement about who is to be party to the agreement in the first place.[3] In trying to reach a consensus about whether to use animals as food, I wouldn't consider whether the animals would assent to the arrangement. We might rule animals out on the grounds that they can't actually take part in discussions about moral principles,[4] But many people would vehemently disagree. There are those whose intuitions about eating animals are roughly the same as my intuitions about eating babies. In addition, if we rule out animals because they can't take part in moral agreements, we must also rule out retarded people, senile people, little children, and fetuses, all of whom are regarded by many, if not most, people as entitled to the protection of moral rules. Of course, all of these people are still people, so we can appeal to our natural tendency to feel sympathy for those who are sufficiently like us; but there are plenty of groups who draw the boundaries around "us" too narrowly.[5]

If all these difficulties make it seem impossible to find some kind of fulcrum on which to place the levers of morality, there are still two options. One is to give up and conclude that there is no justification for our moral instincts. Even if we have them, they're not really any more about morality than is the instinct to dominate other people; they're really just part of our built-in strategy for dealing with other creatures. We can call this *nihilism*.

Curiously, Paul Churchland (1995, pp. 292–293) refers to this position as "moral realism," and describes it thus:

The child's initiation into [moral] practice takes time, time to learn how to recognize a large variety of prototypical social situations, time to learn how to deal with those situations, time to learn how to balance or arbitrate conflicting perceptions and conflicting demands, and time to learn the sorts of patience and self-control that characterize mature skills in any domain of activity. After all, there is nothing essentially moral about learning to defer immediate gratification in favor of later or more diffuse rewards.

So far as the child's brain is concerned, such learning, such neural representation, and such deployment of those prototypical resources are all indistinguishable from their counterparts in the acquisition of skills generally. There are real successes, real failures, real confusions, and real rewards in the long-term quality of life that one's moral skills produce. As in the case of internalizing mankind's scientific knowledge, a person who internalizes mankind's moral knowledge is a more powerful and effective creature because of it. . . .

This portrait of the moral person as a person who has acquired a certain family of cognitive and behavioral *skills* contrasts sharply with the more traditional accounts that picture the moral person as one who has agreed to follow a certain set of *rules*. (emphasis in original)

At least Churchland takes a position on the question of morality; most modern writers on philosophy and cognitive science are willing to write volumes on tiny nuances of the mind-body problem while remaining oblivious to the major damage cognitive science is poised to wreak on our moral traditions. One pictures a philosopher on the Titanic preoccupied with the question of whether he can be sure the iceberg exists.

But the position Churchland takes just won't work. Any scheme that makes morality into an *opportunity* instead of a *constraint* is missing the whole point. By Churchland's criterion, the more socially successful someone is, the more moral he is. It's not clear exactly who we are to count as a "powerful and effective creature." Is he thinking more of Bill Gates, who has the most money in the world, or Elvis Presley, who was perhaps the most admired person in the world during his lifetime? Or perhaps Genghis Khan, who was "powerful and effective" politically and militarily? But exactly who the winner is doesn't matter; obviously they're in the wrong contest. These people may have many praise-worthy attributes, but surely moral virtue is not one of them.

A more sophisticated version of nihilism is *moral relativism,* in which moral judgments are evaluated with respect to various belief systems, but the idea of comparing belief systems is abandoned. Moral relativism is the correct stance for anthropologists, who are observing moral systems from outside, but I don't see how it avoids being nihilistic when applied to one's own moral system. Either I believe my own moral judgments or I don't. If I believe mine then I don't believe frameworks that contradict it. (But see the discussion of epistemological relativism later in this chapter.)

The other option is the one that humanity has traditionally based morality on: the sanction of the divine. No matter how difficult it is to discern moral truth, we can be confident that it exists, and not get discouraged in our search for it, because the world was created by a benevolent God. Our moral instincts point to a concept of *the good,* not "good for me" or even "good for us," but just good. This concept can't be explained in terms of self-interest, even enlightened self-interest. If we meet another intelligent race, it might be good for us if we exterminate them, and good for them if they exterminate us, but either option would be bad. Why? If you say that it would be a great loss for the universe if either were to vanish, then you are taking God's point of view. You may consider it absurd for a bunch of organic molecules to aspire to that viewpoint; in that case you're one bunch of organic molecules I disagree with.

But is the option of relying on God still open to us in the face of the possibility that we are machines? In a widely reported talk, the physicist Steven Weinberg said, "One of the great achievements of science has been, if not to make it impossible for intelligent people to be religious, then at least to make it possible for them not to be religious. We should not retreat from this accomplishment"(Weinberg 1999). Is he being disingenuous? Might it perhaps be the case that it *is* impossible for an intelligent person to be religious? If so, do we just coast on our moral instincts and hope for the best?

God without Dualism

If my theory—or any other materialist theory—is true, then dualism is false. If dualism is true, then it is not too hard to believe in God. Dualism claims that there is a nonphysical realm whose inhabitants (minds) interact continually with the physical world (through human bodies).[6] If you accept that, then accepting that there is a larger Mind that interacts with other parts of the world is an easy step. Why doubt that miracles happen when the human race embodies five billion ongoing miracles every day?

If dualism is false, however, belief in God becomes much more problematic. If consciousness is just virtual consciousness, then physical laws appear to reign supreme in every corner of space and time. If God plays a role in a universe like this, he does it in an indirect way. He never intervenes to push events in a direction they wouldn't otherwise take. The future history of the universe is determined by its past history and physical laws. If God is a causal factor in the story, it is because he created the initial conditions and the laws.

One might suppose that the insights of modern physics save us from this sort of determinism. Given quantum mechanics, it is not clear what we *mean* by the history of the universe. Does the history of the universe correspond to the deterministic evolution of a gigantic wave function (Everett 1957; DeWitt and Graham 1973), or to the randomly distributed events that occur when "measurements" happen? Either view faces severe difficulties. The first view implies that our reality is just one of an infinite number of branches, all equally real. In fact, our version is constantly splitting into new branches, so that there is no such thing as "the" future.

The second view is simply incoherent, since there is no explanation of what a measurement is without appeal to the properties of macroscopic systems, and no way to explain what a macroscopic system is in terms of quantum systems (Putnam 1979). But I don't think quantum mechanics changes the essential desolation of the picture, as I will explain in more detail below.

Many people I talk to don't see why the picture is so "desolate." They think that it just confirms that when it comes to moral judgments the human race is on its own. It's true that the human race's track record on being moral is not great, but then God's track record, if we judge by the number of bloody religious conflicts in history, isn't so great either. In any case, people don't pay much attention to God or to principles anyway. When they do wrong, it's not because they don't know what's right. They usually know what's right but do what they want anyway.

The people I talk to tend to be academics. When I talk to normal people, or at any rate normal Americans, I usually get a very different picture. Most of them take for granted that religion is on to something, even though in our modern tolerant society everyone is supposed to acknowledge that no one religion can claim to be absolutely correct. Almost everyone believes that moral laws ultimately derive from some kind of divine authority. As Ken Wilber says (1998, p. 3), "religion remains the greatest single force for generating *meaning*." My opinion sample is somewhat skewed by the fact that in the United States religion tends to be more prominent than in many other industrial countries. But Americans are probably more like the average world citizen, for whom religion is and always has been the foundation of philosophy, especially ethics.

I think it is fair to say that for most people science appears to be just another among several possible religious stances, albeit one with certain peculiar features. Like Christianity, it has a priesthood. Like Asian religions, it has a doctrine of mystifying depth that only a few adepts can master. It's easy to make quantum mechanics sound like Buddhism or Taoism, as several popular books have done. Under these circumstances, it's natural to believe that acceptance of science is like acceptance of a foreign religion; tolerating it is the polite thing to do, but you don't have to assume it's literally true.

This attitude has been made respectable under names like "relativism" and "postmodernism." This is a different sense of the word "relativism" than that used above. There it meant a refusal to select among different moral frameworks; here it refers to a broader refusal to grant objective truth to assertions of any sort. The first type is *moral relativism;* the second, *epistemological relativism.* I can't claim to understand the more technical aspects of postmodern literary criticism, if the word "technical" can be applied to a discipline that denies that any theories, including its own, actually mean anything. But I think I understand some of the simpler versions of relativism. They tend to be based on the idea that belief systems exist to help cultures cope, so that "truth" for any culture is whatever works for that culture. So feminist history can contradict patriarchal history, and black history can contradict white history, even though all of these histories are true. It is child's play then to hold that science and religion are both true, even though they contradict each other in places.

I don't know of any way to refute relativism, except to scratch my head and look puzzled. I assume that if someone is attracted to it, it's because they are interpreting it in one of two ways. The first is best explained in the context of contradictory scientific theories, such as Newtonian mechanics and quantum mechanics. They are both true, even though they contradict each other, because the former is a simplified version of the latter that works fine when dealing with objects too big and complex for the superposition effects of quantum mechanics to matter. In other words, the former is never anything but approximately true, and, when looking at subatomic particles, not even that.

This kind of contradiction is not always so tidily dealt with. Currently quantum mechanics and general relativity theory contradict each other, and physicists do not know how to fix the problem. The former works for subatomic systems and the latter for supergalactic ones, but they make assumptions about the forms of physical laws that are hard to reconcile. Consequently, when reasoning about situations involving both cosmological and subatomic scales, such as the Big Bang, they are forced to switch back and forth between the two frameworks in an ad hoc way.

In spite of appearances, this is not relativism. We do not have different camps of physicists who insist that their theory is "true for them," but not necessarily for anyone else. A single physicist can deploy quantum mechanics and relativity on the same problem at the same time, using instinct to decide which theory will work best for which aspect of the problem. However, if the two theories contradict each other, then one conclusion or the other, or maybe both, will have to be discarded. They can't both be true, or one true at one time, the other at another.

Most important, scientists believe that both theories are actually simplifications of a more general theory, the way Newtonian mechanics is a simplification of quantum mechanics. They just don't know what that theory is; they may never know, and they will still go on believing that there is such a theory.[7] If in fact both theories are literally true, and they contradict each other, then physicists might end up believing two contradictory empirical facts, such as, "the universe will eventually collapse," and "the universe will expand forever." To accept such a conclusion is to deny that there is one physical reality, which would make physics the study of nothing in particular.

The other way relativism might be true is for different theories to use the same terms to mean different things. Lately many people seem to think "reticent" is a synonym for "reluctant." They can truly say that yonder talkative chap is reticent, even though it is also true that he is anything but. It is quite difficult to define terms like "God," so it may not be surprising that two people could say "God exists" and "God does not exist" and both speak truly, in a sense. Or one could say "God is female" and the other "God is male," and the difference could be reconciled by saying that each is referring to a different image of God; in a case like that, they might agree that they're both wrong.

The problem is that neither of these benign ways of interpreting relativism will help us resolve the most thorny contradiction, which is this: religious people believe that God intervenes in the day-to-day happenings in the universe, and science denies any such thing. There is not much hope in resolving this contradiction by looking for differences in the way the two camps use the word "God" and "intervene." Either God overrules physical laws on occasion, or he never does.

It is important to realize that science does not *intrinsically* deny divine intervention. The enterprise of science was carried on for hundreds of years by people who believed unquestioningly in divine intervention. Science began by assuming that *some* aspects of the universe were governed by immutable laws. It might perfectly well have found places and times where the laws lapsed; but it didn't. The more it investigates, the more it finds the same pattern: everything everywhere is governed by the same, mathematically precise laws of physics. Everything that happens is ultimately explained by the rigidly law-governed behavior of lots and lots of elementary particles.

Sometimes people say that religion is concerned with matters of the spirit, and science with empirical matters, so they can't actually conflict. But if scientists had found evidence of divine intervention in the world, no one would have ruled that inadmissible or meaningless. They would have said, *of course* the existence of God is an empirical question, and scientists have found evidence of his existence. So they can't now say, oh well, you won't find scientific evidence of the existence of God; he trades in other sorts of evidence.

I fear that the conclusion is inescapable that the reason most people see no conflict between religion and science is that most people don't understand science. They take dualism for granted, and assume that scientific explanation stops at the skull; what goes on inside it is not entirely explained by the laws of physics, but requires positing a spirit or soul that interacts with the brain. But as I have explained, there is reason (if not yet indisputable reason) to believe that the functioning of the brain is all ultimately physical and computational.

One might ask, how can you be sure that physical law covers all of space and time? We can only examine a tiny piece of it; isn't there plenty of room for God to slip in a miracle or two every day? I raised a similar point about the brain in chapter 1: the brain is so complex that it will never be possible to rule out the possibility that a nonphysical mind affects some of the events in it. The problem is that the better we understand how the brain works the less there is for the mind to do. Similarly for divine intervention. When we examine the world closely, we never find any evidence of divine intervention. The parts of the world we don't examine closely appear to work about the same as the parts we do. The simplest hypothesis is that exactly the same processes are present in both cases.

Various twentieth-century theologians have tried sophisticated strategies for making God's intervention consistent with what we know about the laws of physics, notably Polkinghorne (1998) and Peacocke (1984) (see Drees 1996 for discussion). One way God could intervene would be to take advantage of the unpredictability of the world to insert undetectable little nudges into it. Kenneth Miller (1999) argues eloquently that the unpredictability of quantum-mechanical systems sets limits to what science can ever tell us about the behavior of the world, leaving room for God to act on it. Polkinghorne finds scope of divine action in the phenomenon of *chaos*. A chaotic system is one that, although deterministic, is fundamentally unpredictable because very slight perturbations cause arbitrarily large changes in its behavior. Hence the changes God makes could be so small as not to violate conservation of energy and still have macroscopic effects.

It is tempting to seize on modern physics as giving God a place to hide in the world, but we should resist the temptation. Miller's picture of quantum mechanics seems to be that it accounts for 90% of the behavior of a system, leaving 10% unaccounted for, which is plenty of room for God to act. But this is not right. What quantum mechanics says is that the possible events obey certain probability distributions, and that there is *no* other influence on them. An action by God would have to *change* the probabilities, which would be detectable as a violation of physical laws. To take a crude example, suppose a fiendish mad scientist decides to test for God's presence by setting up an apparatus that beams some sort of lethal radiation in the general direction of two people. The mad scientist has placed a magnetic field in the path of the beam, which makes each particle in the radiation beam veer to the left or to the right.[8] Which direction a particle takes is, in the usual quantum way, totally unpredictable. A particle has a 50% chance of going left and a 50% chance of going right. Now the evil scientist places a saint on the left and a sinner on the right. Picture Gandhi and Stalin. If God decides to save Gandhi and give Stalin what he deserves, he will have to change the probabilities set by physics.

I suppose that Miller, Polkinghorne, and others would object that this is not the situation they have in mind. Suppose we don't send a beam of lethal particles toward the two human guinea pigs, but send just one really energetic particle. Furthermore, we carefully avoid repeating the experiment with several pairs of good and bad people. Now statistics can't enter the picture. We send the particle, it goes right, Stalin is vaporized, and those who want to see God's hand at work can say that he spared Gandhi because of his goodness.

If this is the idea, then quantum mechanics is not really giving us any leverage. We still have to assume that God acts only when his presence cannot be detected. If that's his modus operandi, he could perfectly well act in the deterministic world of classical physics. Whether a system is chaotic in the technical sense or not, in practice we can never measure the state of the world with complete accuracy. God can sneak in and violate whatever laws of physics he wants so long as he does it when we're not looking. Such a "God of the gaps" (Drees 1996) may be consistent—just barely—with the facts, but it imposes an even more stringent set of conditions on the ways God can intervene. If, as most theologians posit, God wants to be involved in the day-to-day running of the universe, why go to the trouble of creating a universe that works just fine without that involvement, and then having to skulk around it poking here and there in an undetectable way? He could have created a universe that behaved more or less the way Aristotle thought it did, through which he roamed changing things right and left. But instead he created something that, as far as we can tell, has run pretty well with no further intervention after the Big Bang. Some may argue that he created an apparently purely physical universe in order to test our faith; these are the same sort of people who argue that the fossils of the dinosaurs were created by God to test our faith in Genesis. To my mind, there's something awfully unsavory about a God who would play such a game, in which he knows which of several shells the pea is under and can manipulate the evidence to point in an arbitrary direction.

It may sound as if I am an atheist, or at best a *deist,* one who thinks of God as creating the world and then abandoning it. Actually, I am neither. I find the world to be morally incomprehensible without being able to adopt God's view of it, and physically inexplicable unless there is something outside of it that explains why it exists. I realize perfectly well that just saying the word "God" does not solve either problem. What it does is acknowledge the *holiness* surrounding them, and express the faith that they are linked.

The only way to reconcile God's silence with his existence is to assume that he poured himself into the world when he created it. His intervention in the world consists in creating laws of physics that allow complex physical systems to evolve that understand those very laws; in making it possible for weird creatures to evolve from monkeys and grasp the need for an overarching set of moral principles. We can't of course talk of evolution as having us, or anything else, as a goal. Still, we know that intelligent life evolved on at least one planet, probably many more. How many of those species have the concepts of sacredness, or good and evil? Perhaps all of them do, in which case the discovery of God is, in every part of the universe, an inevitable aspect of the discovery of intelligence. When matter organizes itself into smart objects, these objects will always be aware of huge missing pieces in the puzzle the world presents to them. God is the biggest missing piece, or maybe the answer in the back of the book. We may think that belief in God is a transient stage in the development of civilization, and that, if we survive our own technological achievements, we'll outgrow that belief. I doubt it. We will always be painfully aware of our finiteness, and will always yearn for the Infinite.

The place where God intervenes in the world is therefore *us*. If his will is to become effective in the world, it will be because we carry it out. I realize that much harm has been done by people who claim to be acting on God's behalf. However, I don't think that relieves me of an obligation to think about what God wants me to do, which, I assure you, is often different from what I would do if I thought God's opinion was irrelevant. Furthermore, those who think religion is on balance a force for evil (Weinberg 1999) are not thinking things through. We take the values of our civilization for granted, without realizing how hard it was for the monotheistic religions to instill those values in our ancestors. It's hard to picture the human race without religion. The closest I can come is to imagine a world based on the moral outlook of pre-Christian Rome. In that framework, religion is essentially a system of magic spells to persuade one god to counteract the plots of another. The elite of the society don't really believe in that or any other system. I submit that if mankind had stopped at that stage of religious development it would have been impossible for anything like a modern democratic civilization to evolve. The Roman Empire was essentially the Mafia in togas. They could never get beyond the idea that society is a zero-sum game.

In affirming that we are the main entry point of God into the universe, I don't want to reject entirely the possibility that he built more specific interventions into the structure at various points. It is proper to be grateful to him that the universe is the way it is, and in particular to thank him for our existence and our occasional abilities to partake in his divinity. It is reasonable to pray for strength to act according to his will; it might be that you are praying to yourself, but the proper way of addressing the divine in yourself may be to speak to God. Praying that God act in the world independently of his creatures in order to cause the future to turn out a certain way is presumably futile.

Many people are offended by a God who would turn us loose in such an uncaring world. This is typically known as the Problem of Evil: Why would a good, omnipotent God allow bad things to happen? I think the answer is fairly obvious. The only way for us to exist is for us to exist in the world as it is. We are as we are because of a long evolutionary process based ultimately on the behavior of physical particles. The physical world is a set of axioms, and we are a theorem.[9] We could not exist in another context. We imagine that evil could simply go away, but this is an incoherent fantasy. Any given bad thing that happens we can imagine not happening. If it didn't, the world would be a bit better. Hence we imagine we can eliminate *all* bad things by getting rid of them one by one. The question is whether the inhabitants of the resulting world would be recognizable as human beings. They might look like us, but they would be lacking all the misfortune that, in struggling against, we define ourselves by. It might be better if those people (a hearing Beethoven, an easy-going Lenin) existed instead of us. But to wish it is to wish for nonexistence. Perhaps it was immoral for God to create a universe such as this, but if we're going to exist this is the kind of universe we must exist in, governed by rigid physical laws and subject to considerable pain; and in which the sentient beings must be silent sometimes to hear the voice of God.

Religious intuitions, like all other mental events, are the work of various brain structures. That in itself does not mean that the experience of holiness is a hallucination. After all, the ability to do mathematics depends on some brain structures too, but that doesn't mean numbers are an illusion. But what about robots' brain structures? They'll certainly be able to reason about numbers, but it's all too easy to imagine a robot that is dead to the possibility of God. That's why I put "spirituality" at the very end of the list in figure 6.1. I explained earlier that mental attributes such as humor and aesthetics could not be authentic if they were just simulated. We might want robots to tell jokes and to laugh at them, but it would be hard to say that a robot really thought a joke was funny. We want robots to be aware of and respect our moral beliefs, but that would not really make them moral; an unloaded gun is just as amoral as a loaded one. Similarly, we might want robots to notice and respect religious things, but it would be hard to believe that the feelings of awe we implant in them are authentic.

As I mentioned above, I expect many people to be taken in by robot simulacra, if robots ever become sophisticated enough to play the role pets play in human ecology. That would be relatively harmless. Much worse would be the possibility that human beings might come to be viewed as "tunable" with respect to moral and spiritual issues. If we know how to tweak someone's brain to change their fundamental beliefs, we may cease to believe that there is such a thing as a fundamental belief.

When?

There is a large gap between what is currently known about human thinking and what we will have to know to verify (and correct) the theory of consciousness outlined in chapters 3, 4, and 5. The gap is so large that perhaps the best attitude toward it is not to worry about it.

Those who worry about long-term phenomena such as the sun using up all its fuel and the ability of the human race to genetically reengineer itself might want to know exactly what time scale I have in mind for the creation of truly intelligent robots. The answer is that I don't have one. I doubt that anything like intelligent robots will exist in my lifetime, but I'm not that young and my health isn't that good. However, I do expect to see the terms of the debate begin shifting. Machines that can see and hear are becoming increasingly common, and that means that people will begin to take robots into account as "presences" of a new kind. These machines will be quite sensitive to some of the needs of the humans in their vicinity, and stupidly blind to others. But they will have to be taken into account; to deal with them, their behavior must be predicted, and increasingly it will be predicted by taking what Dennett (1978*b*) calls the "intentional stance." That is, the simplest way to predict their actions will be to assume they're rational and to make inferences from what they believe and what they are trying to accomplish, making due allowance for their usually inadequate understanding of the situation. It will be like dealing with an animal, but an animal that can carry on a simple conversation. That's hard to visualize, but I am confident that people will smoothly adapt to the presence of creatures like that.

The main problem people will have, I suspect, is overestimating the mental capacities of robots. People will know how stupid they are, but not necessarily how little they experience. People tend to believe that almost any organism that can move has experiences; it won't take much autonomy on the part of their machines to trigger their "animate organism" detectors. So even if it seems absurd to many now that a robot could ever feel anything, I suspect that in a few years intuitions will swing in the opposite direction, and it will take a lot of persuading by computer scientists and philosophers to convince people that their old family robot doesn't actually experience anything. By the time robots actually do have experiences, if they ever do, it will be an anticlimax.

In the years ahead, it will be much more important to focus on avoiding philosophical decadence than enjoying continued technological progress. The process of dethroning humanity that began with Copernicus is nearing completion. It is not necessary that this process cause the devaluation of humanity, but it is all too possible. We must look for a coherent synthesis of our religious intuitions and our scientific discoveries, so that as the very definition of what it is to be human changes, we will have a hope that our moral intuitions will not degenerate; or if not a hope, at least a prayer.

Notes

Chapter 1

1. No one is quite sure what the number is. 10^{11} is a conservative estimate. 10^n is 10 to the nth power, i.e., a 1 followed by n zeros. 10^{11} is 100 billion.

2. It repolarizes after every depolarization; each cycle takes about one millisecond.

Chapter 2

1. For the most part, AI researchers have, quite rightly, preferred to work on much narrower technical issues. On the rare occasions when they have taken a broader view, the results are not always worthwhile (Moravec 1988; Kurzweil 1999).

2. The name of an early program with very broad ambitions (Newell and Simon 1961; Ernst and Newell 1969).

3. I could contrast my view with that of Jerry Fodor: "If someone . . . were to ask why we should even suppose that the digital computer is a plausible mechanism for the simulation of global cognitive processing, the answering silence would be deafening" (1983, p. 129). My bet would be that "global cognitive processing" will turn out, like other kinds of processing, to be a collection of modules, none of which does anything particularly mystifying.

4. Actually, we'll need to represent slightly more than just the positions of all the pieces, because of various subtleties in the rules of chess. For instance, you can't castle after moving your king, even if the king has moved back to its original square. So somehow you have to record whether the king has ever moved. None of this need concern us.

5. Programs tend to be broken into many little chunks called *subroutines* or *subprocedures*. Each chunk typically does a few operations itself, but delegates most of its work to subordinate chunks, which themselves delegate most of their work. When subroutine R_1 delegates a piece of its work to subroutine R_2, we say R_1 *calls* R_2.

6. The actual field has two values at every point, the velocity in the x and y directions. Also, the full mathematical treatment requires t to become infinitesimally small, so that the relationship between spatial and temporal change becomes a differential equation.

7. I don't want to leave the impression that a cell of the type shown literally infers the flow field at a certain point. The truth is more complex. For one thing, the relationship between the velocity at a point and the response of the cell system of figure 2.3c is somewhat indirect. A given velocity value may not stimulate any detector fully, but will cause partial stimulation of detectors that are tuned to nearby values; this is sufficient for accurate motion perception. For another, there are technical reasons that the flow field cannot be computed locally at all no matter how precisely the spatial and temporal changes are measured; any one local measurement is ambiguous. It is only well defined when the measurements from the whole image are combined and integrated.

8. After John von Neumann, the same guy who invented game theory with Oskar Morgenstern.

9. I.e., you're not in New England.

10. In assuming my brain could have labels for bundles of facts, I am mixing computer talk with psychological talk and brain talk. I argued previously that we are justified in ascribing the presence of symbols to neural systems and will return to the issue in Chapter 5.

11. The BBS issue consists of several reviews of (Penrose 1989), mostly negative.

12. Of course, a chess program contains subroutines that are algorithms for making legal moves, algorithms for verifying checkmate, algorithms for detecting a draw, etc.

13. Personal communication.

Chapter 3

1. Because of the particular way the nervous system is constructed, there are constraints on the bogus location the message can mention. For example, a neuroma in the leg can cause a signal to be sent along any of several neurons in the sciatic nerve. The location of a pain is encoded by which neuron in that bundle is active. Hence the perceived location of the pain is constrained to be somewhere in that leg, and not, for instance, in the other leg.

There is another classic problem, Sellars's "grain" problem (Sellars1965; Metzinger 1995*b*), which, to the degree I understand it, has essentially the same solution as the externalization problem. Sellars noted that when we think of something as colored, we think of it as "homogeneously" colored, either on its surface or through its entire extent. How could a property like that actually be a property of a bunch of neurons, which are not homogeneous at all? If you imagine dividing a colored patch into smaller and smaller bits, you imagine them remaining colored no matter how small they get. But if you imagine dividing groups of neurons, you eventually get to pieces that are not groups of neurons. Sellars thought this showed that phenomenal colors can't ultimately be properties of neurons. But if the brain is a computer, all we have to explain is how a brain might manipulate representations of homogeneous things. The representational machinery itself need not be homogeneous.

2. This distinction is closely related to Block's distinction between "access consciousness" and "phenomenal consciousness" (Block 1997b).

3. Thanks to Aaron Sloman for pointing this out to me.

4. "I" is identical with the symbol "R" I introduced ad hoc at the beginning of this chapter.

5. Which is why the police can often reconstruct files you thought you deleted from your hard disk; if you want to commit the perfect crime, don't keep any evidence on a computer system, even temporarily.

6. Compare Robert Kirk's formulation (Kirk 1994) that something be present to the "general assessment processes."

7. In the same galaxy as Twin Earth.

8. I shouldn't misrepresent Rey's actual conclusion, which is not quite the same as mine. Instead, he says we seem to have a choice between saying consciousness doesn't really exist at all, or continuing to search for some further "arcane condition" that is true of people but not of his hypothetical machine.

Chapter 4

1. There is an interesting indeterminacy here. My theory is that consciousness is a matter of the brain's modeling itself as conscious. In this formula there is no mention of time. If we try to add a temporal component, we have two places to bring time in: at time t_2 the brain models itself as (conscious at time t_1). If $t_1 \neq t_2$, then which variable represents "the" time at which the conscious event occurred? It would seem that if the self-model had a delay occasionally (or continuously), then the past would be constantly revised, in a sense. That is, at some or all time points, the system would be nonconscious (or not conscious of some particular event) when the time point occurred, and then become conscious at that time point *retroactively*. If this model turns out to be correct, then our pretheoretic notions about consciousness are going to need some revision. See Dennett and Kinsbourne (1992) for a discussion of this issue, which I am going to neglect. It obviously has implications for the case of the overlooked whirr.

2. Carruthers believes that consciousness requires the ability to express judgements about experiences using language. In chapter 3 I attempted to put some distance between cognizance and linguistic reportability; Carruthers is happy to equate them.

3. As Chalmers points out, if the zombie world were physically impossible, materialism might still be false, because phenomenal experience might be an irreducible feature of physical events that is not itself physical.

4. It's off the topic, but I feel compelled to point out that many people would disagree with the presupposition that "God" does not name a phenomenon that needs explaining.

5. Also, he apparently makes the same mistake as Shapiro, discussed above, viz., equating judgments made by my self-model with judgments of "mine."

6. China, coincidentally enough.

Chapter 5

1. Technically, it would be preferable to use the logicians' notation $(\lambda v \cdot 2v)$ to refer to this function, making use of the lambda-calculus, in which the notation $(\lambda x \cdot E)$ refers to a function whose argument is x and whose value is E. However, Greek symbols can be intimidating, and in context it will always be clear what the argument is.

2. The requirement that the system be incorporable in a larger system must be interpreted counterfactually: "If it were incorporated, it would behave as follows." The system may of course already be a part of a larger system, in which case the requirement of approximateness would apply to the larger system.

3. In general, $t_1 < t_2$, because we want to be on the safe side. If the scanner detects a light level in the range $[t_1, t_2]$ it should turn on a warning light and complain that something's wrong. However, this has nothing to do with the proposed analysis of the symbol site.

4. The exact technical requirements on d are not terribly important, but we must at least require that for every state $x \in S$ and every $\epsilon > 0$, there is an infinite number of neighbor states x' such that $d(x, x') < \epsilon$.

5. In mathematical terms, $N(R) = \{R' : M_{12}(R') = M_{12}(R)\}$ contains a neighborhood of R under the metric d, that is, an open ball around R. We might also want to require that the diameter of $M_{12}(R)$, that is, the maximum distance between two of its points, be small. Better yet, what we really should do is provide a probability distribution on $M_{12}(R)$ and replace the diameter with a constraint on the variance of that distribution.

6. At least until quantum-mechanical effects become important, at which point it is hard to say what the proper analysis would be: either causality becomes too distorted for the concept of symbol to make sense, or everything becomes discrete. We won't worry about such issues here.

7. Epilogue: They live happily ever after.

8. Technically, we need to assume that the distances satisfy the "triangle inequality," that for any three cities A, B, and C, the distance from A to C is no greater than the distance from A to B plus the distance from B to C.

9. I'm assuming there is no low-dimensional vector space of possible Disney characters in which Grumpy and Doc are points.

10. The allusion is to variable binding in logic-based representations. A more realistic example is afforded by the human brain, where there seem to be two subsystems of the visual system, one for recognizing the type of perceived objects, the other their location. If more than one object is in view, the brain must make sure the type of each object is properly matched up with the corresponding location.

11. Of course, "cow" can mean "female seal," can be used as a verb, can be used metaphorically, etc. Ignore all that. Most semantic theories make even the straightforward, bovine sense of the word come out meaning things like "cow, or horse seen under bad lighting conditions."

12. Some females have made the intriguing suggestion that this is the *only* neuron in the male brain.

13. John Allman, personal communication.

14. In Fodor's original example, it was a chess game, not a weather station, but the weather station works better with the point I'm making here.

15. We can't leave a tautology contradicted. I have to explain why, in spite of its obviousness, the statement that we can only know things as they appear is false. The bug is that it assumes that there is a well-defined concept of the way things appear, which is given prior to all theorizing about the way things are. This is simply false. The theory of the way things appear is just another empirical theory. Judgments about the way things appear are no different from judgments about the way molecules behave. In fact, they ultimately *are* judgments about the way molecules behave, namely, those in information-processing systems. As soon as the mind is assumed part of the world, then we can no longer view the world as something created by the mind (as Berkeley thought) or as something hidden behind the veil of the senses (as Kant thought). We once thought heavenly bodies were unreachably remote; then we realized we were living on one.

Chapter 6

1. The only exception would seem to be if a group of people could agree to abide by a program's decision, on the grounds that they all share a set of principles and think the program will apply them more consistently or neutrally than any available person. This scenario is not as plausible as it might seem to be at first. There is no reason to think that a program is inherently more consistent than a person; to think so is to fall into the formalism fallacy discussed in chapter 2 of confusing the formal system embodied by the program with the domain it reasons about. Consistency with respect to legal insight is not a formal property of a program, but a reputation that the program can earn only by making wise decisions about a series of cases.

2. Of course, if the robot claims sincerely to *feel* guilty, we won't be able to deny it, but feeling guilty is only one component of guilt.

3. Utilitarianism is not immune from this problem either, of course, because we have to decide *whose utility* to take into account.

4. William James argues somewhere that we are justified in using dogs in medical experiments, because even though the dog can't understand the situation, if it could it would surely agree that the interests of an animal are negligible compared to those of a human. This was not one of his better arguments.

5. Rawls (1971) proposed a clever idea for getting around some of these problems, namely, to suppose that principles were valid if they would be agreed to by participants *before they find out what role they are to play* in society. The idea is that you will take more heed of the rights of, say, women if once the rights are in place you might discover that *you* are a woman. Alas, this idea doesn't solve all the problems, because part of the disagreement is over the question of whether one of the things you might discover you are is a fetus or a dog.

6. Not all versions of dualism make this claim. Chalmers (1996) argues for "property dualism," in which certain physical objects have experience-like properties. It's not clear how God fits into that kind of scheme.

7. The current most attractive candidate is string theory (Greene 1998).

8. We defer all the details to the mad scientist, with thanks for his or her invaluable contribution to philosophy.

9. We are not a theorem of the form "Necessarily there are people," but of the form "Possibly there are people." We're not the only theorem of this form, either; there are probably many others on other planets.

References

Anderson, A. R., ed. (1964). *Minds and Machines*. Prentice-Hall.

Armstrong, D. M. (1968). *A Materialist Theory of the Mind*. Routledge & Kegan Paul.

Asimov, I. (1950). *I, Robot*. Gnome Press.

Baars, B. J. (1988). *A Cognitive Theory of Consciousness*. Cambridge University Press.

Baars, B. J. (1996). *In the Theater of Consciousness: The Workspace of the Mind*. Oxford University Press.

Baillargeon, R., Spelke, E., and Wasserman, S. (1985). "Object permanence in five-month-old infants." *Cognition* **20**, 191–208.

Banks, M. and Salapatek, P. (1983). "Infant visual perception." In M. Haith and J. Campos, eds., *Handbook of Child Psychology: Infancy and Developmental Psychobiology*. Wiley.

Bar-Hillel, Y. (1960). "The present status of automatic translation of languages." *Advances in Computers* **1**, 91–163.

Barzel, A. (1998). "The perplexing conclusion: The essential difference between natural and artificial intelligence is human beings' ability to deceive." *J. of Applied Phil.* **15**(2), 165–178.

Block, N. (1978). "Troubles with functionalism." In N. Block, ed., *Readings in the Philosophy of Psychology*. Harvard University Press, pp. 268–306. 2 vols.

Block, N. (1997*a*). "Inverted earth." In Block et al. (1997), pp. 677–693.

Block, N. (1997*b*). "On a confusion about a function of consciousness." In Block et al. (1997), pp. 375–415.

Block, N., Flanagan, O., and Güzeldere, G., eds. (1997). *The Nature of Consciousness: Philosophical Debates*. MIT Press.

Boddy, M. and Dean, T. (1989). "Solving time-dependent planning problems." In *Proc. Ijcai*. Vol. 11, pp. 979–984.

Bradley, F. (1893). "Appearance and reality." In J. Allard and G. Stock, eds., *Writings on Logic and Metaphysics*. Clarendon Press, pp. 115–225.

Brentano, F. (1874). *Psychology from an Empirical Standpoint*. Routledge and Kegan Paul. Translated by A. Rancurello, D. Terrell, and L. McAlister, 1973.

Bruce, V., ed. (1991). *Face Recognition*. Lawrence Erlbaum Associates. (Book version of special issue of *European J. of Cognitive Psych.*)

Cardie, C. (1997). "Empirical methods in information extraction." *AI Magazine* **18**(4), 65–79.

Carnap, R. (1942). *Introduction to Semantics*. Harvard University Press.

Carnap, R. (1947). *Meaning and Necessity: A Study in Semantics and Modal Logic*. University of Chicago Press.

Carruthers, P. (1996). *Language, Thought, and Consciousness: An Essay in Philosophical Psychology*. Cambridge University Press.

Chalmers, D. (1996). *The Conscious Mind: In Search of a Fundamental Theory*. Oxford University Press.

Charniak, E. (1993). *Statistical Language Learning*. MIT Press.

Chase, W. G. and Simon, H. A. (1973). "The mind's eye in chess." In W. G. Chase, ed., *Visual Information Processing*. Academic Press.

Chomsky, N. (1957). *Syntactic Structures*. Mouton.

Churchland, P. M. (1990). "Eliminative materialism and propositional attitudes." In Lycan (1990), pp. 206–223.

Churchland, P. M. (1995). *The Engine of Reason, The Seat of the Soul: A Philosophical Journey into the Brain*. MIT Press.

Churchland, P. S. (1986). *Neurophilosophy: Toward a Unified Science of the Mind-Brain*. MIT Press.

Churchland, P. S. and Sejnowski, T. J. (1992). *The Computational Brain*. MIT Press.

Clark, A. (1993). *Sensory Qualities*. Clarendon Press.

Crick, F. and Koch, C. (1990). "Towards a neurobiological theory of consciousness." *Sem. Neurosci.* **2**, 263–275.

Crick, F. and Koch, C. (1998). "Consciousness and neuroscience." *Cerebral Cortex* **8**, 97–107.

Davis, E. (1986). "A logical framework for solid object physics." *Technical Report* 245. NYU Dept. of CS.

Davis, E. (1990). *Representations of Commonsense Knowledge*. Morgan Kaufmann.

Dawkins, R. (1989). *The Selfish Gene* (2nd edition). Oxford University Press.

deGroot, A. (1965). *Thought and Choice in Chess*. Mouton.

Denes, P. B. and Pinson, E. N. (1973). *The Speech Chain: The Physics and Biology of Spoken Language*. Anchor Press/Doubleday.

Dennett, D. (1978*a*). *Brainstorms*. Bradford Books/MIT Press.

Dennett, D. (1978*b*). "Toward a cognitive theory of consciousness." In Dennett (1978*a*), pp. 149–173. Originally in Savage (1978).

Dennett, D. (1978*c*). "Where am I?" In Dennett (1978*a*), pp. 310–323.

Dennett, D. (1979). "On the absence of phenomenology." In D. Gustafson and B. Tapscott, eds., *Body, Mind, and Method*. Kluwer Academic Publishers.

Dennett, D. (1991). *Consciousness Explained*. Little, Brown and Company.

Dennett, D. and Kinsbourne, M. (1992). "Time and the observer: The where and when of consciousness in the brain." *Behavioral and Brain Sciences* **15**(2), 183–201.

Desimone, R. (1991). "Face-selective cells in the temporal cortex of monkeys." *J. of Cognitive Neuroscience* **3**, 1–8.

DeWitt, B. S. and Graham, R. N., eds. (1973). *The Many-worlds Interpretation of Quantum Mechanics*. Princeton University Press.

Drees, W. B. (1996). *Religion, Science, and Naturalism*. Cambridge University Press.

Dretske, F. I. (1981). *Knowledge and the Flow of Information*. MIT Press.

Eccles, J. C. (1970). *Facing Reality: Philosophical Adventures by a Brain Scientist*. Springer-Verlag.

Eccles, J. C. (1973). *The Understanding of the Brain*. McGraw-Hill Book Company.

Engelson, S. P. and McDermott, D. V. (1992). "Error correction in mobile robot map learning." In *Proc. IEEE Conf. on Robotics and Automation*, pp. 2555–2560.

Ernst, G. W. and Newell, A. (1969). *GPS: A Case Study in Generality and Problem Solving*. Academic Press.

Everett, H. (1957). "'Relative state' formulation of quantum mechanics." *Rev. Mod. Phys.* **29**(3), 454–462.

Feigenbaum, E. A. and Feldman, J., eds. (1963). *Computers and Thought*. McGraw-Hill Book Company, Inc.

Flanagan, O. (1992). *Consciousness Reconsidered*. MIT Press.

Fodor, J. (1975). *The Language of Thought*. Thomas Y. Crowell.

Fodor, J. (1981*a*). "Methodological solipsism considered as a research strategy in cognitive psychology." In Fodor (1981*b*), pp. 225–253.

Fodor, J. (1981*b*). *Representations*. Bradford Books/MIT Press.

Fodor, J. (1983). *The Modularity of Mind*. MIT Press.

Fodor, J. (1986). "Banish disContent." In J. Butterfield, ed., *Language, Mind, and Logic*. Cambridge University Press, pp. 420–438. Also in (Lycan 1990).

Fodor, J. (1988). *Psychosemantics: The Problem of Meaning in the Philosophy of Mind*. Bradford Books/MIT Press.

Fodor, J. and Pylyshyn, Z. (1988). "Connectionism and cognitive architecture: A critical analysis." In S. Pinker and J. Mehler, eds., *Connections and Symbols*. MIT Press, pp. 3–72.

Gallistel, C. R. (1990). *The Organization of Learning*. MIT Press.

Garey, M. R. and Johnson, D. S. (1979). *Computers and Intractability: A Guide to the Theory of NP-Completeness*. W.H. Freeman.

Gazzaniga, M. S. (1998). *The Mind's Past*. University of California Press.

Goodman, N. (1951). *The Structure of Appearance* (2nd edition). Harvard University Press.

Greene, B. (1998). *The Elegant Universe: Superstrings, Hidden Dimensions, and the Quest for the Ultimate Theory*. W.W. Norton.

Gunderson, K., ed. (1975). *Language, Mind, and Knowledge: Minn. Stud. in Phil. of Sci.*

Hager, G. D. (1997). "A modular system for robust hand-eye coordination using feedback from stereo vision." *IEEE Trans. on Robotics and Automation* 13(4), 582–595.

Hammeroff, S. R. (1994). "Quantum coherence in microtubules: A basis for emergent consciousness?" *J. of Consciousness Stud.* 1, 91–118.

Hans, J. S. (1993). *The Mysteries of Attention*. State University of New York Press.

Harnad, S. (1990). "The symbol grounding problem." *Physica D* 42, 335–346.

Haugeland, J. (1985). *Artificial Intelligence: The Very Idea*. MIT Press.

Hofstadter, D. R. (1979). *Gödel, Escher, Bach: An Eternal Golden Braid*. Basic Books.

Hofstadter, D. R. and Dennett, D. C. (1981). *The Mind's I: Fantasies and Reflections on Self and Soul*. Basic Books.

Jackendoff, R. (1987). *Consciousness and the Computational Mind*. MIT Press.

Jackson, F. (1982). "Epiphenomenal qualia." *Phil. Quart.* 32, 127–136.

Jelinek, F. (1997). *Statistical Methods for Speech Recognition*. MIT Press.

Johnson-Laird, P. N. (1983). *Mental Models*. Harvard University Press.

Kant, I. (1956). *Critique of Practical Reason*. Bobbs-Merrill. Lewis White Beck (trans.).

Kirk, R. (1994). *Raw Feeling: A Philosophical Account of the Essence of Consciousness*. Oxford University Press.

Kriegman, D. J. and Taylor, C. (1996). "Vision-based motion planning and exploration for mobile robots." *IEEE Trans. on Robotics and Automation*.

Kripke, S. (1972). "Naming and necessity." In D. Davidson and G. Harman, eds., *Semantics of Natural Language*. Reidel, pp. 253–355.

Kuipers, B. and Byun, Y.-T. (1991). "A robot exploration and mapping strategy based on a semantic hierarchy of spatial representations." *Robotics and Autonomous Systems* 8, 47–63.

Kunz, C., Willeke, T., and Nourbakhsh, I. R. (1997). "Automatic mapping of dynamic office environments." In *Proc. IEEE Conf. on Robotics and Automation*, pp. 1681–1687.

Kurzweil, R. (1999). *The Age of Spiritual Machines: When Computers Exceed Human Intelligence*. Penguin Books.

LaForte, G., Hayes, P. J., and Ford, K. M. (1998). "Why Goedel's theorem cannot refute computationalism." *Artificial Intelligence* 104(1–2), 211–264.

Lenat, D. B. and Guha, R. (1990). *Building Large Knowledge-Based Systems*. Addison-Wesley.

Lerdahl, F. and Jackendoff, R. (1983). *A Generative Theory of Tonal Music*. MIT Press.

Lettvin, J., Maturana, H., McCulloch, W., and Pitts, W. (1951). "What the frog's eye tells the frog's brain." *Proc. IRE* 47(11), 1940–1959.

Levine, J. (1983). "Materialism and qualia: The explanatory gap." *Pacific Phil. Quarterly* 64, 354–361.

Levine, J. (1997). "On leaving out what it's like." In Block et al. (1997), pp. 543–555.

Lewis, D. (1990). "What experiences teaches." In Lycan (1990), pp. 499–519.

Lucas, J. (1961). "Minds, machines and Goedel." *Philosophy* 36, 112–127. Reprinted in (Anderson 1964), pp. 43–59.

Lycan, W. G. (1987). *Consciousness*. MIT Press.

Lycan, W. G. (1990). *Mind and Cognition: A Reader*. Basil Blackwell.

Lycan, W. G. (1996). *Consciousness and Experience*. MIT Press.

Lycan, W. G. (1997). "Consciousness as internal monitoring." In Block et al. (1997), pp. 755–771.

Mataric, M. J. (1990). "A distributed model for mobile robot environment-learning and navigation." *Technical Report* 1228. MIT AI Lab.

McCune, W. (1997). "Solution of the Robbins problem." *J. of Automated Reasoning* 19(3), 263–276.

McDermott, D. (1987). "A critique of pure reason." *Computational Intelligence* 3(3), 151–160.

McDermott, D. (1999). "A vehicle without wheels." *Behavioral and Brain Sciences*. Commentary on "A connectionist model of phenomenal experience," Gerard O'Brien and Jon Opie.

McGinn, C. (1991). *The Problem of Consciousness*. Basil Blackwell.

Mead, C. (1989a). "Adaptive retina." In C. Mead and M. Ismail, eds., *Analog VLSI Implementation of Neural Systems*. Kluwer Academic Publishers, pp. 239–246. Proceedings of a workshop on Analog Integrated Neural Systems.

Mead, C. (1989b). *Analog VLSI and Neural Systems*. Addison-Wesley.

Metzinger, T. (1995a). "Faster than thought: Holism, homogeneity, and temporal coding." In Metzinger (1995b).

Metzinger, T., ed. (1995*b*). *Conscious Experience.* Ferdinand Schoningh.

Miller, K. R. (1999). *Finding Darwin's God.* HarperCollins.

Milner, P. M. (1999). *The Autonomous Brain: A Neural Theory of Attention And Learning.* L. Erlbaum Associates.

Minsky, M. (1968). *Semantic Information Processing.* MIT Press.

Minsky, M. (1986). *The Society of Mind.* Simon and Schuster.

Moravec, H. (1988). *Mind Children: The Future of Robot and Human Intelligence.* Harvard University Press.

Muller, R., Kubie, J., and Saypoff, R. (1991). "The hippocampus as a cognitive map (abridged version)." *Hippocampus* 1(3), 243–6.

Nagel, E. and Newman, J. R. (1958). *Goedel's Proof.* New York University Press.

Nagel, T. (1975). "What is it like to be a bat?" *Philosophical Review* 83, 165–180. Reprinted in Nagel, 1991. *Mortal Questions.* Cambridge: Cambridge University Press.

Nemirow, L. (1990). "Physicalism and the cognitive role of acquaintance." In Lycan (1990), pp. 490–499.

Newell, A. and Simon, H. (1961). "GPS: A program that simulates human thought." *Lernende Automaten,* pp. 279–293. In Munich: R. Oldenbourg KG. Reprinted in Feigenbaum and Feldman (1963).

Newell, A., Shaw, J., and Simon, H. A. (1958). "Chess-playing programs and the problem of complexity." *IBM J. of Res. and Devel.* 2, 320–335.

Nietzsche, F. (1886). *Beyond Good and Evil.* The Modern Library. Translated by Walter Kaufmann 1968.

Nozick, R. (1993). *The Nature of Rationality.* Princeton University Press.

O'Brien, G. and Opie, J. (1999). "A connectionist theory of phenomenal experience." *Behavioral and Brain Sciences* 22, 127–148.

Peacocke, A. (1984). *Intimations of Reality: Critical Realism in Science and Religion.* University of Notre Dame Press.

Pearl, J. (2000). *Causality: Models, Reasoning, and Inference.* Cambridge University Press.

Penrose, R. (1989). *The Emperor's New Mind: Concerning Computers, Minds, and the Laws of Physics.* Oxford University Press.

Penrose, R. (1994). *Shadows of the Mind: A Search for the Missing Science of Consciousness.* Oxford University Press.

Pinker, S. (1994). *The Language Instinct.* Morrow.

Poincaré, H. (1982). *The Foundations Of Science.* University Press of America.

Polkinghorne, J. C. (1998). *Belief in God in an Age of Science.* Yale University Press.

Puddefoot, J. (1996). *God and the Mind Machine.* SPCK.

Putnam, H. (1963). "'Degree of confirmation' and inductive logic." In P. Schilpp, ed., *The Philosophy of Rudolf Carnap*. The Open Court Publishing Company.

Putnam, H. (1975). "The meaning of 'meaning'." In H. Putnam, ed., *Mind, Language, and Reality: Philosophical Papers, Vol. 2*. Cambridge University Press, pp. 215–271. (Originally in Gunderson (1975))

Putnam, H. (1979). "A philosopher looks at quantum mechanics." In H. Putnam, ed., *Mathematics, Matter and Method. Philosophical Papers* (2nd edition). Cambridge University Press.

Putnam, H. (1988). *Representation and Reality*. MIT Press.

Putnam, H. (1992). *Renewing Philosophy*. Harvard University Press.

Quine, W. V. (1960). *Word and Object*. Wiley.

Rabiner, L. and Juang, B.-H. (1993). *Fundamentals of Speech Recognition*. PTR Prentice Hall.

Rawls, J. (1971). *A Theory of Justice*. Harvard University Press.

Reichardt, W. (1961). "Autocorrelation, a principle for the evaluation of sensory information by the central nervous system." In W. Rosenblith, ed., *Sensory Communication*. Wiley.

Rey, G. (1997). "A question about consciousness." In Block et al. (1997), pp. 461–482.

Rorty, R. (1965). "Mind-body identity, physicalism, and categories." *Review of Metaphysics* **19**(1), 24–54.

Rosenthal, D. (1986). "Two concepts of consciousness." *Phil. Studies* **49**, 329–359.

Rosenthal, D. (1993). "Higher-order thoughts and the appendage theory of consciousness." *Phil. Psych.* **6**, 155–166.

Rosenthal, D. (1997). "A theory of consciousness." In Block et al. (1997), pp. 729–753.

Russell, S. and Wefald, E. (1991). "Principles of metareasoning." *Artificial Intelligence* **49**(1–3), 361–395.

Sacks, O. (1987). *The Man Who Mistook His Wife for a Hat*. HarperCollins.

Savage, C. W., ed. (1978). *Perception and Cognition: Issues in the Foundation of Psychology, Minn. Studies in the Phil. of Sci.*

Savage, L. J. (1954). *Foundations of Statistics*. Wiley.

Searle, J. R. (1983). *Intentionality: An Essay in the Philosophy of Mind*. Cambridge University Press.

Searle, J. R. (1992). *The Rediscovery of the Mind*. MIT Press.

Searle, J. R. (1997). "The explanation of cognition." In J. Preston, ed., *Thought and Language*. Cambridge University Press, pp. 103–26.

Sekuler, R., Anstis, S., Braddock, O. J., Brandt, T., Movshon, J. A., and Orban, G. (1990). "The perception of motion." In L. Spillman and J. S. Werner, eds., *Visual Perception: The Neurophysiological Foundations*. Academic Press, pp. 205–230.

Sellars, W. (1965). "The identity approach to the mind-body problem." In W. Sellars, ed., *Philosophical Perspectives*. Charles C. Thomas, pp. 370–88. (Originally published in *Rev. of Metaphysics* 18)

Shannon, C. (1950a). "A chess-playing machine." *Scientific American* 182(2), 48–51. Reprinted in James R. Newman 1956 *The World of Mathematics* 4, New York: Simon and Schuster, pp. 2124–2133.

Shannon, C. (1950b). "Programming a computer for playing chess." *Philosophical Magazine* 7-41(314), 256–275. Reprinted in D. N. L. Levy ed. (1988) *Computer Chess Compendium*. New York: Springer-Verlag, NY.

Shapiro, L. (2000). "Saving the phenomenal." *Psyche.*

Shoemaker, S. (1981). "The inverted spectrum." *J. of Philosophy* 74(7), 357–381.

Shoemaker, S. (1997). "The inverted spectrum." In Block et al. (1997), pp. 643–662.

Silman, J. (1993). *How to Reassess Your Chess* (3rd edition). Siles Press.

Smolensky, P. (1988). "On the proper treatment of connectionism." *Behavioral and Brain Sciences* 11, 1–74.

Soderland, S., Fisher, D., Aseltine, J., and Lehnert, W. (1995). "Crystal: Inducing a conceptual dictionary." In *Proc. AAAI*. Vol. 14, pp. 1314–1319.

Stich, S. (1978). "Autonomous psychology and the belief-desire thesis." *The Monist* 51(4), 573–591.

Stich, S. (1983). *From Folk Psychology to Cognitive Science*. MIT Press.

Styles, E. A. (1997). *The Psychology of Attention*. Psychology Press.

Tagare, H., McDermott, D., and Xiao, H. (1998). "Visual place recognition for autonomous robots." In *Proc. IEEE Conf. on Robotics and Automation*.

Tarski, A. (1956). *Logic, Semantics, Metamathematics*. Oxford University Press.

Tesauro, G. (1995). "Temporal difference learning and TD-gammon." *Communications of the ACM 3*.

Thrun, S., Burgard, W., and Fox, D. (1998). "A probabilistic approach to concurrent mapping and localization/ for mobile robots." *Machine Learning/ Autonomous Robots 5*.

Turing, A. (1953). "Digital computers applied to games: Chess." In B. V. Bowden, ed., *Faster than Thought*. Pitman, pp. 288–295.

Tye, M. (1995). *Ten Problems of Consciousness*. MIT Press.

van Gulick, R. (1997). "Understanding the phenomenal mind: Are we all just armadillos? Part II: The absent qualia argument." In Block et al. (1997), pp. 436–442.

von Neumann, J. and Morgenstern, O. (1944). *Theory of Games and Economic Behavior*. Princeton University Press.

Weinberg, S. (1999). "A designer universe?" *New York Review of Books* 46(16), 46.

Weisberg, R. W. (1993). *Creativity: Beyond the Myth of Genius.* W.H. Freeman and Company.

Wilber, K. (1998). *The Marriage of Sense and Soul: Integrating Science and Religion.* Random House.

Williams, B. (1976). *Problems of the Self.* Cambridge University Press.

Winograd, T. (1972). *Understanding Natural Language.* Academic Press.

Index

absent qualia, 144–148
access
  normal vs. introspective, 108
algorithms, 82, 189
appearance, 106
Armstrong, David, 95
artificial intelligence, 29–91
attention, 142

backgammon, 42, 46
Bar-Hillel, Yohoshua, 71
bats, 159
Bayes's Theorem, 63, 75
behavior, 22
behavioral explanation
  necessity of, 22, 146
belief, 132
  false, 205
binding problem, 195
Block, Ned, 134, 143, 157, 163,
  214, 245
brain,
  See neuroscience

Carnap, Rudolf, 44, 69
Cartesian theater, 123, 211
categorical imperative, 228
causality, 170, 198
Chalmers, David, 20, 93,
  144–148, 248
chess, 31
Chinese Room argument, 161–163
Churchland, Paul, 20, 186, 188, 192

codes
  neural, 13, 15
cogito, 212
cognitive science, 8, 29
cognizance, 106–111,
  113, 126
  and language, 126–130
color, 112–116
computation, 46, 167
  approximate, 173
  complexity of, 67, 87, 195
  definition of, 171, 173, 175
  observer-relativity of, 168
computationalism, 25
computer
  compared to brain, 37
  definition, 167, 170
computers, 143, 162
connectionism,
  See neural nets
consciousness
  first-order theories of, 139
  hard problem of, 20, 93
  higher-order theories of, 135,
    137, 142
  phenomenal, 93
  varieties of, 93
  virtual, 131, 162, 164
creationism, 237
creativity, 89

decodings, 167, 169, 172, 186
  discrete, 173

deduction, 65
Dennett, Daniel, 26, 117, 123, 141,
    147, 151, 211, 223, 241
depolarization, 13
Descartes, René, 211, 212
divine intervention, 234
dualism, 147, 235
  and the brain, 10, 94
  belief in by robots, 101
  definition, 5
  mind-body link, 16
  versus computation, 15

eliminativism, 20
emotions
  robotic analogues of, 104
epiphenomenalism, 17
episodic memory, 125
epistemology, 210
evil
  problem of, 239
evolution, 2, 50, 172, 201
experience
  externalization of, 95
explaining vs. explaining away, 95
explanatory gap, 133

fiction, 132, 157, 206, 208, 212
first- and second-order theories, 22
formalism fallacy, 82, 83, 247
free will, 8, 96–100, 153, 205
functionalism, 25, 135

game trees, 32
games, 31, 42, 46
generality of AI, 30, 36
genetic engineering, 227
Gödel's Theorem, 81
GOFAI (good old-fashioned AI), 39,
    43, 45
grammar, 149
grammaticality, 150

hidden Markove models, 76
Hofstadter, Douglas, 27

"I" symbol, 207, 245
induction, mathematical, 86
inference, 46
  deductive, 68, 77–79
information extraction, 70,
intentional stance, 241
intentionality, 198
interpretation of formal languages,
    44, 208
intractability, 67, 190, 191
introspection, 137
inverted spectrum, 154–158
  intrasubjective, 156

Jackson, Frank, 150

language, 64, 87, 109, 181, 196
  natural, 64
language of thought, 65, 195
laws of robotics, 223
learning, 41, 55, 87, 125
life, as necessary for consciousness,
    24, 163
Lycan, William, 26

map learning, 55
Mary the neuroscientist, 150–154
materialism
  arguments against, 144, 150
meaning,
  See semantics
mental images, 6, 95
mentalese,
  See language of thought
metrics on symbols, 187
mind-body problem, 18
Minsky, Marvin, 27
miracles, 235
model
  definition, 118
models
  mental, 96
  self-fulfilling, 3, 121–123
moral instincts, 226
moral rules, 228

morality
  foundations of, 225–231

neural nets, 40, 50, 188, 189
  compared with computers, 192
  simulation on digital computers, 41
neuroscience, 9, 13, 24, 124, 188
neurotransmitters, 9
NP-completeness, 190

observer-relativity, 203

Penrose, Roger, 81
perception, 105–108
  errors in, 105
personal identity, 163, 164
persons
  identity of, 214
phenomenal consciousness
  definition, 20, 159
phenomenal objects, 158
pixels, 50
pleasantness
  quale of, 102
precursors (of symbol sites), 184
preferences, 101, 103–104
probability, 61, 75
process theories, 20
pronouns, 64, 65

qualia, 6, 132
  comparison of, 135, 141, 149–161
  function of, 115, 142, 149
  of emotions, 104
  robotic analogues of, 102
  unnoticed, 137–139
  what they're like, 150, 153, 154, 159
qualities
  primary and secondary, 6, 211
quantum mechanics, 236

reasons vs. causes
  of behavior, 7
  of perceptual judgments, 112
reference,
  See semantics

relativism, 230, 233–234
religion, 231–240
representation, 117
  notations for, 65, 66
  of knowledge, 87, 195
robot consciousness, 217, 241
robot judges, 220
robot navigation, 61
robots, 47, 51, 197
  aesthetics of, 218–221
  emotions of, 222
  goals of, 100
  morals of, 217, 222, 223
  navigation, 55
  place recognition, 57
  preferences of, 101
  reasons for acting, 101
  visual control of, 54
Rosenthal, David, 26
rules, 44, 192

self
  unity of, 121
self-model, 3–5, 88, 97, 118–130,
    143, 148, 152, 162, 203, 206
semantics, 39, 43, 44, 144, 168, 171,
    186, 196–198, 209
  causal theory of, 46, 198, 209
  compositional, 194
sensor fusion, 105
skepticism, 140, 212
solipsism, 212
speech, 72
speech recognition 72, 77
symbol sites, 182
symbols, 42, 44, 168, 180
  analog, 187
  discrete, 188
  tokens of, 184
  types of, 185
synapses, 9
syntax, 69

Tarski, Alfred, 44
tickles, 116
time, 138

translation of natural language, 71
Traveling Salesman Problem, 190
Turing machines, 182
type-token distinction, 181

utilitarianism, 228

vehicle theories, 20
verificationism, 157
vestibular-ocular reflex, 176
vision, 14, 47
  depth maps, 52
  robotic, 105
  stereo, 52, 107
visual field
  as object of perception, 111

"what it's like," 159–161

zombies, 145